Anatomy of a Failed Embargo

Anatomy of a Failed Embargo

U.S. Sanctions Against Cuba

Donna Rich Kaplowitz

BOULDER
LONDON

Published in the United States of America in 1998 by
Lynne Rienner Publishers, Inc.
1800 30th Street, Boulder, Colorado 80301

and in the United Kingdom by
Lynne Rienner Publishers, Inc.
3 Henrietta Street, Covent Garden, London WC2E 8LU

Library of Congress Cataloging-in-Publication Data
Kaplowitz, Donna Rich, 1962–
Anatomy of a failed embargo : U.S. sanctions against Cuba / Donna Rich Kaplowitz.
Includes bibliographical references and index.
ISBN 1-55587-616-1 (alk. paper)
1. Economic sanctions, American—Cuba. 2. United States—Foreign economic relations—Cuba. 3. Cuba—Foreign economic relations—United States. 4. United States—Commerce—Cuba. 5. Cuba—Commerce—United States. 6. Embargo. I. Title.
HF1500.5.U5K36 1998
337.7291073—dc21 97-32754
CIP

British Cataloguing in Publication Data
A Cataloguing in Publication record for this book is available from the British Library.

Printed and bound in the United States of America

The paper used in this publication meets the requirements of the American National Standard for Permanence of Paper for Printed Library Materials Z39.48-1984.

5 4 3 2 1

To my father,
Arthur Rich,
who was here at the beginning,
and whose passion for justice continues to inspire me

Contents

Acknowledgments

No work of this magnitude can materialize without substantial assistance from a great number of people. I am grateful to Wayne Smith, who first inspired me to conduct research on the Cuba sanctions a decade ago. Little did he know that he would ignite an interest that I will carry with me through my life. I am also indebted to Philip Brenner, who taught me how to sculpt my youthful indignation and passion for justice into scholarly work. Riordan Roett also helped me to cultivate my intellectual pursuits.

Parts of this work were made possible by research and travel grants from the Ford and Arca Foundations. Funding from the Cuban Studies Program at Johns Hopkins University and the Latin American and Caribbean Studies Program at Michigan State University also helped support my research.

Many government officials on both sides of the Florida straits have assisted in this work. Clara David of the U.S. Treasury Department has been a consistent and cheerful source of information over the years. Catherine Mann of the U.S. Treasury Department and Kathleen Scanlon at the U.S. Commerce Department were both interested in my research and eager to help.

Manuel Davis and Miguel Nuñez of the Cuban Interests Section helped facilitate my numerous trips to Havana, and never complained when I pestered them about my visas. In Cuba, I received assistance from too many people to name. The Foreign Trade Ministry, the Center for the Study of the United States (CESEU), the Center for the Study of the Americas (CEA), the Cuban Chamber of Commerce, and the Institute of Advanced International Relations (ISRI) were all extremely helpful in the preparation of this work.

Closer to home, family and friends gave me aid and comfort in countless ways. My brother-in-law Roger Gerstle read earlier versions of the manuscript despite the fact that his interests lie in far different horizons. My sister and brother, Marjorie Rich and Daniel Rich, entertained my children when I was computer-bound. Much appreciation goes to my grandmother, Ruth Shwam, whose genuine interest in the details of the embargo and skepticism over U.S. policy inspired me when I needed encouragement. Finally, my mother had the foolish sense to teach me that I could "do it all."

I am grateful to Kelly Campbell, Nitsan Kaplun, and most especially Missy Trimmer, who loved my babies while I spent long hours in my study, listening to Ariel and Andrew laugh on the other side of the door.

Last, but not least, I thank my husband, Michael Kaplowitz, for his tireless intellectual and personal support. His critical eye edited much of my writing, often in the wee hours of the morning when his own work was waiting and the children were temporarily asleep. Michael also spent more than his share of days and nights washing bottles, changing diapers, and fathering babies so that I could write. Finally, thank you Michael, for your fierce loyalty, and for believing, all along, that I could do it. Now it's your turn.

When you hear [a State Department official] explain what Cuba would have to do [to get the embargo lifted], that to me is what black folks had to answer in Mississippi when they had to take a test to vote. They asked them how many bubbles were in a bar of soap, and if they passed that, they went on to the next question. The goalpost has not just been moved forward. They have taken the goalpost away.

—Congressman Charles Rangel, March 17, 1994

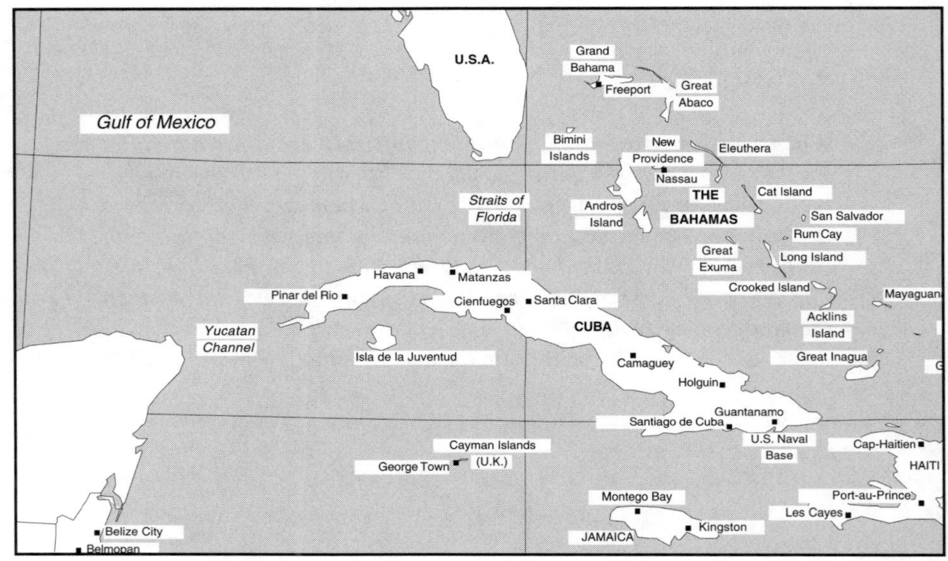

Cuba and Vicinity

1

Introduction

When the United States first imposed an embargo on Cuba, Dwight D. Eisenhower was president, more than half of the present population of Cuba was not yet born, and Bill Clinton was a teenager. Today, we find ourselves in a different world. Yet an embargo policy conceived more than a century ago remains in place. The Cuba embargo is considered a "model embargo" in its thoroughness. It has virtually denied Cuba access to the U.S. import and export markets; and it has often interfered with access to worldwide markets as well. Nevertheless, this most exhaustive of embargoes has failed to achieve many of its main goals, most importantly the ouster of Fidel Castro.

The Cuba embargo as a case study reflects the intricacies of the modern world. Embedded in the case are aspects of struggles for independence; complex relationships among national (Cuba), regional (OAS), and global (United Nations) sources of power; and both North-South (Cuba vs. the United States) and East-West (Cuba and the Soviet Union vs. the United States) tensions. It is particularly interesting because it includes both of the elements that gave rise to sanctions as a popular twentieth century policy tool: Cuba and the United States had an asymmetrically interdependent relationship before the advent of sanctions, and the two countries became opponents in the East-West conflict.

This book provides a comprehensive historical analysis of the U.S. embargo against Cuba and analyzes and explains *why* the embargo has failed to achieve its major foreign policy objectives, despite its impressive duration and exhaustive scope.

An Evolving Embargo

The U.S. sanctions against Cuba, initiated in 1960, are the second oldest ongoing U.S. embargo policy; only the embargo against North Korea, which began in 1950, predates the Cuba sanctions.[1] The U.S. embargo of Cuba has spanned more than three decades, ten U.S. presidents, and a changing international political and economic climate. The Cuba embargo has successfully prohibited virtually all direct and indirect commercial relations between individuals subject to U.S. jurisdiction and Cuba or its nationals for more than a third of a century. Furthermore, the U.S. sanctions policy has, during various incarnations, prevented trade between Cuba and much of the Western Hemisphere.[2]

There have been five distinct periods of the Cuba embargo.[3]

1. 1960–1962: development of unilateral U.S. embargo against Cuba.
2. 1962–1970: constant efforts at closing loopholes, and expanding the scope of the embargo to include hemispheric and global participation.
3. 1971–1980: brief effort at dismantling parts of the policy most offensive to allies and U.S. citizens.
4. 1981–1989: systematic tightening of the bilateral embargo.
5. 1989–1996: expanded efforts at globalization of embargo. Widespread anti-embargo sentiment among U.S. allies.

During the 1960s and early 1970s, the embargo was slowly but continuously strengthened until it became virtually absolute. By 1964, all imports, exports, and finance between Cuba and the United States were outlawed. The embargo became multilateral with the expulsion of Cuba from the Organization of American States (OAS) in 1962 and the subsequent OAS decision to join the United States in embargoing the island in 1964.

During the mid-1970s, there was a brief attempt at reconciliation between the two nations and a commensurate move toward dismantling parts of the sanctions policy. In 1975, the OAS, with tacit U.S. approval, lifted the regional ban on trade with Cuba. That same year, the United States significantly altered its sanctions policy by permitting trade between subsidiaries of U.S. corporations in third countries and Cuba. Two years later, President Carter lifted certain travel restrictions and paved the way for thousands of U.S. tourists to visit the island for the first time since the 1959 revolution.

The 1980 and 1984 elections of Ronald Reagan to the U.S. presidency and the 1988 George Bush victory were accompanied by a systematic tightening of the Cuba embargo. By the eve of President Bush's departure from office, the U.S. sanctions against Cuba were once again nearly complete. This was in good part due to the fact that Cuba became an issue in the 1991 presidential campaign. When then-candidate Bill Clinton announced his support for legislation tightening the embargo during a campaign stop in South Florida, President Bush was forced to follow suit lest he appear "soft on communism." Bush signed the Cuban Democracy Act into law in October 1992, ushering in a new era of effort to make the embargo span the globe. This period climaxed in 1996, when President Clinton signed the Helms-Burton legislation into law, further expanding the embargo extraterritorially.

In contrast to the U.S. extraterritorial embargo of the 1960s, during the more recent period the United States no longer enjoyed the support of regional or international organizations for its embargo policies. This change is best illustrated by the consistent United Nations votes condemning the embargo between 1992 and the present, and by the extensive international condemnation of the Cuban Democracy Act and the Helms-Burton bill.[4]

The Embargo's Objectives

Because the U.S. sanctions against Cuba have succeeded in blocking substantial trade with the island, the policy is often considered an example of successful *implementation* of a trade embargo. However, successful implementation does not necessarily correspond with successful attainment of policy goals. Sanctions theorists Gary Clyde Hufbauer and Jeffrey Schott, who have studied more than one hundred sanctions cases in recent history, write, "At most there is a weak correlation between economic deprivation and political willingness to change. The *economic* impact of sanctions may be pronounced, both on the sender and on the target, but other factors in the situation often overshadow the impact of sanctions in determining the *political* outcome."[5]

An important and probative question is whether the Cuba sanctions policy succeeded in achieving the goals for which it was invoked or any of the policy goals that were subsequently established for it. The objectives of the embargo have changed over time and have not always been obvious, even to Cuba scholars.[6] This book identifies six major foreign policy goals of the Cuba embargo: overthrow Castro, retaliate for nationalizations of U.S. property, contain the Cuban revolution, break Soviet-Cuban ties, demonstrate U.S. opposition, and change the internal situation in Cuba. Each objective, and the degree to which it has been achieved, are discussed in turn.

Overthrow

The primary and long-term goal of the embargo has been the ouster of Cuban President Fidel Castro.[7] The U.S. defeat at the Bay of Pigs in April 1961 led President John F. Kennedy to seek methods that did not rely solely on military force to oust Castro.[8] The Cuban economy seemed an obvious point of vulnerability for the new regime, particularly because Cuba had enjoyed extensive economic relations with the United States before the revolution. At the time of the embargo's implementation, U.S. policy planners believed that economic hardship resulting from an embargo would foment enough internal dissent to lead to Castro's ouster. Former U.S. Ambassador Philip Bonsal writes, "[The] new American policy . . . was one of overthrowing Castro by all the means available to the United States short of the open employment of American Armed Forces in Cuba."[9] *New York Times* correspondent Herbert Matthews reported that the United States calculated that Cuba "would suffer so greatly [under an embargo] that the Castro regime would be fatally weakened."[10] Likewise, Robert Hurwitch, who was serving at the time as the State Department's officer in charge of Cuban affairs, noted that policymakers hoped the effect of the embargo on the Cuban economy "might translate itself to open active opposition to the regime."[11]

Rather than inciting internal rebellion, however, the embargo proved to be a rallying point for the Cuban people. President Castro blamed the economic ills that the Cuban people suffered on the United States and thereby gained support for his own policies.[12] Clearly, almost forty years after the embargo was originally imposed, the objective of removing Castro from power has not been achieved.

Retaliation for Nationalizations

Another reason the United States invoked the embargo was to retaliate against Cuba's nationalizations of U.S. property and specifically to obtain a favorable settlement on some $1.8 billion in U.S. claims against the island.[13] (See Appendixes 3 and 4 on p. 212.) The U.S. State Department in 1960 announced that the embargo had been imposed to "defend the legitimate economic interests of [U.S.] citizens . . . against the aggressive, injurious and discriminatory policy of Castro's regime."[14]

However, rather than forcing the Cuban government to compensate U.S. citizens and settle their claims, the embargo virtually ensured that U.S. companies would not be paid. In order to reimburse the original owners of the nationalized property, Cuba had planned to issue bonds that could be repaid out of Cuba's annual export earnings from trade with the United States; the Cuban government estimated that 25 percent of these earnings would go to pay off claims.[15] The United States believed, however, that Cuba's proposal was insufficient. Since the early 1960s, Cuba has been prepared to negotiate the claims issue with the United States, but the United States has refused to discuss it.[16]

In 1996, in an effort to appease individuals with claims against Cuba, President Clinton expanded the embargo to include a provision that allows owners of properties confiscated in Cuba to sue, in U.S. courts, entities "trafficking" in those properties. This expansion of the embargo—aimed at indirectly damaging Cuba by punishing its foreign trading partners—has indeed dampened the foreign investment climate in Cuba, but it has also provoked widespread international condemnation of the embargo. Meanwhile, it has not compensated individuals who lost property on the island.

Containment

When it became evident by the mid-1960s that the Castro government was not going to collapse immediately under the pressure of the U.S. embargo, U.S. policymakers shifted the embargo objectives to *containment* of the Cuban revolution. Writing on Cuba in 1972, Lynn Bender noted that with the shift in goals from ouster to containment, the embargo's objectives became increasingly nebulous:

> Still absent was a clear definition of the *ultimate* goal pursued by U.S. policy toward the Castro regime—a problem that even today is yet to be fully and satisfactorily resolved. . . . The United States did come to the realization during this phase that the containment policy alone would not bring about the collapse of the Castro regime . . . but also harbored the expectation that, in the long run, its over-all policy would be effective in creating the necessary conditions for the *eventual* overthrow of Castro.[17]

The ultimate—if unstated—objective remained the ouster of the Castro government.

One of the specific goals subsumed by the containment objective was to deprive the Cuban government of hard currency earnings that could finance Cuba's "export of revolution."[18] In 1962, the U.S. Congress passed a joint resolution on this point, declaring, "The United States is determined to prevent by whatever means may be necessary, including the use of arms, the Marxist-Leninist regime in Cuba from extending, by force or the threat of force, its aggressive or subversive activities to any part of this hemisphere."[19]

Although the embargo has cost the Cuban government—by its own estimate—about $38–40 billion over the last three decades,[20] it did not prevent the Cubans from supporting revolutionary movements. On the contrary, Cuba was most active in supporting militant left-wing groups in Latin America during the early years of the U.S. embargo (1960–1968), which were the most difficult economically for Cuba. In fact, it may be argued that the U.S. embargo imbued Cuba's internationalist zeal with even greater urgency, born of Cuba's need to compensate for the perceived threat and concrete economic disturbance the embargo produced on the island.[21]

It is interesting to note that not only did the United States want to curb Cuba's efforts to export revolution, but the Soviet Union was also anxious to do so. Between 1962 and 1968, Soviet and Cuban foreign policies diverged over the question of support for revolutionary movements: Havana supported leftist movements while Moscow sought normal relations with all nations. Sergio Roca has commented, "Despite Moscow's leverage over Havana, the Cubans persisted on the *Camino Revolucionario* both at home and abroad. If Premier Castro managed, in large measure, to maintain his political and ideological independence from the Soviet Union, what degree of compliance with U.S. aims could Washington have expected?"[22]

Moscow was eventually more successful than Washington in exerting economic pressure on its wayward ally, using its "oil weapon" to bring Cuba back into the fold of current Soviet foreign policy, and to force Havana to tone down its anti-Soviet rhetoric. By the late 1960s, Cuba was heavily dependent upon the Soviet Union and virtually excluded from Western trade by the U.S. embargo. In late 1967 and early 1968 the Soviet Union capitalized on the island's economic vulnerability by delaying oil shipments to Cuba and postponing the 1968 annual trade agreement negotiations.[23] Political scientist Anna Schreiber concludes: "Soviet pressure on Castro has probably had more influence [than the U.S.] in limiting Cuban efforts to export revolution."[24] Indeed, for a number of years after the oil slowdown, Castro followed Soviet foreign policy wishes and was apparently rewarded. For example, in the Soviet trade pacts of 1969 and 1970, Cuba received better terms than it had previously.[25]

The nature and timing of Soviet success through a mere threat of economic sanctions suggests why the United States was unable to obtain its objectives after years of sanctions policy. First, the U.S. embargo faced great odds because Cuba was able to turn to another source, the Soviet Union, for most of its needs. Later, when Moscow threatened economic coercion, there was no other suitable nation to whom Cuba could turn.[26] Second, the Soviet Union had specific goals for its sanctions policy whereas the United States' goals were nebulous, changing, and difficult to obtain. Sanctions are most effective when goals are specific and focus on minor policy changes in the target nation.

Break Cuban-Soviet Ties

Another goal of the U.S. embargo was to increase the cost of and ultimately break Soviet-Cuban relations.[27] To be sure, the embargo did increase the cost of the Soviet-Cuban relationship; by 1979, Moscow's annual aid to Havana amounted to about 6 percent of its total hard currency exports.[28] By 1992, Moscow estimated that it had invested \$60 billion to \$80 billion in Havana since 1962, and that Cuba's debt to the Soviet Union was between \$20 billion and \$30 billion.[29] However, far from threatening Soviet-Cuban ties, the U.S. embargo locked Cuba more tightly into the Soviet Union's trade and assistance sphere. Moreover, the U.S. embargo of Cuba may have contributed to the deepening division between the superpowers and may have thus exacerbated the conditions leading up to the Cuban Missile Crisis. Schreiber notes: "U.S. economic coercion hastened the development of a clash between the superpowers over Cuba. . . . Castro provided the United States and the Soviet Union with a new arena in which to act out their potentially explosive antagonism. The missile crisis of October 1962 exemplified the dangers inherent in such a situation."[30]

During the early part of this decade, after the Soviet Union disintegrated into a loose confederation of independent states, the relationship between the former superpower and Cuba likewise disintegrated. This "break" in relations, however, has nothing to do with the U.S. embargo: Russian officials have said, in fact, that normalization of relations between the United States and Cuba would speed Russia's complete pullout from the island.[31]

Symbolism

Other analysts and policymakers argue that the primary goal of the Cuba embargo is *symbolic or demonstrative;* that is, to demonstrate to the Castro government, the U.S. public, and/or the world at large, U.S. opposition to the Cuban state.[32] Moreover, the embargo has functioned as a declaration of the belief of successive administrations in the right of the United States to exercise its influence in the affairs of Latin America—in a sense, a modernization of the Monroe Doctrine of 1823.[33] In 1964, Undersecretary of State George Ball commented that two of the goals of the embargo were symbolic: showing the Cuban people that Castro does not serve their interests, and demonstrating to the Western Hemisphere states that communism does not belong here.[34] More recently Ambassador José Sorzano reiterated the symbolic importance of the embargo in testimony before the U.S. Congress: "I believe that the purpose of the embargo is not to overthrow Castro. . . . Embargoes are symbolic measures that also have real impact. They are symbolic in the sense that they proclaim to the world United States repudiation of the practices of a particular regime."[35]

While the symbolic or demonstrative goal was probably an important objective early on in the embargo, with the passage of time it no longer seems compelling. The symbolic argument may simply be an excuse for those who seek to maintain a policy that has failed to achieve any of its other stated goals.[36] In fact, the embargo has done more to damage U.S. prestige than to demonstrate U.S. anticommunism.

When the embargo was initiated, U.S. policymakers hoped it would demonstrate to the young Cuban government the high level of U.S. enmity, thereby forcing a change in Cuban revolutionary policy favorable to U.S. interests. After more than three and a half decades, the Cuban government surely recognizes U.S. enmity but has not changed its policies as a result.

Rather than proving to the Cuban people that communism was not in their interest, as George Ball had hoped thirty years ago, the embargo appears to have cemented in their minds precisely the opposite: that the United States is not their friend. If it is primarily aimed at Cuba, the symbolic goal has long since lost its purpose.

Furthermore, if the embargo was invoked in response to demands by the U.S. public for retaliation against Castro three decades ago, this has become a moot point. In a 1988 Gallup poll, a plurality of those surveyed indicated that they favored reestablishing diplomatic and economic relations with Cuba.[37] Although the embargo has undoubtedly successfully served to placate a selective U.S. audience—principally, certain elements of the Cuban-American community who advocate tightening the embargo at every opportunity—the U.S. public as a whole appears to support normalization of relations with the island rather than heightened hostility.

As previously noted, one of the demonstrative or symbolic goals of a policy that punished Cuba was to demonstrate to other nations of the Western Hemisphere that their well-being required correct relations with the United States and maintaining distance from the Communist bloc. In the past three decades, revolutionary movements worldwide have come and gone; revolutionary governments in the Western Hemisphere have been born and have died.[38] There is little to suggest that the example the United States made of Cuba has had much impact on the emergence or disappearance of those movements. Although it probably had some tempering effects on the economic model pursued by the Sandinista government, certainly its impact on the Sandinista regime was not sufficient to make that government acceptable to the United States.

Finally, the embargo damaged U.S. prestige worldwide. In 1992, 1993, 1994, 1995, 1996, and 1997 the United Nations voted overwhelmingly to condemn the embargo.[39]

Theorist David Leyton-Brown has suggested that the symbolic "purpose for economic sanctions can be judged to have been fulfilled successfully if public opinion broadly supports the action, regardless of whether any other objectives are met."[40] In the Cuba case, any symbolic value the embargo may once have had is overwhelmed by the fact that the very existence of the policy has led to domestic disapproval and international condemnation.

Change Internal Situation in Cuba

In the 1990s, U.S. policymakers added a new objective for the U.S. embargo: to change the domestic situation in Cuba. In March 1990, Assistant Secretary of State Bernard Aronson enunciated new conditions for a change in U.S. policy toward the island: "If Cuba holds fully free and fair elections under international supervision, respects human rights and stops subverting e can expect relations between our two countries to ıntly."[41] This major policy shift was due in large part to the viet Union no longer existed as a threat to U.S. national ears about Soviet expansion through Cuba into Latin rthward to Texas, no longer rang true to the U.S. public. ıba's foreign policy had in large part ceased to be a threat to curity: Cuba pulled its troops out of Africa and focused on political and trade relationships with its former enemies. iticians had to find new reasons to justify the embargo.

go's raison d'être is now embedded in the Helms-Burton 996. Helms-Burton spells out twelve precise characteristics government in Cuba must demonstrate before the embargo

Failed Goals

Most Cuba scholars and sanctions theorists agree that the embargo has thus far failed to achieve its major foreign policy goals. According to Cuba scholar Jorge Domínguez, "In a broad strategic sense, U.S. policies toward Cuba have failed. Punitive U.S. policies toward Cuba have not deterred the Cuban behavior to which the United States objected, and have often rallied Cubans to support their government."[42] Sanctions expert Margaret Doxey concludes that "the general ineffectiveness of the [Cuba] embargoes has long been apparent."[43] Even U.S. congressmen acknowledge the failure of the embargo policy; the late congressman George Crockett, former chair of the Subcommittee on Western Hemisphere Affairs of the Committee on Foreign Affairs, has stated, "The economic embargo against Cuba has also been a failure. While it might have proved a hardship on the Castro Government at its inception, the Cubans have learned to live with the embargo—and to get around it—and it serves no purpose other than to leave that market to our Japanese and European competitors."[44]

A minority of analysts argue that the embargo has been effective, basing their arguments on the fact that it is difficult to measure "effectiveness." David Baldwin, a champion of this school, claims that the damaging impact of the embargo may have forced Castro to rearrange his priorities and focus on domestic development, thereby limiting Cuba's foreign adventurism.[45] Of course, it is impossible to know what Cuba's foreign policy would have looked like had the embargo never been invoked. Perhaps Castro would have been more ambitious; perhaps, on the other hand, he would have been more responsive to U.S. interests. Closer ties with the United States may have enticed Castro to stay within the United States' good graces. What *is* clear, though, is that the U.S. government did not believe that the sanctions were effective enough to be removed. The removal of sanctions is an indication that the sender nation believes the policy has been successful.

Hence, despite the thoroughness of the embargo as a policy instrument, the embargo has been highly ineffective in achieving its foreign policy goals. This work identifies and explores three main factors (and numerous secondary factors) that explain why the Cuba embargo failed to achieve its objectives: (1) Cuba was able to circumvent the embargo by turning to the Soviet Union; (2) Castro was able to develop effective countermeasures, most importantly by using the U.S. sanctions policy to rally national support; and (3) the goal of the sanctions policy (ousting Castro) was too difficult to achieve through an embargo policy.

The following chapters explore the embargo in depth. Each chapter examines the evolving domestic economic situation in Cuba, providing a historical analysis of the U.S. embargo against the island during each period in question.

Notes

1. The U.S. sanctions against Vietnam were also long term, dating back to 1975, but were lifted in early February 1994. See *New York Times,* February 3, 1994, p. A1; *New York Times,* January 29, 1995, p. A4.

2. Losman, *International Economic Sanctions,* p. 46; Doxey, *Economic Sanctions and International Enforcement,* Second Edition, p. 40.

3. The periodization in this book is the author's. Some Cuba scholars divide the embargo into five periods. Philip Brenner offers this breakdown: (1) 1960–1962: a de facto unilateral U.S. embargo; (2) 1962–1964: a de jure unilateral U.S. embargo; (3) 1964–1975: a multilateral hemispheric embargo, which in effect involved European countries; (4) 1975–1992: a unilateral embargo that was weak because of trade with third-country subsidiaries; (5) 1992–present: a strong unilateral embargo, but complicated by international hostility to the embargo. (Personal correspondence with the author, January 25, 1994.)

4. In 1992, 59 countries voted in favor of the Cuban resolution condemning the embargo, 3 voted against, 71 abstained, and 42 did not appear for the vote. See *CubaINFO,* Vol. 4, No. 14, December 4, 1992, pp. 1–2. See also *Cuba Business,* Vol. 7, No. 9, November 1993, p. 1. Every subsequent year, more countries voted with Cuba.

5. Hufbauer and Schott, *Economic Sanctions Reconsidered,* Second Edition, p. 94.

6. See Bender, *The Politics of Hostility,* pp. 26–27.

7. Brenner, *From Confrontation to Negotiation,* pp. 13–14. Brenner writes: "Thus the Eisenhower, Kennedy and Lyndon Johnson administrations in short order firmly planted the first two roots of U.S. policy toward revolutionary Cuba: overthrow the Cuban government and isolate it."

Zimbalist, "Dateline Cuba," p. 154. Zimbalist writes: "Since the beginning of the embargo in 1960, the United States has sought to depose the Castro government by imposing heavy economic costs on the Cuban people. That policy has been a failure for 33 years."

Ferro-Clerico and Smith, "The United States Trade Embargo," p. 82. Smith writes: "The U.S. had several objectives in moving toward and finally implementing a full trade embargo. First, beginning in March of 1960, the U.S. began to work for the downfall of the Castro regime."

See also Roca, "Economic Sanctions Against Cuba," p. 98; and Green, "Strategies for Evading Economic Sanctions," p. 68.

8. Schreiber, "Economic Coercion," p. 393.

9. Bonsal, *Cuba, Castro and the United States,* p. 135. Ambassador Bonsal was the last accredited U.S. ambassador to Cuba, serving there during the Castro regime to the break in relations on January 3, 1961. In fact, recently declassified documents on Operation Mongoose reveal that the United States had plans to use military force against Cuba through the mid-1960s.

10. Matthews, *The Cuban Story,* pp. 250–251.

11. Morley, *Imperial State and Revolution,* p. 192.

12. Schreiber, "Economic Coercion," p. 404. Schreiber writes: "The policy of economic coercion has given Castro a scapegoat to divert attention from internal problems and the errors of the regime. . . . The regime has made U.S. economic coercion a rallying point for the people as it attempts to bolster spirits and increase productivity."

13. This is a disputed figure. The Foreign Claims Settlement Commission presented this number to the U.S. Congress in 1972 based on 5,911 approved claims. The 1993 value, calculated at an annual interest rate of 6 percent, was $5.3 billion. This figure does not take into account Cuban counterclaims, which Cubans suggest would include U.S. compensation for damages arising from the embargo, the Bay of Pigs, and attacks by exile groups. This amounts to about $40 billion. See Foreign Claims Settlement Commission of the United States, *Final Report of the Cuban Claims Program;* and Ritter, "The Compensation Question: Who Compensates Whom, Why, How?"

14. "Text of the U.S. Announcement of Embargo," *The New York Times,* October 20, 1960.

15. R. Hart Phillips, "Castro Decrees Seizure of Rest of U.S. Property: Cites Cut in Sugar Quota," *New York Times,* August 8, 1960.

16. *The Economist,* "Cuba: Saying Boo to Helms-Burton," October 19, 1996, p. 49.

17. Bender, *The Politics of Hostility,* pp. 26–27.

18. Schreiber, "Economic Coercion," p. 403; Ferro-Clerico and Smith, pp. 80–81.

19. Public Law 87-733, quoted in Brenner, *From Confrontation to Negotiation,* p. 14. See also the 1964 statement by Undersecretary of State George Ball in which he outlines objectives of the embargo, including "to reduce the will and ability of the present Cuban regime to export revolution and violence to other American states." Quoted in Bender, *The Politics of Hostility,* p. 29.

20. Instituto de Investigaciones Económicas, Juceplan, *El Bloqueo Económico a Cuba,* p. 16. See also Zimbalist, "Dateline Cuba," pp. 155–156; *Cuba Business,* Vol. 7, No. 9, November 1993, p. 2; author's notes from McGill University—University of Havana, Conference on Cuban Foreign Trade, May 6, 1996, Havana, Cuba.

21. Schreiber, "Economic Coercion," p. 394; Ferro-Clerico and Smith, "The U.S. Trade Embargo," p. 82. For an opposing point of view, see Baldwin, *Economic Statecraft,* pp. 179–181.

22. Roca, "Economic Sanctions Against Cuba," p. 98.

23. For more information, see LeoGrande, "Cuban Dependency," p. 26.

24. Schreiber, "Economic Coercion," p. 403.

25. Ibid., p. 403.

26. Ibid., p. 402.

27. Ferro-Clerico and Smith, "U.S. Trade Embargo," pp. 80, 82.

28. Theriot, *Cuba Faces the Economic Realities of the 1980s* (Government Report), p. 18.

29. Juan O. Tamayo, "Russia Reverses Policy, Courts Cuba on Trade," *The Miami Herald,* October 10, 1992, p. 1A. Ernest Preeg notes that Cuba's debt to the Soviet Union is denominated in rubles. He calculates that in late 1992, the dollar value for Cuba's Soviet debt was less than $100 million. See Preeg, *Cuba and the New Caribbean Economic Order,* p. 40.

30. Schreiber, "Economic Coercion," pp. 394–395.

31. Nikolayenko, "An Official Statement of the New Soviet Policy in Latin America," p. 61. See also Schreiber, "Economic Coercion," p. 402.

32. Ferro-Clerico and Smith, "U.S. Trade Embargo," p. 80.

33. Schreiber, "Economic Coercion," pp. 394, 405.

34. Doxey, *Economic Sanctions and International Enforcement,* p. 41. See also Roca, "Economic Sanctions Against Cuba," pp. 88–89.

35. U.S. Congress, House. *Cuba and the United States: Thirty Years of Hostility and Beyond.* Statement of Ambassador José Sorzano, pp. 23–24.

36. Theorists Bienen and Gilpin warn about precisely this: "Sometimes policymakers claim the goals of a particular sanctions policy are symbolic in nature when, in fact, they are covering up a failed attempt at foreign policy goals." Bienen and Gilpin, "Evaluation of the Use of Economic Sanctions to Promote Foreign Policy Objectives, with Special Reference to the Problem of Terrorism and the Promotion of Human Rights," p. 3. (Note: This is an unpublished report in manuscript form, and not all the pages are numbered. On subsequent footnotes, if no page number is given, it is not oversight, but merely reflects that the manuscript does not have page numbers throughout.)

37. "A plurality of Americans (47 percent) favored restoring diplomatic and economic relations with Cuba. . . Forty-one percent of Americans opposed such a change with 13 percent uncertain." Also interesting is the fact that 63 percent of those polled did not think Cuba was a serious threat to U.S. security. See Christopher Marquis, "Poll: Most Back Bush's Cuba Stand, But 47 Percent Favor Restoring Ties," *The Miami Herald,* February 11, 1992, p. 1B.

38. Nicaragua and Grenada are examples of revolutionary governments. Most recently, the Zapatista movement in Mexico became an example of a revolutionary movement in the Western Hemisphere.

39. "U.N. Passes Cuban Resolution against U.S. Embargo," *CubaINFO,* Vol. 4, No. 14, December 4, 1992, pp. 1–2. See also *Cuba Business,* Vol. 7, No. 9, November 1993, p. 1; *CubaINFO,* Vol. 6, No. 14, November 3, 1994, p. 4; *CubaINFO,* Vol. 8, No. 15, November 21, 1996, p. 3; and *CubaINFO,* Vol. 9, No. 15, November 13, 1997, p. 1.

40. Leyton-Brown, *The Utility of Economic Sanctions,* p. 306.

41. Bernard Aronson, assistant secretary of state for inter-American affairs, testimony, U.S. Congress, *Cuba in a Changing World: The United States–Soviet–Cuban Triangle,* p. 93; *CubaINFO,* March 20, 1990, Vol. 2, No. 5, p. 1.

42. Domínguez, "Obstacles and Prospects for Improved U.S.-Cuban Relations: A U.S. Perspective," p. 24. See also Jorge Domínguez's statement before the U.S. Congress, *Cuba and the United States: Thirty Years of Hostility and Beyond,* pp. 43–44.

Other analysts have also concluded that the Cuba sanctions have not been effective. As Sergio Roca put it, "At present, the U.S. policy of containing Cuban support of international revolutionary activities by using economic sanctions appears to be futile. In general terms, Cuba is not harmed and U.S. interests are not advanced by the continued application of Washington's economic sanctions." Roca, "Economic Sanctions Against Cuba," p. 102.

Similarly, sanctions theorist Donald Losman concludes, "It would appear that American economic pressures have had little impact upon Castro's domestic orientation and his foreign policies despite its great economic effectiveness." Losman, *International Economic Sanctions,* p. 44. Anna Schreiber writes, "While the U.S. has achieved some of its objectives through the policy of economic coercion, it has failed to achieve others. Some of the effects of the policy have been clearly detrimental to U.S. interests." Schreiber, "Economic Coercion," p. 394.

43. Doxey, "Sanctions Revisited," p. 69.

44. Statement of Hon. George W. Crockett, Jr., U.S. Congress, *Cuba and the United States: Thirty Years of Hostility and Beyond,* p. 2.

45. Baldwin, *Economic Statecraft,* pp. 179–181.

2

Cuba: Ideal Climate for an Embargo?

When a victorious Fidel Castro entered Santiago on January 2, 1959, he told the crowd that this time there would be a *real* revolution for a just society. Referring back to Cuba's first experience with revolution in 1898 when the United States snatched victory from the victors, Castro said: "The Revolution will truly come to power. It will not be like in 1898, when the North Americans came and made themselves masters of our country. . . . For the first time the republic will be entirely free and the people will have what they deserve."[1] From Castro's first moment as leader of Cuba, he vowed to return Cuba to the Cubans.

Because there are numerous excellent volumes on Cuban history, a complete examination of U.S.-Cuban relations before the revolution will not be presented here.[2] A brief review highlighting key moments in the relationship follows, demonstrating that even before Cuba's birth as an independent nation and then through subsequent epochs, U.S. political interest and economic domination have shaped the Cuban experience.

Cuba is the largest island in the West Indies with a total area of 44,218 square miles. (See Appendix 1 on p. 210.) It stretches 745 miles from east to west and lies ninety miles off the U.S. coast at the entrance to the Gulf of Mexico. Consequently, it has always been of strategic interest to the United States. Thomas Jefferson called Cuba "the key to the Gulf of Mexico" and tried to purchase the island from Spain in 1808. In 1823, John Quincy Adams described Cuba as a ripening fruit that would inevitably fall into the lap of the United States. Cuba's importance to U.S. national interests, Adams asserted, was greater than that of any other foreign territory.[3]

As early as 1823, with President James Monroe's enunciation of his famous doctrine, U.S. influence shaped Cuba's political landscape. The Monroe Doctrine stated that the United States supports the political status quo throughout the New World. Thus, it defended the rights of the newly independent republics against foreign interference at the same time that it maintained the rights of Spanish domination over Cuba.

Since the early nineteenth century, the United States has tried many ways to acquire control over Cuba or to ensure its allegiance; the Cubans, however, have had other ideas. Cuba's first war of independence against Spain began in 1868. It raged for ten years and ended with the Treaty of Zanjon, which provided a brief peace but not independence. The second war for Cuban independence began in 1895 and is known in the United States by the telling misnomer "the Spanish-American war." The young Cuban poet and journalist José Martí led the struggle, not only for Cuba's independence from Spain, but for social justice and racial equality as well. Slavery had been abolished in Cuba in 1886, and the Cuban revolutionaries received support from the newly freed slave population. Martí also emphasized the need to free Cuba from any foreign power, be it Spain or the United States. Though he was killed in one of the first battles of the revolution, his death did not stop the independence movement, and Martí's ideas are still acclaimed in Cuba.

Under the guise of defending Cuban sovereignty, the United States wanted to fill the vacuum that would be created by the imminent Spanish defeat. The explosion of the *U.S.S. Maine* in the Havana harbor in February 1898 provided a rallying point for U.S. public support behind the Cuban independence movement, and Congress immediately voted to appropriate $50 million toward the war effort. Colorado Senator Henry M. Teller amended the declaration of hostilities to disclaim any intention to exercise sovereignty over the island. Thus, when U.S. forces entered the war on April 25, the stated objectives were to restore the peace and then to leave the government of the island in the hands of the Cuban people. These were welcome words to the Cuban revolutionaries, who had warned that without such a declaration of intent, they would fight the U.S. army as they fought the Spanish.

Relations between the U.S. and Cuban allies, however, were poor from the start. Many of the Cuban officers and soldiers were Afro-Cuban and the issue of race divided the allies. Theodore Roosevelt described the beleaguered Cuban forces as "a crew of as utter tatterdemalions as human eyes ever looked on . . . [who] would be of no use in serious fighting."[4]

Less than three months after the United States entered the war, the Spanish surrendered. A few days later, U.S. troops staged a victory parade in Santiago and did not invite Cuban troops to participate; in fact, the U.S. commander, General William R. Shafter, forbade Cuban forces from even entering the city. Six decades later, as Fidel Castro triumphantly entered Havana in January 1959, he noted, "There is no General Shafter here now to prevent our victory march."[5]

Cuba: A U.S. Protectorate

Though Cuba was theoretically granted full sovereignty after the war in accordance with the Teller Amendment, in fact the United States imposed protectorate status on the island and ruled it through proxy between 1901 and 1933. Shortly after the cessation of hostilities, Washington Senator Orville Platt introduced legislation allowing the United States to intervene in Cuba whenever it wished in order to protect life and property and "assure Cuban independence." In effect, the Platt Amendment gave the United States the right to determine Cuban foreign relations and domestic policy. The Cubans had little choice: either they accepted the Platt Amendment as an appendix to their constitution or U.S. military occupation would continue indefinitely. During Cuba's constitutional convention of 1901, though no one supported the Platt Amendment, the majority of those in attendance recognized that Cuba would have to bow to U.S. law and thereby win limited sovereignty or continue under foreign military rule.

U.S. domination has shaped Cuban history. As historian Ramon Eduardo Ruiz notes, "No Cuban nationalist has ever forgotten that humiliation. On the eve of independence, the Cuban had confronted truth: in theory he was a free man, but in practice he was a vassal of the United States. It was out of such experiences that Cuban attitudes toward the United States evolved."[6]

With U.S. protectorate status established, the United States immediately demanded and received a reciprocal trade agreement with the new Cuban government. During the three decades of protectorate status, Cuban presidents who ruled the island answered more to Washington than to Havana. U.S. investments in Cuba increased 536 percent from 1913 to 1928:[7] by 1929, U.S. interests in Cuba amounted to $1.5 billion, almost 30 percent of U.S. investments in all of Latin America.[8]

Fifty percent of American investments in Cuba were in the sugar industry; U.S.-owned sugar mills grew from 15 percent of Cuban production in 1906 to 75 percent by 1929.[9] Moreover, U.S. capitalists provided funds to expand the industry enormously. Annual sugar production rose from 300,000 tons at the time of Cuban independence to a record crop of 5.9 million tons in 1925.[10] By 1929, Cuba supplied 45 percent of the world's sugar and 50 percent of U.S. sugar imports.[11] The United States had become the most important market for Cuban exports and supplied 75 percent of Cuban imports.[12] U.S. bankers, managers, and technicians owned and operated the Cuban sugar industry.

Cuban sugar production expanded eighteen-fold in the first three decades of this century. But at what expense? As sugar increasingly dominated the Cuban landscape, Cubans were forced to import most of their food. Nearly all their rice, eggs, and poultry, and half their beans and meat came from abroad. Tomatoes, green peppers, cucumbers, and okra, grown domestically, were all for export.[13]

Cuba's reliance on the export of sugar had both positive and negative results. Cubans lost their status as landowners and now served predominantly as labor for international investors. At the time of independence, most Cuban land was in private domestic hands—land ownership was widespread. With the emergence of the sugar industry and its accompanying giant sugar mills, Cuban land slipped into the hands of foreign—mostly U.S.—enterprises. In fact, the unwieldy mills were so expensive to build and operate that even U.S. investors were forced to find financing from large bankers and from the stock-buying U.S. public. U.S. investors demanded a voice in the island's political affairs commensurate with their investments, and U.S. policy toward Cuba shifted from its original strategic concerns to the protection of U.S. property.[14]

As long as sugar sold well on the international market, the island prospered. Most economic indicators suggest that Cubans enjoyed a better standard of living than their Caribbean and Latin American neighbors. However, the price of sugar dropped from its high of 22.5 cents a pound in 1920 to less than one cent a pound in 1932.[15] Cuban sugar production dropped precipitously from over 5 million tons in 1925 to less than 2 million tons in 1932–1933, as a result of global depression, expanding sugar industries in Europe and Asia, and a U.S. tariff policy. The industrialists' response was to lower the wages of employees in the cane fields and factories.[15] Because other sectors in the Cuban economy were dependent on the sugar economy, almost all wages across the island therefore saw a commensurate decline. Dependence on a single crop brought the Cuban economy to its knees.

The Grau Revolution

President Gerardo Machado was elected to office in 1925 on a campaign promise to bring about the moral regeneration of the government and to fight for abrogation of the Platt Amendment. However, far from championing a new morality, the Machado government brought graft and corruption to new heights. Moreover, rather than challenging the Platt Amendment, it presided over the consolidation of foreign ownership of Cuban land.[17] Machado also had the unfortunate opportunity to rule Cuba during the years of world economic depression. A year after the 1929 Wall Street crash, Cuban foreign trade dropped to one-tenth its 1929 level, and U.S. bankers retreated from all major new investments on the island. Unemployment rose, and defaults and bankruptcies were common. In 1932 and 1933, Cuba's sugar income dropped by 75 percent of its total earnings during the 1920s.

Opposition to the unpopular president grew as economic conditions declined. In particular, Machado's opponents blamed Cuba's social injustices on its dependence on U.S. business interests.[18] In this volatile context, perceived as inhospitable to U.S. business, the United States eventually withdrew support for Machado.[19] This sequence of events, coupled with deepening social conflict and economic crisis on the island, led to Machado's ouster by a group of junior officers in the Cuban army, under the leadership of Colonel Fulgencio Batista. Machado resigned on August 12, 1933, flying into exile in possession of five revolvers and several bags of gold.

In the wake of the coup, Batista threw his support to Dr. Ramón Grau San Martín, a former University of Havana professor and chief of the Partido Revolucionario Cubano, also known as the Auténticos, who were committed to making an "authentic" Martíano revolution. Though Grau's tenure as president of Cuba lasted only 120 days, they were days that would change Cuban history. Grau proposed and enacted wide-ranging social and economic programs aimed at benefiting the island's working class. The eight-hour day, a minimum daily wage for cane cutters, the establishment of a Department of Labor, a reduction in electricity rates, and the initiation of an agrarian reform program were among Grau's efforts.[20] In addition, he denounced the Platt Amendment, purged Machado's followers from his government, and granted autonomy to the university.[21] Finally, Grau confronted U.S. business interests on a number of occasions. He suspended payments on an $86 million public works loan negotiated by the Machado government with Chase National Bank, and intervened in the enterprises of the Cuban-American Sugar Company.

Not surprisingly, the newly inaugurated Franklin D. Roosevelt administration in Washington was not enamored with Grau's changes. After three decades of U.S. investment in Cuba, U.S. investors controlled nearly two-thirds of the sugar economy, and held major interest in the telephone service, light and electrical services, and the banking industry. U.S. currency was the legal tender.[22] There was too much at stake for the United States to watch idly as Cuba continued on its reform course. U.S. businessmen asked Washington to intervene on their behalf.[23]

Claiming that Grau had "communistic tendencies," the Roosevelt administration refused to recognize his government and sent Sumner Welles as a special emissary to Cuba, charged with convincing Colonel Batista that Grau would never receive Washington's approval.[24] Moreover, Welles let it be known that once Cuba had a "stable" regime, the United States was ready to cancel the Platt Amendment and provide economic assistance. Batista, who did not want confrontation with the United States, forced Grau out of office and replaced him with Colonel Carlos Mendieta in January 1934.[25] Recognition from the United States came immediately.

Although Cuban nationalists charged that U.S. intervention had once again denied Cuban sovereignty, Grau's demise cannot be laid solely in the hands of the U.S. government. His brief regime had been unable to stabilize the downward economic spiral, restore political stability, or build a strong supporting coalition.[26] Grau's tenure was simply too abbreviated to suggest with any degree of certainty what course his government might have followed.

The Batista Era and a New Form of U.S. Involvement

The United States remained true to its word and abrogated the Platt Amendment after Grau fell. With the annulment of Platt, U.S. rights to occupy the naval base at Guantánamo Bay also ended. Nevertheless, a new treaty was negotiated and signed in 1934 that allowed the United States to rent the Guantánamo base until the treaty was abrogated or modified with the consent of both the United States and Cuba. In other words, the agreement allowed the United States to remain on Guantánamo until it decided it would be willing to leave.[27] The seeds of future conflict were sown into that treaty.

U.S. economic aid was soon forthcoming through the Jones-Costigan Act of May 1934, which assigned sugar quotas to foreign producers and granted Cuba approximately 28 percent of the U.S. market. The Reciprocity Act of August 1934 swiftly followed, with lowered tariffs on raw Cuban sugar and preferential treatment for thirty-five Cuban products. Conversely, the Cuban government gave preferential treatment to four hundred U.S. items. Such an arrangement limited possibilities for Cuban industrial development and discouraged agricultural diversification, except in those areas which did not involve competition with U.S. economic interests on the island.[28] Nonetheless, the Cuban economy did improve. Quotas and lower duties helped revive the stalled sugar economy. The United States profited as well; Cuban imports from the United States rose nearly 60 percent in 1934–1935.[29]

The underlying economic troubles besetting the island, however, remained unchanged. Nothing was done to diversify Cuba's monocrop economy, and Cuba's dependence on sugar deepened. Moreover, the few independent sugar producers remaining went bankrupt during the difficult years of the early 1930s, leaving intact only the giant mills backed by U.S. capital. Rather than becoming more autonomous, with the changes of 1934 Cuba became increasingly dependent on the United States.

Between 1934 and 1940, under Batista's tutelage, a series of puppet presidents ruled the Cuban island. They responded more often to

Washington's interests than to Cuban ones. Between 1934 and 1937, presidential power changed hands four times.[30]

In 1940, Batista ran for and won the presidential elections, under a coalition supported by the Communist party of Cuba and the Revolutionary Union Party. Batista ruled Cuba from 1940 to 1944 and again from 1952 until he was forced to flee in January 1959. Among the most significant events during Batista's first tenure was the creation and adoption of the Constitution of 1940, a document that emphasized the quest for social justice through economic reform. Though this constitution was one of the most progressive in Latin America—it went far beyond the revolution of 1933—it was stronger in general philosophy than on specific issues.

The Auténticos Take the Helm

Batista was defeated in 1944 with the election of his longtime political rival, Grau San Martín. Nevertheless, Batista left office confident that the former revolutionary movement had lost steam, and with the belief that his long tenure both behind the scenes and as executive left Cuba in a stable situation.

Grau came to office at the height of the wartime economic boom. Between 1942 and 1947 the United States purchased all Cuban sugar at a relatively high price and imposed low duties. Wartime prosperity only fed corruption, however, and the advent of the Cold War in Europe reverberated on the island with the crumbling of old coalitions. Grau's Auténtico party was not spared these divisions. The Auténticos had won power by coalescing with the Conservative Republican party and the Communist party, but in 1947 Grau broke ties with the Communists.[31]

Grau's second term proved to be the opposite of his first in nearly every way. Rather than being the reformer he attempted to be during his first term, he disregarded even the reforms he was authorized to make under the Constitution of 1940. Worse yet, he succumbed to traditional political avarice. Cuba's treasury was not bankrupt by the end of Grau's term only because Cuba's sugar harvests were good and world market prices for the crop were so high that, as Wayne Smith notes, "not even Grau could steal the money as fast as it came in."[32]

Despite Grau's corruption, his party won the elections of 1948 with the victory of Carlos Prío Socorrás. A new opposition party, the Ortodoxos, had been created in 1946, and though both parties emphasized the principles of social and economic development, the Ortodoxos also demanded a new administrative morality. Prío was not a newcomer to the Cuban political scene. He had spent his student days in the midst of the anti-Machado struggle, serving as secretary general of the Havana Directorio Estudiantil. He was founder of the Auténtico Party and had participated in the drafting of the 1940 constitution. Finally, Prío had served as secretary of labor under the previous Grau administration.

Prío governed the island during an important political juncture. The end of World War II revived the old problem of sugar overproduction, which, in combination with the appearance of new sugar producers in the international market, threatened the Cuban economy. Faced with these challenges, Prío proved incapable of any real change, and his tenure was marked more by mismanagement and graft than anything else.[33]

The Cuban sugar quota became Washington's preferred diplomatic weapon to force resolution of bilateral economic disputes during the Auténtico Party's tenure. The U.S. executive branch cajoled the U.S. Congress into allowing it to manipulate the sugar quota for political purposes. Morris Morley, a political economist, notes: "American economic aggression culminated in Section 202(e) of the Sugar Act of 1948 which allowed the Secretary of State to change the sugar quota of any country that 'denies fair and equitable treatment to the nationals of the United States, its commerce, navigation or industry.'"[34] Though the bill was repealed within a year, it foreshadowed Washington's proclivity to turn to economic warfare when dealing with its closest island neighbor.

Batista Returns, 1952–1958

If the Cuban people got political change in 1952, it was probably not exactly what they had envisioned. Fulgencio Batista returned from retirement on Key Biscayne to run for president and, three months before the election, staged a bloodless coup d'etat ensuring his victory and sealing Cuba's fate with his own. President Prío and his cabinet went into exile in Miami without protest within several hours of Batista's coup. Batista quickly declared himself provisional president and appointed his men to all the high military posts. In his official explanation for the coup, Batista said he had evidence that Prío was preparing to steal the elections. Batista, however, never explained why elections were not held after he became provisional president. Cuba became a classic Latin American military dictatorship.

The second Batista regime quickly proved to be nothing like the first—resembling, in fact, the Machado dictatorship more than the Batista government of the 1940s. First, Batista suspended the constitution and dissolved all political parties. Additionally, to secure U.S. support, he adopted a McCarthyite position on communism. He drove the local Communists underground with the creation of a Bureau for the Repression of Communism (BRAC), and he broke relations with the Soviet Union.[35] Needless to say, this played well in Washington and pleased the local conservatives. If much of Cuba acquiesced to Batista's seizure of power in

1952, his growing hardline tactics led over time to increasing popular discontent on the island.

Enter: Fidel Castro

Public opposition to Batista was centered in the hands of Fidel Castro, who in 1952 was a young lawyer, fresh out of the university, and full of youthful idealism. Angered that Batista never allowed the elections of 1952 to take place, Castro vowed to see a return to democracy on the island. He led the Cuban revolution's opening battle with the July 26, 1953, guerrilla attack on the Moncada Barracks in Santiago, Cuba. Though the Moncada assault was a military failure, and though most of the revolutionaries involved were either killed in the conflict or imprisoned, the battle is remembered as a political victory. Through it, Fidel Castro was able to gain widespread support and recognition, defending himself at his trial with the historic speech that became a rallying cry for revolution: "History Will Absolve Me."

By the time Castro and his followers attacked the Moncada Barracks, the Cuban population had become disillusioned with the Batista regime. Government corruption had reached new heights and organized crime from the United States had found hospitable territory on the island. Most of Havana's main nightclubs, in fact, were under mob control. Once recognized as a "populist," Batista was increasingly viewed as a corrupt military dictator more interested in appeasing U.S. business interests than in improving the lot of the majority on the Cuban island. Castro, therefore, had little trouble gaining support for his movement. As he served his jail term on the Isle of Pines, backing for his release mounted. On May 6, 1955, Batista made a serious mistake: he allowed Castro and his fellow revolutionaries to be released from prison. For the next seventeen months, Castro and more than a hundred followers—including the famous Argentine doctor Ernesto "Che" Guevara—lived in self-imposed exile in Mexico. There, the revolutionaries plotted their return to Cuba and trained for the battles ahead.

Castro mounted his return to Cuba, as promised, before the end of 1956. However, the revolutionaries once again met with military failure: their yacht, *Granma,* got lost in the midst of bad weather, and worse yet, Batista's army awaited them upon their arrival in Cuba. The fourteen survivors of the *Granma* headed for the Sierra Maestra, where local peasants aided them in regrouping and gaining strength. Though Batista announced he had squashed the opposition, Castro used *New York Times* reporter Herbert Matthews to send out the message that the movement had considerable strength. Castro duped Matthews into believing he had a large contingent of followers by marching the same group of men past Matthews numerous times. Matthews then published articles in the *Times* indicating that Castro had considerable support. International and domestic aid flowed to Castro as a result. By mid-1957, Ché had opened up a front in the central Sierra Maestra, and in early 1958, Raúl Castro led a group to the Sierra Cristal mountain range. Meanwhile, Juan Ameida opened up yet another front in the eastern ranges of the Sierra Maestra, and Camilo Cienfuegos moved toward Havana.

Batista unwittingly aided the revolutionary effort by increasing repression on the general populace. He arrested thousands of young people, and tortured many. The more repressive Batista became, the more support Castro could count upon. Wayne Smith, then third deputy in the U.S. embassy in Cuba, reported that "by the end of 1958, it is fair to say that 95 percent of the Cuban population was in opposition to Batista."[36] Two years later, Fidel Castro marched triumphantly into Havana, a hero among a majority of the Cuban population.

U.S. Policy Toward Batista

While initially tentative, the United States greeted Batista's coup d'etat with sympathy. Impressed with Batista's promises to attract private foreign capital and his strong anticommunist sentiment, the United States offered formal diplomatic recognition almost immediately. Shortly thereafter, however, U.S. government misgivings began to grow. The level of corruption in Batista's government soon eclipsed that of his predecessors, which led U.S. Treasury and State Department officials to express their concern. U.S. economic interests on the island, however, overshadowed U.S. government distress over Batista's fiscal and monetary policies, and for the most part the U.S. government was willing to turn a blind eye toward Batista's debauchery.[37] Moreover, Ambassador Earl T. Smith (1957–1959), an Eisenhower political appointee, was closely aligned with U.S. business interests on the island and therefore vociferously opposed decreasing U.S. support for Batista.

In Morley's careful review of U.S. government documents from the period, he notes that in 1957 divisions increasingly arose within the U.S. government—both on the island and in Washington—about how to deal with the growing Cuban guerrilla movement. The U.S. consulate in Santiago mirrored U.S. business's concern about the growing threat from the revolutionaries, advocating the evaluation of new strategies to deal with possible future events. The U.S. embassy in Havana, on the other hand, preferred to look the other way. Similar divisions plagued Washington. The Pentagon advocated an interventionist position if necessary to prevent a guerrilla victory, in contrast to the State Department's desire to maintain diplomatic relations with the island without meddling in Cuba's domestic difficulties. The Treasury Department, meanwhile, was increasingly disgruntled about Batista's balance of payments problems and spiraling inflation.[38]

Only in early 1958, on the eve of the revolution, did Washington realize the degree of support enjoyed by the opposition movement in Cuba and undertake a serious reconsideration of policy. At that point Castro counted a wide range of interest groups among his followers, including such strange bedfellows as conservative businesspeople and nationalist guerrillas. Evaluation of the situation led Washington to recognize that some action was needed to secure U.S. interests on the island in the face of increasing social turmoil. From the start, however, U.S. decisionmakers disagreed both on the goal and the methods to achieve it.

Most U.S. policymakers believed that Batista had become a liability for U.S. interests on the island. There was also unanimity in Washington against Castro's rise to power. In order to get rid of Batista while prohibiting a guerrilla victory, a plan evolved to aid the creation of an interim or transitional government composed of anti-Castro and anti-Batista forces. Much debate ensued, however, over specific methods and timeframes to achieve this plan. Hesitant to take any action that would be considered "intervention" in Cuban affairs, the State Department bypassed one opportunity after another in early 1958 to openly express the belief that Batista should resign, or even to lend support to those on the island who called for a transitional government.[39] Instead, the United States chose to publicly place full confidence in the elections scheduled for November 1958.

The U.S. government was divided as well on the actual composition of an interim government. Ambassador Smith believed that people linked to Batista should be able to remain in power, while the State Department thought that only a total housecleaning of all Batista associates would be acceptable in Cuba. Wayne Smith notes: "Ambassador [Earl] Smith and the Department of State thus proceeded from different assumptions and worked toward different goals. They continued to do so, thwarting one another's efforts, until it was too late to do anything but watch Castro march into Havana."[40] The disagreement stymied U.S. action. With Castro gaining support daily, however, Washington had to do something concrete to turn the increasingly untenable situation around.

Debate crystallized around the imposition of an arms embargo against Batista. The Cuban military had long been dependent on the United States for support; by the end of Batista's tenure, Cuba had received more than $16 million in military equipment and arms, and the Cuban armed forces also received training from the U.S. military.[41] Since U.S. military involvement on the island was so intense, and since the Batista forces used U.S.-supplied military equipment against the Cuban population, military aid became the logical fulcrum from which to exert pressure. However, the Department of Defense argued with the State Department over imposition of an arms embargo on ideological and strategic grounds. Taking account of Cuba's strategic location, Batista's support for U.S. regional and global policies, and the possibility that an arms embargo could foreshadow serious rupture between the two countries, the Pentagon concluded that good relations should be maintained at any cost. The State Department, on the other hand, believed that U.S. interests—primarily the protection of U.S. business concerns on the island—were gravely threatened under current conditions and would best be insured by avoiding "an explosion."[42] The State Department carried the day, and on March 14, 1958, an arms embargo was announced.

The arms embargo was little more than a public slap on the wrist for Batista, which is probably all it was intended to be. In fact, the U.S. government was so ambiguous about its policy that its military mission in Havana remained after the imposition of the embargo to train Batista's troops in their "final offensive" against the guerrillas. The Cuban military forces in any case did not need extensive U.S. aid to wage guerrilla warfare; they far outnumbered Castro's forces, they were better armed and equipped than their opposition, and whatever weapons they did not have could be purchased on the international arms market.

What they could not purchase, however, and what they needed most, was common sense and commitment. On the matter of commitment, Wayne Smith notes, "[t]he common Cuban soldier became increasingly demoralized as he realized he was fighting for an unpopular cause and defending a dictator whose corrupt system was hated by the vast majority of Cubans."[43] And so lacking in common sense was Batista's army that in December 1958, at the very end of the war, it sent an armored train to fight the rebels in Las Villas. Even a civilian could figure out that you cannot conduct effective warfare against a guerrilla army from a train bolted to its tracks.

The embargo, then, was not Batista's most serious handicap. To be sure, he was irritated by the embargo, and it certainly did not *help* him retain support among the Cuban populace. But the goal of the embargo was never in any event to shift the balance of forces in Cuba to favor the Cuban guerrillas. On the contrary, it was a haphazard policy constructed in the midst of a crisis, pulled and tugged by a government divided over its own goals. The State Department had to take some action to publicly portray its "concern" about the volatile situation near its border, and the 1958 arms embargo against Cuba suited this purpose. Unfortunately, it completely failed to help produce an interim government in Cuba friendly to U.S. interests but not aligned with either of the warring parties.

Revolutionary victory in Cuba cannot be blamed, however, on a poorly executed U.S. policy. Castro's success was probably inevitable by the time the United States took action. It is fair to say, though, that if anything, the embargo aided Castro's cause. Worse yet, the failed U.S. policy toward Batista foreshadowed a poorly conceived and poorly executed embargo policy in the decades to follow.

Ambivalence and lack of clarity characterized U.S. policy right through Batista's final days. Stuffed ballot boxes and tombstone votes gave Batista's candidate Rivero Aguero a hollow victory in the November elections. Faced with blatant fraud, Washington ordered Ambassador Smith to inform the Cuban government that U.S. support for the president-elect would depend upon the new government's ability to win acceptance among broad sectors of the Cuban populace. More importantly, Smith was to convey Washington's doubts that any internal solution could be worked out as long as Batista was in the country. The implicit directive that Batista resign should have been clear. However, Ambassador Smith declined to deliver the instructions, and in fact sent telegrams to Batista and Rivero congratulating them on their victory.[44] The U.S. directive was only conveyed after Ambassador Smith returned to Washington for consultations (presumably about the instructions), at which point Deputy Chief of Mission David Braddock, acting in Smith's place during his absence, communicated the message. Finally, upon his return to Havana, on December 17, 1958, Ambassador Smith himself let Batista know he could no longer count on U.S. support. Batista fled the island less than two weeks later, just after midnight on January 1, 1959.

Cuba in 1959

The Cuba Fidel Castro inherited was not terribly poor relative to conditions generally in Latin America; Cuba had been among the top three Latin American countries in living standards in 1950. The essential problem was that Cuba had become a static society. Cuba's GNP was roughly the same level in 1950 as it had been in 1925, because population had increased while sugar production had not. The stagnant economy led to widespread frustration and a commensurate desire to rejuvenate the island.[45] The Castro government attempted to do this through radical transformation. What follows is a sectoral analysis of Cuba at the time of the revolution.

Income and Land Distribution

Though statistics indicate that Cuba was well off relative to other Latin American countries, gross inequalities in Cuban income distribution produced this impression, masking the difficult situation endured by the majority of the Cuban population in the 1950s. For example, Cuba's per capita income in the 1950s was about $500—higher than all other Latin American countries except oil-exporting Venezuela. However, in 1958, 9 percent of all farm owners possessed 62 percent of the land, while 66 percent of the population owned 7 percent of the land.[46] Landless farm workers and their families constituted the majority of the rural population—just over a third of the country's 7 million people in the mid-1950s—and they earned 5 to 10 percent of the national income.[47] Historian Hugh Thomas illustrates the disparate income distribution by estimating that there were more millionaires in Cuba, per capita, than in any other country in Latin America, and that in 1954, more Cadillacs were sold in Havana than in any other city in the world.[48]

Education

Cuba's education system in the 1950s was dismal. According to sociologist Nelson P. Valdés, a quarter of the Cuban population was illiterate; illiteracy in rural areas reached 42 percent, whereas in urban areas it was only 12 percent.[49] Valdés also notes that Cuba had a higher percentage of children enrolled in primary school in 1923 than in the mid-1950s, when Cuba occupied seventeenth place in primary school enrollment in all of Latin America. At that time, more than half of the total population of the island had never gone to school beyond the third grade.

Health Care

Inequalities in health care availability mirrored those in income distribution and education. Though Cuba had the highest ratio of hospital beds to population in the Caribbean, 80 percent of them were in the city of Havana. Similarly, more than 60 percent of all physicians in 1958 practiced in Havana, where there was one doctor for every 420 people. In Oriente province, on the other hand, each doctor served 2,550 people.[50] Not surprisingly, 91 percent of the Cuban rural population suffered from malnutrition in 1956.[51] The infant mortality rate in Cuba in 1958 was 33 per 1000 live births.[52]

Housing

The rural-urban divide was also reflected in housing distribution at the time of the revolution. In the mid-1950s, 63 percent of all homes were located in urban areas, while 57 percent of the population lived in cities.[53] Sixty-two percent of all Cuban homes had thatched roofs and dirt floors, and 53 percent had no baths. Nine percent of the rural homes had electricity, compared with 87 percent of urban homes. Ninety-six percent of rural homes had no refrigeration, while 62 percent of urban homes lacked refrigeration. Two percent of the rural population had running water in their homes; 55 percent of urban households had this convenience.[54]

Land Cultivation

In the late 1950s, sugar dominated the Cuban economy, as it had for the first half of the century. Sugar companies controlled 75 percent of all

Cuban land and kept two-thirds of their land uncultivated. Sugarcane was planted on more than half of the land that was under cultivation. In the harvest season sugar companies employed about 25 percent of the island's labor force (between 400,000 and 500,000 workers), leaving all but 25,000 of them unemployed during the remaining eight months of the year. Sugar and its by-products constituted about 25 percent of Cuba's GNP.[55] Cuba's sugar yields were notoriously low: of the eighteen top sugar-producing nations, Cuba ranked seventeenth.[56] Because so much land was devoted to sugar, Cuba imported almost a third of the food it consumed—including such staples as rice, lard, vegetable oils, beans, potatoes, dairy products, eggs, vegetables, fruits, fish, poultry, and pork. Food constituted one-quarter of Cuba's total imports in 1954.[57]

Sugar and its by-products (primarily alcohol and molasses) accounted for 84 percent of Cuba's total exports. Tobacco, minerals, and coffee accounted for most of the remaining 16 percent.

Cuban GNP

The Cuban National Bank reported that during the period 1950–1958 the Cuban GNP grew at an average rate of 4.6 percent annually. According to these figures, the increase in inflation-adjusted GNP per capita was about one percent during the 1950s.[58] Therefore, the Cuban economy showed slow growth in the immediate prerevolutionary period.

Cuban Economy Vulnerable to Sanctions

The situation described above made Cuba highly vulnerable to a U.S.-initiated policy of economic sanctions. A target state is considered particularly vulnerable to sanctions if: (1) the sender nation controls a particularly important commodity for the target nation; (2) the sender nation imports a large percentage of the target's important export; (3) the target is dependent on one or a few export items; and (4) if the target economy is highly dependent on foreign trade.[59] All of these factors characterized the Cuban economy and made it vulnerable to U.S. economic coercion. They are examined in detail below.

U.S. controls important commodity. Edward Boorstein, a scholar of the Cuban economy during its nascent revolutionary stage, writes that the central economic fact about Cuba prior to the revolution was neither Cuba's dependence on sugar, nor the monopoly of the *latifundia,* nor the weakness of the industrial system, but the overwhelming domination of the economy by U.S. companies.

The data supports Boorstein. U.S. investment in Cuba just prior to the revolution was "possibly the second largest in Latin America," according to Mesa-Lago.[60] Embargo theorists have found that if the sender nation accounts for at least a quarter of the target's total trade, the chances of embargo success are greater. In the decade preceding the Cuban revolution, about two-thirds of Cuba's foreign trade was with the United States, by this measure rendering Cuba exceptionally vulnerable to U.S.-instigated economic aggression.[61] Cuba imported 60 to 65 percent of its total needs from the United States at an average annual cost of $428 million.[62] By 1955, almost 69 percent of Cuba's exports went to the United States. Moreover, in that same year, U.S. interests on the island produced about 40 percent of Cuba's raw sugar; U.S. companies controlled over 90 percent of Cuban public utilities; and U.S. capital controlled about 50 percent of the public service railways. U.S. branch banks, furthermore, held 25 percent of all bank deposits.[63] Not surprisingly, Cuba's dependence on U.S. suppliers led to a negative trade balance. By 1958, its cumulative trade deficit was $374 million.[64]

In sum, at the time the embargo was originally invoked, the United States had a high degree of control over the supply of most Cuban imports, rendering the island vulnerable to external economic pressures.

U.S. imports large percentage of Cuban export. By the mid-1950s, more than two-thirds of Cuba's exports went to the United States.[65] In 1958, the United States purchased 58 percent of Cuba's annual sugar exports alone.[66] Furthermore, U.S. sugar quota policies determined the health of the Cuban economy from year to year. Benjamin, Collins, and Scott note that the U.S. quota was key to the Cuban economy: "Every year the U.S. Congress made the single most important decision to the Cuban economy—the 'quota' of Cuban sugar that could be imported into the U.S. market at the relatively high prices of the U.S. domestic producers. . . . Cuba's economy was not only dependent on a single crop but on a single customer."[67]

Hence, by any measure, the United States imported a large percentage of Cuba's most important export, sugar. At the time the embargo was originally invoked, the United States constituted a critical market for Cuba, rendering Cuba ostensibly vulnerable to an embargo policy.

Cuba: A monocrop economy. The Cuban economy has always been focused on the export of sugar. Cuba has always ranked as *the,* or one of the, world's leading sugar exporters.[68] In the forty years prior to the Cuban revolution, sugar and its by-products (primarily alcohol and molasses) accounted for more than 80 percent of Cuban exports. For example, out of total export earnings of $617.3 million in 1960, sugar contributed $467.5 million—more than 75 percent—while tobacco, the next most important export, contributed only $63 million.[69] The Cuban economy was focused on the export of a single item and was therefore, in this regard as well, vulnerable to sanctions.

Cuba's dependent economy. As a typical developing nation, Cuba has always been highly dependent on foreign trade. This dependence was exaggerated in the Cuba case because so much of Cuba's land was devoted to the cultivation of an export crop, sugar. Hence, before the revolution and continuing to the present, Cuba has had to import much of the food, petroleum, and industrial products it requires.[70]

Between the mid-1950s and the 1960s, annual imports equaled from 22 to 32 percent of Cuban GNP, while exports accounted for 16–31 percent.[71] In 1958, for example, more than 57 percent of Cuba's GNP went to foreign trade. In comparison, in other small, medium-income Latin American countries, imports comprised approximately only 25 percent.[72] To further put Cuban trade into perspective, U.S. imports and exports as a percent of GNP amounted to less than 10 percent.[73] Highly dependent on foreign trade, Cuba was therefore by this criterion also vulnerable to economic sanctions.

Relationship Between Cuba and the U.S. Further Suggests Sanctions Success

Cuba was also vulnerable to a policy of economic sanctions based on its relationship to the United States prior to the embargo. Sanctions theorists have noted that the greater the differential of the GNP between the sender and the target, the greater the chance of embargo success: a ratio greater than 50 to 1 significantly improves chances of a successful embargo. The ratio of the U.S. GNP to Cuba's GNP at the time the embargo was originally invoked was 173 to 1.[74]

In addition, sanctions invoked against allies have a greater chance of success than those imposed on adversaries.[75] Prior to the Castro regime, the United States was involved in nearly every aspect of Cuban government, beginning from Cuba's birth as a nation-state. Though the client-state relationship was fraught with antagonisms typical of such arrangements, the level of involvement between the two states could be classified only as "friendly."[76]

Conclusion

From this brief examination of the Cuban economy prior to the invocation of U.S. sanctions, it is evident that Cuba was highly vulnerable to economic aggression from the United States. The United States provided more than 60 percent of Cuba's imports prior to the sanctions, thereby controlling the supply of many essential goods. At the same time, the United States imported more than two-thirds of Cuba's exports, rendering Havana dependent on U.S. purchases. Significantly, the United States consumed more than half of Cuba's most important export: sugar. This domination was reinforced by the fact that the U.S. Congress set the Cuban sugar quota annually, furthering Cuba's dependence on the United States. Finally, Cuba's vulnerability was enhanced through its status as a close ally of the United States prior to the invocation of the embargo; Cuba had more to lose from a U.S.-sponsored embargo than from economic aggression by any other nation. For all of these reasons, then, the Cuban economy was a logical point upon which the United States could exert pressure to effect change on the island. Nevertheless, other factors proved to have far more influence on the course of events than the raw economic data provided above. The following chapters demonstrate how the actors involved proved crucial in shaping the outcome of the embargo.

Notes

1. Smith, *Portrait of Cuba,* pp. 51, 86.
2. See, for example, Lou Perez, *Cuba Between Empires, 1878–1902* (Pittsburgh: University of Pittsburgh Press, 1978); Philip Foner, *A History of Cuba and Its Relations with the United States,* two volumes (New York: International Publishers, 1962 and 1963); Thomas, *Cuba: Pursuit of Freedom;* Ruiz, *Cuba: The Making of a Revolution;* Smith, *The United States and Cuba: Business and Diplomacy, 1917–1960.*
3. Smith, *Portrait of Cuba,* p. 41.
4. Quoted in ibid., p. 51.
5. Ibid., p. 51.
6. Ruiz, *Cuba: The Making of a Revolution,* p. 33.
7. Smith, *The United States and Cuba,* p. 29.
8. Ibid., p. 29.
9. Smith, *The United States and Cuba,* p. 29.
10. Ruiz, *Cuba: The Making of a Revolution,* p. 42.
11. Smith, *The United States and Cuba,* p. 175.
12. de Lima-Dantas, "Historical Setting," p. 27. See also Morley, *Imperial State and Revolution,* p. 32.
13. Ruiz, *Cuba: The Making of a Revolution,* pp. 45–46.
14. Ibid., p. 50.
15. Ibid., pp. 48–49.
16. Morley, *Imperial State and Revolution,* p. 33.
17. See Smith, *The United States and Cuba,* pp. 120–136.
18. de Lima-Dantas, "Historical Setting," p. 29.
19. Smith, *The United States and Cuba,* pp. 146–147; Ruiz, *Cuba: The Making of a Revolution,* p. 87.
20. Morley, *Imperial State and Revolution,* p. 34.
21. de Lima-Dantas, "Historical Setting," p. 31.
22. Ruiz, *Cuba: The Making of a Revolution,* p. 93.
23. Ibid., p. 93.

24. Smith, *The United States and Cuba,* pp. 154–155.
25. Smith, *Portrait of Cuba,* p. 60.
26. Ruiz, *Cuba: The Making of a Revolution,* p. 85.
27. Smith, *The United States and Cuba,* pp. 156–157.
28. Ruiz, *Cuba: The Making of a Revolution,* p. 95; Morley, *Imperial State and Revolution,* p. 36.
29. Ruiz, *Cuba: The Making of a Revolution,* p. 95.
30. de Lima-Dantas, "Historical Setting," p. 32.
31. Ibid., p. 34.
32. Smith, *Portrait of Cuba,* p. 66.
33. Morley, *Imperial State and Revolution,* pp. 36–37; de-Lima Dantas, "Historical Setting," p. 34.
34. Morley, *Imperial State and Revolution,* p. 38.
35. Ruiz, *Cuba: The Making of a Revolution,* p. 111.
36. Smith, *Portrait of Cuba,* p. 84.
37. Morley, *Imperial State and Revolution,* p. 56.
38. Ibid., p. 57.
39. In February 1958, the Cuban bishops had approached Ambassador Smith for U.S. support in their endeavor to try mediation between Batista and Castro. U.S. support was denied. A month later, the Cuban Joint Committee of Civic Institutions—composed of forty-two religious, professional, and fraternal organizations—issued a statement demanding Batista's resignation and the imposition of an interim government. Once again, the United States refused to lend support to the joint committee's statement. For more details, see Smith, *The Closest of Enemies,* pp. 22–23.
40. Smith, *The Closest of Enemies,* p. 21.
41. Morley, *Imperial State and Revolution,* p. 58.
42. Ibid., p. 61.
43. Smith, *Portrait of Cuba,* p. 84.
44. For a thorough discussion of these events, see Smith, *The Closest of Enemies,* p. 35.
45. Thomas, *The Cuban Revolution,* p. xxiii.
46. Chonchol, "El primer bienio de reforma agraria (1959–1961)," p. 469, and cited in Benjamin, Collins, and Scott, *No Free Lunch,* p. 3.
47. Leyva, "Health and Revolution in Cuba," p. 458.
48. Thomas, *Cuba: The Pursuit of Freedom,* p. 1107.
49. Valdés, "The Radical Transformation of Cuban Education," p. 423.
50. Goldston, *The Cuban Revolution,* p. 58, cited in Leyva, "Health and Revolution in Cuba," p. 472.
51. Leyva, "Health and Revolution in Cuba," p. 458.
52. Leyva notes that this number is deceptively low because Cuban statisticians before the revolution failed to record infants who died before they were registered as born. Leyva, "Health and Revolution in Cuba," p. 490.
53. Koth, *Housing in Latin America,* p. 32, cited in Leyva, "Health and Revolution in Cuba," p. 465.
54. Much of this information comes from Leyva, "Health and Revolution in Cuba," pp. 464–469.
55. Boorstein, *The Economic Transformation of Cuba,* p. 2.
56. MacEwan, *Revolution and Economic Development,* p. 17, cited in Benjamin, Collins, and Scott, *No Free Lunch,* p. 8. See also Boorstein, *The Economic Transformation of Cuba,* p. 3.
57. Boorstein, *The Economic Transformation of Cuba,* p. 3.

58. Carmelo Mesa-Lago, "Revolutionary Economic Policies in Cuba," in Brenner et al., *The Cuba Reader,* pp. 63–64.

59. Bienen and Glipin, "Evaluation of the Use of Economic Sanctions," p. 9; Galtung, "International Economic Sanctions," p. 23; Hufbauer and Schott, *Economic Sanctions Reconsidered,* p. 30.

60. Mesa-Lago, "Revolutionary Economic Policies in Cuba," p. 64.

61. Morley, *Imperial State and Revolution,* p. 51. A 1951 World Bank "Report on Cuba" says that 80 percent of Cuba's imports came from the United States. See Benjamin, Collins, and Scott, *No Free Lunch,* p. 11.

62. Morley, *Imperial State and Revolution,* p. 51. See also Smith, *The United States and Cuba,* p. 166.

63. Smith, *The United States and Cuba,* pp. 166–167.

64. Business International Corporation, *The Cuban Revolution,* p. 11, cited in Morley, *Imperial State and Revolution,* p. 51.

65. Thomas, *The Cuban Revolution,* p. 407.

66. Buzzanell, "Cuba's Sugar Industry—At the Crossroads," p. 5. See also Arthur T. Downey, "United States Commercial Relations with Cuba: A Survey," in U.S. Congress, report, *U.S. Trade Embargo of Cuba,* p. 588.

67. Benjamin, Collins, and Scott, *No Free Lunch,* p. 11. See also Mesa-Lago, "Revolutionary Economic Policies in Cuba," p. 64.

68. Buzzanell, "Cuba's Sugar Industry—At the Crossroads," p. 5.

69. Doxey, *International Sanctions in Contemporary Perspective,* p. 62.

70. Boorstein, *The Economic Transformation of Cuba,* p. 3.

71. U.S. Congress. *U.S. Trade Embargo of Cuba,* p. 585. Another study says that some 36 percent of Cuba's GNP was generated by exports in the 1949–1958 period. See Mesa-Lago, *The Economy of Socialist Cuba,* pp. 7–32.

72. Zimbalist, "Dateline Cuba," p. 152.

73. See Bienen and Gilpin, "Evaluation of the Use of Economic Sanctions to Promote Foreign Policy Goals," p. 10.

74. Hufbauer and Schott, *Economic Sanctions Reconsidered,* Second Edition, p. 87.

75. Hufbauer and Schott, *Economic Sanctions Reconsidered,* Second Edition, pp. 47, 99–100.

76. Hufbauer and Schott give the relationship a "3"—the highest score on their 1–3 scale, indicating the degree of warmth, prior to the sanctions episode, in overall relations between Cuba and the United States. Hufbauer and Schott, *Economic Sanctions Reconsidered,* Second Edition, pp. 58–59.

3

Origins of a Unilateral Embargo: 1960–1962

Pinpointing a precise starting date for the Cuba embargo involves some arbitrariness and subjectivity. For four years beginning in July 1960, the United States applied increasingly severe economic measures against Cuba. Similarly, it is unclear which nation—Cuba or the United States—started the spiral of antagonism that ultimately led to one of the most restrictive and longest lasting embargoes in modern history. Philip Brenner writes, "There continues to be a debate about whether the United States 'pushed' Cuba into the arms of the Soviet Union, or whether the revolutionary leadership had long been committed to Marxism-Leninism. . . . The simple answer is that because Cuban history did not begin in 1959, both sides of the debate have validity."[1]

The period between 1960 and 1962 ushered in the unilateral embargo policy against Cuba that remains more or less intact today, almost forty years later. While the period is characterized by the progressive tightening of the unilateral embargo, U.S. efforts to include allies and neighbors also began in these early days. Nonetheless, U.S. efforts to multilateralize the embargo did not gain focus and momentum until after 1962; this first period of the extraterritorial embargo lasted until the early 1970s. Because the story of the making of the multilateral embargo is rich and detailed, Chapter 4 is devoted entirely to that time period.

Agrarian Reform, 1959–1961

Between January 1959 and February 1961, Cuba underwent rapid economic transformation from a capitalist market economy to a centrally planned socialist economy. The cornerstone of this transformation was Cuba's Agrarian Reform Law of May 1959. Both moderate and nationalistic in most respects,[2] the law consisted of several components: (1) individual ownership of land was limited to a maximum of 995 acres; (2) all farms were nationalized (i.e., ownership was transferred from United States to

Cuban public and private hands); (3) foreign ownership of all land was prohibited;[3] and (4) compensation for expropriated holdings was offered in the form of redeemable twenty-year government bonds (with a maximum interest rate of 4 percent). To compute compensation, the basis for valuation of the appropriated properties was the assessed properties' tax value.[4] Because a quarter of Cuba's prime land was owned by U.S. concerns at the time, the agrarian reform law immediately set U.S. interests against Cuban ones. In fact, the Cubans identify the 1959 law as "the beginning of the end of U.S.-Cuban relations."[5]

The U.S. response to the agrarian reform law was mixed. According to Wayne Smith, a junior officer in the U.S. embassy in Havana at the time, the official U.S. response emphasized U.S. acceptance of Cuba's right to such reform.[6] Smith writes, "[I]t was clear to me that Ambassador Bonsal . . . and others on the staff accepted the need for agrarian reform and many other changes in Cuba."[7] On the other hand, the United States also questioned the adequacy of the compensation Cuba was offering for the land it was nationalizing.[8] The United States implied that if adequate compensation was not forthcoming, it would consider several policy options, among them a reduction in the sugar quota, a prohibition on private investment in Cuba by U.S. nationals, and a termination of economic aid.[9] Although official U.S. response to the 1959 reforms was ambivalent at best, Smith disputes the contention that the agrarian reform law can be identified as the turning point in U.S.-Cuban relations.[10]

The law was enacted slowly. Ten months after it was invoked, only six thousand Cuban peasants out of a total of 150,000 had received redistributed land.[11] In November of 1959, when major U.S. agricultural and mining properties in Oriente and Camaguey provinces were expropriated, support was generated in the U.S. executive and legislative branches for reducing or canceling Cuba's sugar quota. At the same time, U.S. State Department and Central Intelligence Agency officials began discussions culminating in President Eisenhower's March 1960 approval of a memorandum advocating covert action and economic sabotage.[12] *New York Times* reporter Herbert Matthews suggests that U.S.-Cuban enmity never recovered from Eisenhower's decision to back CIA actions against Cuba. "From that day on, the United States was caught in an inexorable millrace; something had been started that could not be stopped."[13] Matthews's prediction of inevitable doom was, however, probably premature. At that early date, there still remained some room for maneuver on the part of both governments.

Soviet Aid and Trade, 1960–1961

While the White House decision to approve covert operations against Cuba was of undisputed importance in defining the relationship between the former allies, the new Soviet-Cuban trade agreement of February 1960 was probably of greater significance.[14] Sanctions theory predicts that trade embargoes may unintentionally force the target into the trade spheres of the sender's opponents. Cuba is a case in point. In 1960, a Soviet mission headed by Politburo member Anastas Mikoyan agreed to purchase 425,000 tons of Cuban sugar that year, and one million tons in the four subsequent years.[15] This agreement effectively ended Cuba's dependence on the U.S. annual sugar quota and hence on the United States in general. The Soviet Union also extended $100 million in credits at 2.5 percent interest to Havana for the purchase of oil, equipment, machinery, and other materials over a five-year period.[16] The Soviet-Cuban agreement, however, was not as generous as it appeared. The Soviets had agreed to buy a substantial portion of Cuban sugar, but at prices *below that of the world market.* And though Cuba could have $100 million in credit, the credit could be used only to purchase Soviet goods. Smith points out, "The agreement was useful, but hardly impressive in magnitude or pricing arrangements."[17]

More important than the quantities, however, was the fact that Cuba could get around the U.S. sanctions. By trading with the Soviet Union, Cuba began to deprive the United States of one of its principal weapons against the new Castro regime: the threat of economic sanctions. By 1961, Cuban trade with socialist countries constituted over 70 percent of Cuba's foreign trade, and over 80 percent in 1962.[18] Hence, by that date, Cuban trade had shifted decisively from being U.S.-centered to being Soviet-centered. (See Appendix 2 on p. 211.)

Soviet willingness to assist Cuba should not have come as a surprise to U.S. policymakers in the early 1960s. Three distinct U.S. embargoes during the previous decade had elicited Soviet aid to the targeted nations. When the United States embargoed North Korea in 1950, the Soviets had moved in to help North Korea. The 1954 U.S. embargo of North Vietnam, an effort to impede that country's military effectiveness, likewise resulted in Soviet aid to the North Vietnamese. When the United States embargoed Egypt, furthermore, in 1956, to ensure free passage through the Suez Canal and gain compensation for nationalizations, the Soviets moved in to help the Nassar regime. In fact, the United States had also played the countersanctions game: When the Soviets embargoed Yugoslavia in 1948, the U.S. government attempted to befriend the wayward Tito regime.

As early as 1962, the United States appeared to understand the correlation between its aggression and increasingly close ties between Cuba and the Soviet Union. A July 1962 National Intelligence Estimate on the situation in Cuba found that "Castro's position of leadership was now firmer than had appeared likely earlier in the year" and that "the USSR is becoming more deeply committed to the preservation and advancement of the regime in Cuba."[19]

In an effort to capitalize on Cuba's economic vulnerability, the White House began to organize a stronger retaliation. The State Department began discreetly to block loans and credits from Western Europe to the Castro regime. In March 1960, Washington successfully pressured a consortium of Dutch, French, and West German banks to countermand an apparent agreement to negotiate $100 million in loans to the Cuban government.[20] Moreover, also in early 1960, the U.S. delegation to NATO formally requested "political, economic, and moral support" from member countries for U.S. policy toward Cuba.[21] Many Western European governments provided "full assurances regarding sales and transportation of arms to Cuba," but were less willing to curtail traditional trade. The U.S. government stepped up the pressure by notifying nations receiving U.S. Mutual Security Act assistance that the aid was conditional on an agreement not to purchase Cuban sugar.[22]

The Oil Decision, 1960

Perhaps the most significant aspect of the Soviet-Cuban trade agreement of February 1960 was Cuba's commitment to purchase one-third to one-half of its total annual petroleum imports from the Soviet Union. In essence, Cuba was bartering its sugar for oil from the Soviet Union and conserving its dangerously low foreign currency reserves. In 1960, Cuba spent over $70 million—10 percent of the island's total imports—on the import of petroleum. An exchange of goods for oil was to Cuba's great advantage.[23]

At that time, three major oil companies enjoyed an oligopolistic position in Cuba: Standard Oil of New Jersey, Texaco Oil Company, and Royal Dutch Shell. These companies supplied virtually all of Cuba's fuel: 90,000 barrels a day.

After the February trade agreement, Cuba notified its Western oil partners that they would be expected to process 2 million barrels of Soviet crude annually. The news was initially greeted with resigned pragmatism; as one oil company official explained, "If we didn't take it, we would be taken over, so what would we gain?"[24] Resigned pragmatism, however, quickly gave way to open hostility under tutelage of the U.S. State Department, which had been looking for a pretext to cut the sugar quota. The oil companies were apparently directed to reverse their decision and to refuse to refine Soviet oil:[25] the Cuban expropriations that were certain to follow would provide Washington with the excuse it needed to cut the sugar quota. Hence, after consultations with the State Department, the three oil companies retracted their initial position and announced their refusal to refine Soviet crude in early June 1960. Their turnabout surprised Havana, as heretofore the oil companies had given every indication that, though not pleased, they would agree to Cuban conditions.[26]

Cuba's efforts to attract other U.S. refiners were stymied by the U.S. State Department. Newly approached companies were advised that the U.S.

government would take "a very critical position toward any company that would attempt to capitalize on the difficulties of the presently established companies."[27] As predicted, Cuba nationalized the big three oil companies in late June 1960.

The U.S. responded with a global petroleum boycott of Cuba. The principal goal of the oil embargo was to render the Cuban refineries inoperative. In early July, Standard Oil issued a directive to all tankers to cease dealing with Soviet or Cuban entities or risk losing further business with Standard Oil and its associates. The U.S. State Department also began efforts to pressure other nations to comply with the oil embargo of Cuba.

Escalation of Tensions, 1960

The tension between Cuba and its former superpower ally reached a climax when five events occurred in immediate succession: the United States acted against the Cuban sugar quota; the United States increased its threats of intervention on the island; the United States attempted to gain OAS support for condemnation of Cuba; Cuba continued its trade negotiations with the Soviets and Chinese; and Cuba continued to nationalize U.S. enterprises on the island.

In early July 1960, the United States canceled the remainder of Cuba's 1960 quota for sugar exports to its northern neighbor. The groundwork had already been laid for this action. Several months prior to canceling the quota, Secretary of State Christian Herter presented legislation to the U.S. Congress requesting presidential authority to manipulate foreign sugar quotas. After several White House defeats in Congress, legislation was finally passed granting the president authority to determine the Cuban sugar quota for the remainder of 1960 and to set the 1961 quota "at any level he finds to be in the national interest."[28] Immediately after Congress granted him the authority, Eisenhower issued Presidential Proclamation No. 3355, canceling the 700,000 tons of sugar remaining in Cuba's 1960 sugar quota.[29] Foreshadowing things to come, he stated, "this amounts to economic sanctions against Cuba. Now we must look to other moves—economic, diplomatic, and strategic."[30]

Tensions mounted in the late summer of that year. The United States reviewed a full range of military and paramilitary options including direct U.S. intervention on the island.[31] CIA support, assistance, and training of Cuban exiles for the eventual invasion of Cuba continued.[32] In late August, U.S. Secretary of State Herter convened a special meeting of the OAS in San Jose, Costa Rica, in an effort to persuade the organization to condemn Cuba for endangering the hemisphere. The OAS, however, approved only a much weaker resolution, known as the "Declaration of San Jose," condemning all intervention in the Americas by non-American States.[33] In response, on September 2, 1960, Castro pronounced the "Declaration of Havana," which attacked the United States and the OAS, denounced U.S. intervention in Latin America, accepted assistance from the Soviet Union, and announced Cuba's intentions to establish relations with the People's Republic of China.[34] As sanctions theory accurately predicted, economic aggression against Cuba led hardliners within the Cuban government to gain the upper hand.

By late September the U.S. government had issued a travel advisory against Cuba and urged all U.S. citizens living in Cuba to return home.[35] For its part, Cuba had nationalized the Cuban Telephone and Telegraph Company, the Cuban Electric Company, thirty-six sugar centrales, and all oil refineries.[36] The Soviet Union had agreed to purchase the 700,000 tons of sugar that the United States had canceled, and Cuba was receiving large quantities of old, obsolete weapons from Eastern Europe.[37]

By mid-October 1960, the Cubans enacted a second nationalization law that virtually ended large-scale private sector enterprise on the island. Its impact was major: the banking industry and nearly four hundred foreign and locally owned properties came under government control; a total of 2.7 million acres of sugar lands were expropriated and placed under the jurisdiction of the National Agrarian Reform Institute (INRA); and over 160 U.S.-owned properties, including the $100 million Nicaro nickel mining plant, were expropriated.[38] By the end of 1960, the Cuban economy was, for all intents and purposes, socialized. About 80 percent of Cuba's industrial capacity was controlled by the state—encompassing the strategic industries of sugar, petroleum refining, telephone and electric power, and cement.[39] Carmelo Mesa-Lago notes, "All domestic wholesale and foreign trade and banking, and most transportation, industry, construction, and retail trade, as well as more than one third of agriculture was in state hands."[40] About 30 percent of Cuba's total farmland, including the best lands, was nationalized.[41]

U.S. Imposes Embargo, October 1960

The spiral of antagonism was far from over. In response to Cuba's second nationalization law, the United States imposed a partial embargo, prohibiting all exports to Cuba except nonsubsidized foodstuffs and medicines. The embargo was also extraterritorial in scope. It prohibited the re-exportation from third countries of any commodities or technical data of U.S. origin to Cuba.

The decision to impose an embargo had long been debated in the U.S. State and Treasury Departments. Within a year of Castro's rise to power, "economic warfare" was considered an important policy option. U.S. policymakers believed Cuba would be highly vulnerable to sanctions, since "almost everything, from the large boilers in the sugar mills to ordinary electric sockets, was built and worked according to American designs and specifications."[42] In mid-June 1960, the State Department sent the Treasury Department a report listing a number of economic actions under consideration, including denying Cuba premium payments for sugar and encouraging U.S. creditors to press their claims and obtain liens on Cuban assets in the United States. At follow-up meetings other actions were discussed: (1) a freeze on public and private Cuban assets in the United States; (2) a prohibition on transactions with Cuba; (3) a total ban on Cuban imports; (4) a limitation on U.S. exports to Cuba; (5) an invocation of the Battle Act to prevent shipment of strategic materials to Cuba; and (6) a voluntary embargo against Cuba by private U.S. companies.[43]

In conjunction with these discussions, debate arose over the legal basis for economic actions. The National Security Council favored a new proclamation specifically directed at the Cuban situation. The State Department, however, strongly opposed any such proclamation, as it would imply that Cuba constituted a "threat" to U.S. "national security" and thereby commit U.S. prestige to economic and perhaps other warfare against the island. The State Department preferred extending existing legislation to Cuba—either the Trading with Enemy Act (TWEA) or the Export Control Act of 1949.[44] When the White House announced the embargo on October 20, 1960, it noted that it was acting under the general authority of the Export Control Act. The White House had decided not to label Cuba a threat to U.S. national security.

Target countries often seek antidotes to sanctions by trading with sender nation's enemies. Cuba responded to the embargo by sending Che Guevara (a leading member of the July 26 Movement and head of the National Bank) on a trade mission to socialist countries. Guevara signed agreements for sale to various socialist countries of more than four million tons of sugar in 1961—about a million tons more than had formerly gone to the United States annually—and for the sale to Cuba of a majority of the goods needed to keep the Cuban economy going.[45] Trading with the Soviet bloc was beginning to look even more lucrative for the Cubans than their previous trade with the United States.

On December 19, 1960, President Eisenhower canceled the Cuban sugar quota for the first quarter of 1961.[46] At the same time, the U.S. Commerce Department, in charge of preventing U.S. exports to Cuba, was given additional resources to enforce the new prohibition.[47]

Tensions Mount, 1961

On January 3, 1961, as Castro was addressing an anniversary celebration in Havana, a bomb exploded in the crowd. Castro accused the U.S. embassy of complicity in the bombing and ordered that its staff be reduced to eleven people within thirty-six hours.[48] In an official pronouncement, President Eisenhower claimed that Castro's order had "no other purpose than to render impossible the conduct of normal diplomatic relations," and he immediately severed, accordingly, all diplomatic ties with Cuba.[49] In mid-January 1961, the State Department followed up on the president's action by issuing a ban against all travel to Cuba by U.S. citizens.[50]

By 1962, Cuba's dependence on the United States had dwindled. Imports from the United States plunged from $577 million in 1957 to $23.7 million in 1961, and to less than $1 million in 1962. Cuban exports to the United States amounted to less than 1 percent of Cuba's total exports by 1962. By 1961, Cuban trade with socialist countries constituted over 70 percent of Cuba's foreign trade, and over 80 percent in 1962.[51]

Why the Spiral of Antagonism?

A number of differing theories might account for the disintegration of U.S.-Cuban relations. Not one single reason but rather a combination of factors led to the increasing antagonism and ultimate break between the United States and Cuba. A discussion of several significant hypotheses follows.

Morris Morley suggests that Cuba's internal economic reform and increasingly close links with the Soviet Union were sufficient cause for the divorce. He writes, "For most American policymakers, the structural transformation of the Cuban economy and Havana's expanding links with Moscow were sufficient to justify a confrontation."[52] Morley specifically points to the nationalization of agriculture as "pivotal" for Washington. "It . . . led many senior U.S. officials to the inescapable conclusion that a thorough transformation of the economy was imminent."[53] "As early as March 1960, months in advance of the oil and sugar actions, the White House, National Security Council, and State Department originated a multilayered program of public and covert confrontation designed to "bring another government to power in Cuba."[54]

Wayne Smith, however, argues that the split goes beyond the conflict over Cuba's domestic reforms and lies instead with Castro's global ambitions. Smith argues that "an inchoate shift in [U.S.] hemispheric approach just as [Castro] came to power opened the way to a policy which gave him the benefit of the doubt and promised U.S. acceptance of the socioeconomic reforms he was promising to institute."[55] Smith acknowledges the argument that Castro upped the level of antagonism with the United States; in his effort to "galvanize the Cuban people behind the task of national reformation, it was convenient to have an external threat against which to rally them."[56]

However, Smith posits that the "epicenter" of the problem was not domestic policy. "Castro's turn away from us and toward the Soviet Union was essentially a function of his foreign policy objectives, not of his domestic programs." He argues that Castro's objectives were international in scope: "Foreign policy objectives outweighed all domestic goals and considerations, and the centerpiece of his foreign ambitions was the 'liberation' of Latin America."[57] Castro hoped that the emergence of other revolutionary nations in the hemisphere would give him the support he needed to become a leader of the Third World.[58] Absent other revolutionary nations in Latin America, Castro would have either to give up his foreign policy objectives or to seek an alternative source of support. Only the Soviet Union had the power and will to undercut U.S. influence. Hence, according to Smith, Fidel Castro swung eastward in an attempt to obtain Soviet support in his crusade to become a world leader.

Carla Anne Robbins argues that the 1960 U.S. presidential election campaign contributed significantly to hostility between the nations. Though the Cuba question played a small role in the early days of the campaign, as election day neared, both candidates sought issues around which to mobilize support. When a Senate internal subcommittee report was released indicating that the Republican White House had disregarded early signs of Communist influence in Cuba, Democratic presidential candidate John F. Kennedy claimed that Eisenhower had "lost Cuba" and opened the hemisphere to Communist infiltration.[59] Republican presidential candidate Richard M. Nixon, who was also Eisenhower's vice-president, responded by describing the Castro government as "an intolerable cancer" and put forth the administration's goal of quarantining the Castro regime.[60] The embargo was placed on Cuba a day later.

Not to be outdone, Kennedy characterized the embargo as "too little too late" and advocated armed intervention in Cuba. Despite having called for the same action sixteen months earlier when he first met with Castro in Washington, Nixon called Kennedy's solution "shockingly reckless."[61] Kennedy knew that plans for an invasion were in the works at the time, but that Nixon, as a member of the administration, could not publicly acknowledge the covert activities.[62]

In all likelihood, both Kennedy and Nixon believed that Cuba's domestic reforms, its close alignment with the Soviet Union, and its revolutionary foreign policy constituted a genuine threat to U.S. interests. Nonetheless, Cuba ultimately became a domestic U.S. political issue. Though the break in diplomatic relations would probably have occurred anyway, the presidential campaign magnified the situation. Moreover, candidate Kennedy's accusations served to paint President Kennedy into a corner once in office. As Herbert Matthews writes, "John F. Kennedy, for his part, had committed himself in his electoral campaign to help the exiles and domestic Cuban opposition to overthrow Castro. He was caught in a trap that he himself had laid."[63]

Edward Boorstein concludes that the split between the United States and Cuba was inevitable given the goals of the Cuban revolution. He writes: "The Revolution could have avoided taking radical measures or touching American interests. But this would have meant not meeting Cuba's problems; it would have meant doing practically nothing. . . . The Revolution had no choice: it had to grow or die."[64]

Boorstein argues that the split was inevitable precisely because the United States had such a "stranglehold" on Cuba before the revolution. "Cuba could only solve its problems to the degree that it got rid of imperialism," he asserts. "But imperialism could not be nibbled away. At the slowest conceivable pace, it could only be removed in large chunks."[65] Boorstein contends that it was U.S. "violent" reaction to Cuba's internal reforms that forced Cuba to pursue relations with socialist nations.

> When the United States shut off its market, where could Cuba have turned to sell her sugar except to the Socialist countries? The free world market could not have absorbed the three million tons per year set free by the elimination of the sugar quota, especially with the United States exerting pressure on other countries not to trade with Cuba.[66]

Morley takes this proposition one step further. He argues that even before Castro came to power, the U.S. government was "profoundly hostile" to the July 26 Movement. Morley suggests that Washington was never "ambiguous" or "flexible" toward the Castro regime, but that its selective hostility "blossomed into unqualified refusal to accept the continued existence of the Castro government and its program of social and economic development."[67]

Thomas Paterson agrees. He writes that the United States attempted to avert Castro's emergence as a Cuban leader from very early on.

> When Batista faltered and became ever more repressive, Washington cut back on arms shipments in a vain attempt to coerce him to reform. When he proved incorrigible, the Eisenhower administration schemed to push the unpopular dictator out before Castro could come in. The plots designed to block Castro came too late, and they lacked leaders who could rally the Cuban people behind a viable third force.[68]

It is apparent, then, that a variety of issues contributed to the split between the United States and Cuba. Cuba's domestic economic reforms alienated significant elements of the U.S. business community with important investments on the island. These reforms, combined with Castro's unabashed international goals, inflamed U.S. sensitivities. Moreover, domestic pressures in both Cuba and the United States furthered the conflict. In the United States, Cuba bashing became a major sport in the 1960 presidential campaign, and in Cuba, the United States became a convenient enemy around which to rally national spirit and support for the revolution. No single element is solely responsible for the rupture in relations, but more likely, a combination of events served to make the divorce inevitable.

Early Goals of the Embargo

Despite varying theories accounting for failed relations between the United States and Cuba, most authors agree that by the end of the Eisenhower administration, the goals of U.S. policy toward the island were clear. Morley succinctly states, "United States policy toward Cuba after 1959 had a clear-cut political purpose: to destabilize and overthrow the Castro government."[69] Smith likewise suggests that this was the ultimate goal of U.S. policy. "As Castro's verbal vitriol rose," he writes, "and his ties to Moscow strengthened, the Eisenhower administration, concluding that it simply could not deal with him, wrote him off." It is clear from Eisenhower's actions that his main objective was to remove Castro from the Cuban panorama: When Eisenhower handed the reins of power over to President Kennedy in January 1961, he also handed over plans for the overthrow of Fidel Castro. Four months later, Kennedy accepted blame for Eisenhower's plan and for what has been called "a perfect failure" at the Bay of Pigs in Cuba.[70]

1961: The Bay of Pigs

While Castro greeted the new Kennedy administration with cautious optimism, Kennedy remained committed to both the Eisenhower goal of toppling the revolutionary Cuban government and the Eisenhower method of achieving this goal. Since the Bay of Pigs episode has been closely studied and is tangential to reviewing the U.S. embargo, it will be summarized with only the greatest brevity here.[71] On April 16, 1961, 1,300 CIA-trained and -supplied Cuban exiles invaded Cuba from launching posts in Nicaragua. Within seventy-two hours, the Cuban people, well-trained and prepared for such an invasion, defeated the invading forces. One hundred and fifty of the invaders were killed and nearly 1,200 were taken prisoner. The mission was a failure.

Much scholarly debate has focused on whether Kennedy was to blame for the debacle. As we have seen, for example, Matthews and Morley argue that Kennedy laid his own trap during the election campaign when he committed himself to help the Cuban opposition overthrow Castro. They argue as well that while the president was misinformed by his intelligence organizations, the failure of the invasion was ultimately his responsibility. Matthews writes:

> Inexcusably, the President was misinformed and misled by the CIA, the Pentagon, and the Cuban exiles. . . . The only meaningful choice which the President had was whether or not to back the invasion force with American arms, men, and naval and air forces. When he decided against an American intervention, he doomed the invasion to virtually certain failure.[72]

Other analysts believe that Kennedy's foreign and national security advisers are to blame. Wayne Smith writes, "President Kennedy accepted the responsibility, as he should have, but the blame lay elsewhere. He inherited the operation and had been in office only three months when it was launched. He had to rely on his military and foreign-policy advisers—those in the CIA. All failed him miserably. . . . All said 'go.'"[73]

Smith further points out that the Bay of Pigs mission rested on a "wildly implausible hope": that the invasion would ignite a popular uprising in Cuba. Smith argues that it was precisely the failure of the planners to consult anyone who had first-hand knowledge of Cuba that led to the fiasco. "Consulting [those who knew Cuba] might have made a difference, for they would have killed the notion that a popular uprising would occur."[74] Observers familiar with political reality on the island also knew that Castro was far more popular than U.S. intelligence agencies estimated. Moreover, Castro had already become adept at using U.S. aggression to his advantage.

Sanctions theory predicts that sanctions are weakened when they cause the population in the target nation to unify against a common enemy. This is what happened in Cuba's case. Even before the sanctions were invoked, the Cuban revolutionary leadership was able to augment Cuban unity and nationalism by invoking the threat of a common enemy. The Cuban population proved willing to accept sacrifice predicated on the notion that their loss was due to an external adversary and was surmountable only through cohesion and commitment to the current leadership. U.S. military action against Cuba thus further solidified this commitment to unity. Wherever one chooses to apportion blame for the Bay of Pigs debacle, one of the lasting results of the invasion was to reinforce popular allegiance to the Castro government and to destroy any remaining elements of an anti-Castro underground on the island.

The ultimate outcome of the Bay of Pigs invasion was not a change in the goals of U.S. policy toward Cuba, but a change in the means of achieving them. Morley writes, "The failure to overthrow Castro militarily did not mean that the objective of getting rid of the revolutionary regime would be abandoned. The major lesson that Kennedy drew from the episode was the need to rethink U.S. tactics with a view to pursuing 'a struggle in many ways more difficult than war.'"[75] Paterson agrees with Morley: "The consequences of the escalating contest are now all too familiar. . . . Castro moved Cuba steadily toward Communism and military alliance with the Soviet Union, and President Kennedy launched a multi-track program of covert, economic, diplomatic, and propagandistic elements designed to bring down Castro."[76]

Following the Bay of Pigs invasion, the central goal of U.S. policy toward Cuba remained the ouster of Castro from Cuba; the principal tools now, however, were covert action and embargo. Short of ousting Castro, the United States hoped to isolate and contain the Cuban revolution.[77] As Brenner explains, "Isolation was intended partly to cripple and topple the government and partly to contain Cuba's influence on other countries where social and economic conditions made them candidates for revolution."[78]

After the Fiasco: 1961–1962

The failure of the United States at the Bay of Pigs had important fallout. In Moscow, Nikita Khrushchev watched events unfold on the island and concluded that the new U.S. president was weak. He also gained new respect for the Cuban revolution and sent more up-to-date Soviet weaponry to Cuba.[79] Anticipating Khrushchev's move, Attorney General Robert Kennedy sent a memo to the president two days after the failed invasion, warning: "If we don't want Russia to set up missile bases in Cuba, we had better decide now what we are willing to do to stop it." Robert Kennedy identified three possible courses of action: (1) sending U.S. troops into Cuba—a proposal "you [President Kennedy] have rejected . . . for good and sufficient reasons (although this might have to be reconsidered)"; (2) placing a strict blockade around Cuba—which, as an act of war, "has the same inherent problems" as number (1); and (3) calling on the OAS to prohibit the shipment to Cuba of arms from any outside source.[80]

In the eighteen months between the Bay of Pigs and the Cuban Missile Crisis, U.S. efforts to oust Castro concentrated on economic warfare and covert operations.

The Making of the U.S. Embargo, 1961–1962

In September of 1961, the U.S. Congress passed a measure barring assistance to any country that aided Cuba, unless the president determined that such aid was in the U.S. national interest.[81] This was the first formal legislation regarding the Cuban trade embargo.[82] In early February 1962, Kennedy expanded the embargo by banning all trade with Cuba, except nonsubsidized sale of foods and medicines.[83] He waited until February 1962 to formalize the embargo because it was only then that he obtained international approval.[84]

On January 31, 1962, the OAS voted to exclude Cuba from participation in the inter-American system. When the State Department was contemplating invoking economic sanctions against Cuba, the Treasury Department counseled that "traditional international law and principles do not afford much support for the unilateral imposition of such a blockade." Hence, Treasury advised the State Department that a White House determination to apply an economic embargo could be based legally on the 1954 OAS Caracas Resolution against intervention of international communism in the hemisphere, or on the Trading with the Enemy Act (TWEA).[85] In fact, the State Department met both of these conditions when it decided to invoke the embargo based on the TWEA after the OAS acted to expel Cuba from the organization.

The new U.S. law directed the secretary of the treasury to carry out the trade prohibitions on Cuban imports, and the secretary of commerce to carry out the prohibitions of U.S. exports to Cuba under the Export Control Act of 1949.[86]

Within a week, the Treasury Department promulgated the "Cuban Import Regulations," which detailed the prohibitions on imports of all goods of Cuban origin to the United States. The Treasury Department had argued that its ability to administer an embargo on imports or financial transactions with Cuba would be seriously hampered by litigation problems because the legislation "lacked satisfactory investigative and penal provisions," and Cuban exporters could take advantage of "loopholes" in the Foreign Assistance Act unless the stricter TWEA was invoked.[87]

Secretary of State Dean Rusk told a closed congressional hearing on Cuba at the time that the administration was reluctant to enact more stringent measures to force compliance with the embargo "because that would create some very sharp issues with friendly governments who at the moment lack the legal resources to move promptly to comply." He assured the legislators that the administration was working "behind the scenes" to reduce shipping in the Cuban trade.[88]

The State Department hesitated at first to approve the TWEA because it feared that calling Cuba an "enemy" would cause political disturbances in Latin America. However, the Treasury Department prevailed, and the TWEA was invoked in February 1962 as part of the Cuban Import Regulations. Hence, both of the recommendations provided by the Treasury Department for the invocation of the Cuba embargo were followed: support for the measures was obtained from the OAS (granted by the expulsion of Cuba from the OAS in January 1962), and the TWEA was used as the statutory basis for the embargo.[89]

Between March and September 1962, the Cuba embargo was systematically tightened. Some of the most important elements included (1) a ban on imports of Cuban products of even partial Cuban origin, regardless of where they were manufactured;[90] (2) rescinding Cuba's Most Favored Nation status and the preferences accorded it under GATT;[91] (3) denial of bunkers in U.S. ports to all vessels under charter to the Sino-Soviet bloc engaged in Cuba trade; (4) prohibition on U.S. tourists from bringing products of Cuban origin into the United States; (5) prevention of Cuban vessels from obtaining bunkers and ships' stores in U.S. ports;[92] and (6) the prohibition of ships registered under the U.S. flag from transporting to Cuba commodities on the U.S. embargoed list and U.S. munitions list as well as items controlled by the Atomic Energy Commission. About 360 foreign-flag vessels whose owners agreed not to violate the transportation order were also affected.[93]

Up to this point, U.S. efforts had primarily concentrated on thwarting bilateral trade. Inspired by the initial successes of the bilateral embargo, the United States moved to legislate international aspects of the embargo with the establishment of the Battle Act in October 1962. The Battle Act prohibited U.S. assistance to any country that furnished aid to Cuba or permitted ships and aircraft under its registry to carry strategic items to Cuba.[94] The new extraterritorial legislation immediately raised concerns among U.S. allies. Canada refused to participate in the ban.[95] Black market trade with Cuba grew.[96] To deter it, Commerce Secretary Hodges closed all U.S. ports to ships that carried any supplies to Cuba when on the same voyage they attempted to dock or take on cargo in the United States.[97]

Cuban Response to U.S. Aggression

While there is little doubt that the increasingly harsh economic measures used against the Cuban people did in fact cause great damage to the Cuban economy, decisionmakers crafting the aggressive policy unwittingly played right into Castro's hands. Evidence suggests that even before the embargo was invoked, the Cuban government attempted to use the United States as a threat in an effort to rally the Cuban public behind its internal reform policies. Writing about the early days of the revolution, shortly after the invocation of the agrarian reform laws, Wayne Smith notes, "Why did Castro rebuff or ignore [U.S.] overtures? One reason perhaps was that to galvanize the Cuban people behind the task of national reformation, it was convenient to have an external threat against which to rally them."[98]

Cuban government efforts to rally public opinion behind its anti-embargo position have been a consistent and successful aspect of Cuban domestic policy. The embargo has been skillfully used to explain economic difficulties confronting the island. For example, Castro attacked the U.S. trade embargo at a rally in Havana on February 4, 1962, calling it "another economic aggression." He predicted "long years of sacrifice" and called on Cubans to increase their productivity.[99] The following month, announcing that food and soap would be rationed, Castro stated that the shortages of consumer goods were the result of a "brutal economic blockade" against the island.[100]

Castro continued to tie announcements of further rationing to aggression from the United States. In July 1962, on the ninth anniversary of the attack on Moncada, he remarked, "the only danger that our country faces is the danger of the direct invasion by Yankee armed forces." He then announced that rationing would be extended from food to shoes and clothing.[101]

The Cuban people were receptive to the strong anti-U.S. rhetoric of their government. Especially in the early years of the revolution, they were anxious to find an external scapegoat for their problems, and the United States, long tied to contemptuous upper echelons of Cuban society, provided just that scapegoat, serving, particularly through implementation of the embargo, as a common enemy around which the Cuban population could unify.

Elements outside of Cuba recognized the counterproductive aspects of the embargo. Even news reports in the United States acknowledged that the U.S. embargo provided Castro with popular support. An article in the *Chicago Tribune* noted, "For Castro, his constant attacks on the 'imperialists' to the north are both a personal crusade and a key to his immense popularity. . . . Even the U.S. embargo—universally called 'the blockade' [in Cuba]—is seen as a source of national strength through adversity."[102]

In 1992, the U.S. Army War College issued a report on Cuba focusing on the counterproductive aspects of the embargo:

> U.S. policy is counterproductive and is one of the factors enabling Castro to remain in power. Castro plays the "confrontation game" extremely well. Over the years, he has been highly successful in manipulating the specter of "Yankee threat" to mobilize the Cuban people behind his leadership and policies. In effect, successive U.S. administrations, both Republican and Democrat, have repeatedly played into his hands by enabling him to wrap himself in the cloak of besieged nationalism.[103]

Despite all the warnings, when formulating Cuba policy, the U.S. government failed to take into account Castro's remarkable ability to galvanize popular support in the face of aggression. Nowhere was this lack of insight more harmful than in the decision to launch the Bay of Pigs. The invasion was based on the erroneous premise that Castro lacked popular support; this mistaken premise also guided the use of covert operations after the invasion.

Covert Operations, 1960–1966

The embargo was only one component of a greater policy instrument to oust the Castro government from Cuba; the U.S. government also relied on a covert action program.[104] Despite the embarrassing failure of covert operations at the Bay of Pigs in 1961, covert ops became an increasingly important aspect of U.S. policy toward the island. Between 1960 and 1965, the Western Hemisphere division of the CIA grew by 40 percent, and as late as 1966, almost one-third of all Western Hemisphere Division officers were assigned to the Cuba section. The covert action team against Cuba was headed up in the White House itself, assisted by the Special Group Augmented (SGA), an interagency committee composed of the administration's most senior officials. Counterinsurgency expert Edward Landsdale had responsibility for the covert program, known as Operation Mongoose.

In early 1962, Lansdale clearly enunciated the overall goal of Operation Mongoose. "The U.S. objective is to help the Cubans overthrow the Communist regime from within Cuba and institute a new government with which the United States can live in peace."[105] Lansdale detailed a six-phase schedule for Operation Mongoose designed to culminate in October 1962 with an "open revolt and overthrow of the Communist regime."[106]

Covert operations against Cuba eventually involved about four hundred U.S. nationals at CIA headquarters and at its Miami station, about two thousand Cuban exiles, a private navy of speedboats, and an annual budget of about $50–100 million.[107]

A primary purpose of the covert operations was economic sabotage. Cuba's oil refineries were one area of attack.[108] Other covert operations centered on burning sugarcane fields and on destroying bridges, mining installations, and sugar mills.[109] The island's food supplies and railway system were also targeted. According to the Defense Department, the sabotage activities were not only aimed at specific targets, but also "the more general objective of keeping the Castro regime so off stride and unsettled that it couldn't concentrate its activities in harmful ends elsewhere."[110]

Covert operations also focused on efforts to assassinate the Cuban revolution's senior leaders. Attempts to assassinate Castro took a variety of forms. Poison pills, multiple-men assassination teams, exploding devices placed inside sea shells where Castro regularly went skin-diving, contaminated diving suits, and poison pens were part of the repertoire the CIA drew on to get rid of Castro.[111]

At times, U.S. covert operations against Cuba led to trouble with allies. When Alpha 66, a Cuban exile organization cooperating with the CIA, publicized a 1962 plan to attack all merchant ships carrying supplies to Cuba, Great Britain officially protested the plan to the U.S. government. A spokesperson for the British Foreign Office said that Great Britain "would take a serious view of any attacks on British shipping going about its lawful business."[112] In response, the U.S. government indicated that it was not willing to take action against Cuban exiles that raided ships headed for Cuba and warned foreign shippers that they would run risks in continued trade with Cuba. The spokesperson added that the U.S. government did not sanction such assaults, but "that there were difficulties in guaranteeing the peace in the Caribbean."[113] Moreover, CIA funds continued to support Alpha 66.[114]

CIA-sponsored exile sabotage was officially disbanded by 1964 because of its failure to produce results. Secretary of State Rusk called the efforts "unproductive" and suspected that the exiles were not adverse "to leav[ing] fingerprints pointing to U.S. involvement in order to increase that involvement."[115] Senior presidential advisor McGeorge Bundy questioned the value of the sabotage in achieving U.S. objectives: "policymakers had turned sabotage operations on and off to such an extent that [the program] simply does not . . . appear feasible."[116] In fact, U.S. assassination attempts against Fidel Castro lasted until 1965, and the U.S.-supported counterrevolutionary forces continued to operate until 1966.[117]

Sanctions theorists have predicted that when sanctions are combined with other policies, they enjoy a higher degree of success at obtaining their goals than when used alone. During the early years of the embargo, the U.S. government combined economic sanctions against Cuba with covert operations, quasi-military actions, and overt military operations against the island. Contrary to theoretical predictions, however, in the case of Cuba it seems that companion measures did little to assist the efficacy of the sanctions policy itself. The constant U.S. efforts at sabotage were undoubtedly a nuisance and quite expensive to the Cuban government. But if there were any lasting results of U.S.-sponsored terrorism against the island, it served to unify the Cuban people further around their government. Nowhere was this more true than in the case of the Bay of Pigs invasion, which achieved the opposite of what it was intended to do: it destroyed the domestic anti-Castro force within Cuba.

Conclusions

During this early period of embargo history, enormous changes took place in a number of arenas. First, Cuba underwent an economic transformation of unprecedented scope and speed. Between 1960 and 1962, Cuba's domestic and international economic strategies shifted 180 degrees: formerly capitalist in orientation and U.S.-dominated, they were now socialist in orientation and Soviet-dominated. The United States both provoked and responded to this transformation in an elaborate dance that resulted in a complete break with the island. In these short two years, the United States went from being Cuba's main export market and major source of imports to invoking one of the strictest embargoes in world history against its former ally. By 1962, the scope of the sanctions (export, import, and financial), as well as their objective (ousting Castro), were ordained for at least the next three and a half decades. The United States had also tried both direct intervention and covert operations to achieve this goal. On his side of the Florida straits, Castro had already devised a strategy of using U.S. aggression to unify Cuban support behind his policies. To this day, Castro's ability to galvanize public support remains effective. No other period of Cuba-sanctions history would be as decisive as these first two years in shaping the pattern of U.S.-Cuban relations for the rest of the millennium.

Notes

1. Brenner, *From Confrontation to Negotiation,* p. 11.
2. Domínguez, Cuba, p. 143.
3. Ibid., p. 143.
4. *VII Leyes Del Gobierno Provisional de la Revolucion* (Havana: November 1960), reprinted in Krinsky and Golove, United States Economic Measures Against Cuba, p. 107.
5. See Benjamin, Collins, and Scott, *No Free Lunch,* p. 163. Wayne Smith contends that this was not, in fact, the beginning of the end, but that both sides were willing to negotiate at this point. See Smith, *The Closest of Enemies,* p. 48.
6. The official U.S. response was conveyed to the Cuban government by U.S. Ambassador Bonsal on January 11, 1960. See Smith, *The Closest of Enemies,* p. 54.
7. Smith, *The Closest of Enemies,* p. 48.
8. Robbins, *The Cuban Threat,* p. 87.
9. Krinsky and Golove, *The United States Economic Measures Against Cuba,* p. 107.
10. Smith, *The Closest of Enemies,* p. 48. "What I can say," Smith writes, "is that nothing I saw in the cable traffic between the embassy's own internal discussions and memoranda, led me to believe that the U.S. intended to reject Castro's internal reforms in the same way it had rejected those of Arbenz. On the contrary, I would say that at least within the embassy and in the Bureau of American Republics Affairs back in State, everyone wished not to repeat the mistakes of Guatemala."
11. Benjamin, Collins, and Scott, *No Free Lunch,* p. 162.
12. Welch, *Response to Revolution,* pp. 48–49; Matthews, "The Bay of Pigs," p. 332. See also Robbins, *The Cuban Threat,* p. 85; Morley, *Imperial State and Revolution,* p. 85; and Paterson, *Contesting Castro,* p. 258.
13. Matthews, "The Bay of Pigs," p. 333.
14. Robbins, *The Cuban Threat,* p. 91. Of the increasingly warm Soviet-Cuban relationship, Robbins writes, "Throughout 1960, relations between Washington and Havana became increasingly strained. The long-standing problems of Cuban defiance and American intolerance grew to unmanageable proportions in what were almost weekly crises. Beneath all the specifics was Cuba's new alliance with the Soviet Union."
15. In 1958, Cuba sold 3.24 million tons of sugar to the United States. Hence, the Soviet promise to purchase one million tons of sugar from the island constituted a fairly significant portion of Cuban exports.
16. Memorandum: "Chronology of Important Events in U.S.-Cuban Relations, 1957–1962," the White House, from the document collection at the National Security Archive. See also Boorstein, *The Economic Transformation of Cuba,* p. 27; Morley, *Imperial State and Revolution,* p. 87.
17. Smith, *The Closest of Enemies,* p. 56.

18. Boorstein, *The Economic Transformation of Cuba,* p. 33; Mesa-Lago, "Revolutionary Economic Policies in Cuba," in Brenner et al., *The Cuba Reader,* p. 71.

19. See Kornbluh and Chang, *Chronology of the Cuban Missile Crisis,* National Security Archives, p. 57.

20. Morley, *Imperial State and Revolution,* p. 88.

21. Ibid., p. 122.

22. Ibid., p. 123.

23. Boorstein, *The Economic Transformation of Cuba,* p. 28.

24. Morley, *Imperial State and Revolution,* p. 104.

25. Robbins, *The Cuban Threat,* p. 95.

26. Morley, *Imperial State and Revolution,* p. 104.

27. Ibid., p. 106.

28. Ibid., p. 110. The legislation passed the House in part because it provided for most of the Cuban quota to be apportioned among other foreign producers and sugar-refining interests with powerful friends in the House. After considerable debate in the Senate, where domestic sugar beet interests likewise had friends, the Senate compromised and a joint committee granted presidential authority to determine sugar quotas through March 1961.

29. Presidential Proclamation 3355 was issued under the authority conferred on the president by Section 408 of the 1948 Sugar Act, as amended July 6, 1960, by Public Law 86-592. See Rich, "The U.S. Embargo Against Cuba," chronology.

30. Rich, "The U.S. Embargo Against Cuba," p. 6.

31. Morley, *Imperial State and Revolution,* p. 112.

32. Boorstein, *The Economic Transformation of Cuba,* p. 29.

33. Rich, "The U.S. Embargo Against Cuba," chronology.

34. White House Chronology, p. 17.

35. Smith, *The Closest of Enemies,* p. 57.

36. Boorstein, *The Economic Transformation of Cuba,* p. 31.

37. Smith, *The Closest of Enemies,* p. 52; personal correspondence with Philip Brenner, January 26, 1995. See also Mary McAuliffe, ed., *CIA Documents on the Cuban Missile Crisis* (CIA: October 1992).

38. Morley, *Imperial State and Revolution,* p. 113.

39. Boorstein, *The Economic Transformation of Cuba,* p. 32.

40. Carmelo Mesa-Lago, "Revolutionary Economic Policies in Cuba," in Brenner et al., *The Cuba Reader,* p. 69.

41. Boorstein, *The Economic Transformation of Cuba,* p. 32.

42. Ibid., p. 65.

43. Morley, *Imperial State and Revolution,* pp. 119–120.

44. Ibid., p. 120.

45. Boorstein, *The Economic Transformation of Cuba,* p. 31.

46. Presidential Proclamation 3383, *Department of State Bulletin,* January 2, 1961, p. 18.

47. U.S. Congress, House Investigation and Study of the Administration, Operations and Enforcement of the Export Control Act of 1949, and Related Acts, in Morley, *Imperial State and Revolution,* p. 190.

Congressional appropriations funded an expanded export-control investigation staff for the Bureau of Customs forces in New York, Miami, the Gulf Coast ports, and key Mexican border locations. Every vessel that originated in Europe and docked at a U.S. port and was scheduled to make a stopover in Cuba was searched, whether or not Commerce officials had concrete information about their cargoes. The baggage of travelers and crews was inspected, and sophisticated detection equipment was installed at various airports to minimize smuggling. These enforcement measures led the United States to seize about $500,000 in U.S.-made spare parts and heavy machinery en route to Cuba between January and October 1961. Additionally, U.S.-made machine bearings valued at more than $84,000 were confiscated in transit from Canada through New York to Cuba.

48. Robbins, *The Cuban Threat,* p. 100; Paterson, *Contesting Castro,* p. 258. For a thorough account of this episode, see Smith, *The Closest of Enemies,* pp. 64–65.

49. *Public Papers of the Presidents of the United States: Dwight D. Eisenhower, 1960–1961,* U.S. Government Printing Office, 1961, p. 891.

50. Krinsky and Golove, *U.S. Economic Measures Against Cuba,* p. 111. The State Department issued Public Notice 179, declaring travel by U.S. citizens to Cuba to be "contrary to the foreign policy of the United States" and "otherwise inimical to the national interest." All U.S. passports were declared "invalid for travel to or in Cuba" unless specifically endorsed by the State Department as valid for such travel. This was later overturned by the Supreme Court. The new basis for the travel ban was the embargo—the prohibition on spending U.S. dollars in Cuba.

51. Boorstein, *The Economic Transformation of Cuba,* p. 33.

52. Morley, *Imperial State and Revolution,* p. 113.

53. Ibid., pp. 128–29.

54. Ibid., p. 129. Carla Anne Robbins supports Morley's conclusions. She writes, "It must be remembered that Cuba's early efforts to export revolution were not of major concern to U.S. policy makers. The Eisenhower Administration's hostility to the Castro regime was based on the radicalization of Cuba's domestic policies and on Castro's penchant for anti-American propaganda." Robbins, *The Cuban Threat,* p. 129–130.

55. Smith, *The Closest of Enemies,* p. 47.

56. Ibid., p. 49.

57. Ibid., p. 49.

58. Smith, *Soviet Partner or Nonaligned?* pp. 6, 9–10.

59. *New York Times,* October 16, 1960, cited in Robbins, *The Cuban Threat,* p. 97. See also Matthews, "The Bay of Pigs," p. 332.

60. *New York Times,* October 22, 1960, cited in Robbins, *The Cuban Threat,* p. 97.

61. Matthews, "The Bay of Pigs," p. 332.

62. Morley, *Imperial State and Revolution,* p. 137.

63. Matthews, "The Bay of Pigs," p. 333.

64. Boorstein, *The Economic Transformation of Cuba,* p. 33.

65. Ibid., p. 33.

66. Ibid., p. 34.

67. Morley, *Imperial State and Revolution,* p. 128.

68. Paterson, *Contesting Castro,* p. 242.

69. Morley, *Imperial State and Revolution,* p. 72.

70. See Smith, *The Closest of Enemies,* p. 70.

71. See, for example, Wyden, *Bay of Pigs: The Untold Story.*

72. Matthews, "The Bay of Pigs," p. 334. Morley also blames President Kennedy. "In memoirs and oral history interviews, senior Kennedy administration officials have sought to portray the President as a 'prisoner of events' set in motion during the Eisenhower period over which he had no control. . . . Explanations that minimize White House responsibility complement efforts to blame the CIA for the project's failure. . . . Ultimately these memoirs fail to salvage the Kennedy White House from primary responsibility for the Bay of Pigs." Morley, *Imperial State and Revolution,* pp. 141–143.

73. Smith, *The Closest of Enemies,* pp. 70–71. Only Senator J. William Fulbright was openly critical of the plan.

74. Smith, *The Closest of Enemies,* p. 71.

75. Morley, *Imperial State and Revolution,* p. 145.

76. Paterson, *Contesting Castro,* p. 258.

77. See Smith, *The Closest of Enemies,* p. 80; Brenner, *From Confrontation to Negotiation,* pp. 13–14.

78. Brenner, *From Confrontation to Negotiation,* p. 14.

79. Mary McAuliffe, CIA Documents on the Cuban Missile Crisis (CIA: October 1992).

80. Schlesinger, *Robert Kennedy and His Times,* p. 471.

81. *New York Times,* September 7, 1961; see also "Chronology of Important Events" (Government Report), p. 20.

82. The new legislation fell under section 620(a) of the Foreign Assistance Act (hereafter referred to as FAA) of 1961.

83. "Chronology of Important Events," p. 21.

84. See Ferro-Clerico and Smith, "The United States Trade Embargo," p. 134.

85. See Morley, *Imperial State and Revolution,* p. 188.

86. Department of the Treasury Memorandum, from Raymond W. Konan to Margery Waxman (Government Report). The new law, Presidential Proclamation No. 3447, took effect February 7, 1962.

The president could unilaterally remove the embargo under the same provision, but he would have to determine that such action is "necessary . . . in the interest of the U.S. under section 620 (a)(2) of the FAA of 1961." Unless the president makes this determination, and Cuba has not made compensation for expropriated property, no benefit may be provided to Cuba. If the president does make this determination, he would have the secretary of treasury rescind the Cuban Import Regulations under section 5(b) of the Trading with the Enemy Act of 1917. The president would also have the secretary of commerce amend the Export Administration Regulations and put most exports to Cuba under general license. The Export Administration Regulations denied U.S. vessels the right to carry U.S. goods to Cuba. Furthermore, no U.S. vessel could carry non-U.S. goods to Cuba or even touch a Cuban port.

87. Foreign Assets Control Memo, for the files, "Embargo on Trade with Cuba under the Foreign Assistance Act," Department of Treasury.

88. U.S. Congress, Senate, Committee on Foreign Relations, Briefing on Cuban Developments, January 25, 1962, in Morley, *Imperial State and Revolution,* p. 201.

89. Morley, *Imperial State and Revolution,* p. 195.

90. "Chronology of Important Events," p. 21; Catherine Mann, U.S. Treasury Department, OFAC, Interview, June 8, 1988.

91. Rich, "The U.S. Embargo Against Cuba," p. 9.

92. "Chronology of Important Events," p. 22.

93. Ibid., p. 23.

94. Public Law 187-565, 301(d) called for the following measures: (1) the closing of U.S. ports to all ships of any nation that allowed its vessels to carry military equipment to Cuba; (2) barring U.S. ports to any ships that brought nonmilitary goods from Communist nations to Cuba; (3) penalizing foreign shipowners whose vessels engaged in trade between Cuba and Communist nations by prohibiting them from carrying U.S. government cargo on any of their ships; and (4) prohibiting U.S. ships from any trade with Cuba.

95. *New York Times,* October 5, 1962. See Chang and Kornbluh, *The Cuban Missile Crisis,* p. 101.

96. Rich, "The U.S. embargo Against Cuba," p. 11.

97. Cable from U.S. Embassy, Madrid, to Secretary of State, October 19, 1962, National Security Archive, Cuban Missile Crisis Document Set, Document Number 00704.

98. Smith, *The Closest of Enemies,* p. 49.

99. *New York Times,* February 8, 1962.

100. "Chronology on Cuba" printed in the *Congressional Record,* January 30, 1963.

101. Theodore Draper, "Castro and Communism," in *The Reporter,* January 17, 1963.

102. R. C. Longworth, "Embrace of U.S. Doesn't Reach Washington," *Chicago Tribune,* May 20, 1986, p. C1.

103. U.S. Representative Dave Nagle (D-IA), quoting the U.S. Army War College report, in testimony, U.S. Congress, House Committee on Foreign Affairs, April 2, 1992 (statement distributed at hearing), p. 4.

104. Paterson argues that economic coercion and covert activities were equal aspects of U.S. policy toward Cuba. See Paterson, *Contesting Castro,* p. 259.

105. "The Cuba Project," Program Review by Brig. Gen. Lansdale, Feb. 20, 1962, National Security Archive, Washington D.C.; Church Committee Report, p. 142 in *The Cuban Missile Crisis, 1962,* pp. 23–37.

106. Final Report of the Select Committee to Study Government Operations with Respect to Intelligence Activities, pp. 143–144. See also Chang, *Chronology of the Cuban Missile Crisis,* p. 38. On March 14, 1962, Guidelines for Operation MONGOOSE were approved by the SGA. They read as follows: "Operation Mongoose will be developed on the following assumptions: a) In undertaking to cause the overthrow of the target government, the U.S. will make maximum use of indigenous resources, internal and external, but recognizes that final success will require decisive U.S. military intervention. b) Such indigenous resources as are developed will be used to prepare for and justify this intervention, and thereafter to facilitate and support it." See "Guidelines for Operation MONGOOSE," reprinted in Kornbluh and Chang, *Chronology of the Cuban Missile Crisis,* p. 39.

107. Church Select Committee to Study Government Operations, p. 140; Garthoff, *Reflections on the Cuban Missile Crisis,* p. 17.

108. Morley, *Imperial State and Revolution,* p. 96.

109. U.S. Congress, *Alleged Assassination Plots Involving Foreign Leaders,* p. 146.

110. Testimony of CIA Case Officer, in U.S. Congress, *Alleged Assassination Plots Involving Foreign Leaders,* p. 86.

111. Hinckle and Turner, *The Fish Is Red.*

112. *New York Times,* October 13, 1962; see also Chang, *Chronology of the Cuban Missile Crisis,* p. 107.

113. Garthoff, *Reflections on the Cuban Missile Crisis,* p. 18.

114. Hinckle and Turner, *The Fish Is Red,* p. 155.

115. Morley, *Imperial State and Revolution,* p. 153.

116. U.S. Congress, *Alleged Assassination Plots Involving Foreign Leaders,* p. 177.

117. Ibid., pp. 174–180.

4

Multilateralization of the Embargo: 1962–1970

Though U.S. efforts to expand the embargo beyond U.S. borders began in earnest in 1963, almost from the beginning the U.S. government sought international support and compliance with its Cuba sanctions policy. It was during the 1962–1970 period that the U.S. embargo enjoyed the greatest level of international backing of its entire history. Though the United States has subsequently tried to increase international compliance, particularly in the 1990s, recent multilateral support has never approached its early level. In fact, today the U.S. embargo of Cuba is routinely condemned by the international community in fora such as the United Nations. The following pages analyze how the United States was able to achieve nearly total Western compliance with its Cuba embargo during the 1960s. This chapter also reveals why, despite widespread international compliance with the embargo, the United States still failed to obtain the desired goals.

OAS/International Participation, 1962

In January 1962, the Foreign Ministers of the American Republics, meeting at Punta del Este, declared that as a consequence of its public alignment with the international Communist movement, the Marxist-Leninist government of Cuba would be excluded from participation in the inter-American system. In fact, the Latin American governments were divided over the Cuba issue. It was only after the United States threatened withdrawing Alliance for Progress funds from countries voting against the U.S. resolution that the United States received the necessary votes to pass a watered-down version of the hoped-for outcome. The United States originally wanted both Cuban expulsion from the OAS as well as an OAS-imposed hemispheric embargo on the island.[1] Though the U.S. delegation received only Cuban expulsion from the OAS, this was touted as a major diplomatic victory by the U.S. team.[2]

A month after the Punta del Este decision, the United States scored another diplomatic triumph in an international arena. The Latin American Free Trade Association (LAFTA) voted to exclude Cuba by a vote of 7 to 4, with Mexico and Brazil abstaining.[3]

Following the OAS and LAFTA decisions, the U.S. government began to pressure European allies to take similar measures against Cuba. Though OAS support was crucial to U.S. efforts to internationalize the embargo, successive U.S. administrations placed greater import on NATO compliance. While Latin America, the junior partner in an asymmetrically interdependent relationship, generally respected U.S. demands, some NATO countries were much more hesitant.

Diplomatic persuasion was used at first in the attempt to prevent NATO countries from trading with Cuba. When this proved unsuccessful, the administration took progressively more severe steps to curb European participation in Cuban trade. Most frequently, U.S. reprimands were directed toward individual countries, but occasionally, the U.S. administration requested the NATO council to castigate violators of the embargo, whether or not they were NATO members. In February 1962, State Department Counselor Walt W. Rostow asked the North Atlantic Council to take the Punta del Este decisions into account when formulating policies toward Cuba. Allies were requested to prohibit voluntary trade in strategic materials with Cuba and, in general, to reduce their trade with Cuba.[4]

In September 1962, the United States urged its NATO allies to further isolate Cuba. The following steps were specified: (1) discouraging the charter of commercial ships to the Soviet Union to carry goods to Cuba; (2) prohibiting the use of their countries for the indirect shipment of U.S.-embargoed goods to Cuba; (3) refraining from exporting items of strategic, economic, or military value to Cuba; and (4) preventing the extension of commercial credits to Cuba.[5] Britain's reluctance to place an embargo on strategic goods trade with Cuba prompted Rusk to raise the issue with British Foreign Secretary Lord Home, but no resolution of the disagreement was reported.[6] Rusk also met with Norwegian Foreign Minister Halvard M. Lange to request that Norway cease transporting strategic goods from the Soviet Union to Cuba; he received an equally ambivalent response. On the other hand, the Turkish and West German governments were apparently more cooperative.[7] The West German government adopted a regulation requiring all ships to obtain special permission to carry goods to Communist nations. Similarly, the Turkish government requested Turkish shipowners to terminate cargo movements to Cuba.[8]

Hence, by October 1962 when the Cuban Missile Crisis occurred, the United States government had developed a three-track approach to oust Fidel Castro from power. From April 1961 until October 1962, the U.S. government had carefully and consistently constructed an embargo against the island of Cuba. It had also launched the largest covert operations in the history of the CIA and had instituted carefully calibrated measures to increase the number of nations complying with U.S. efforts to overthrow the Castro government.

Cuban Missile Crisis

The Cuban Missile Crisis has received much attention. This work briefly reviews the event, paying specific attention to its impact on subsequent U.S.-Cuban relations.[9] In fact, U.S. military defeat at the Bay of Pigs, combined with the events of October 1962, led U.S. decisionmakers to concentrate U.S. policy toward Cuba around the extraterritorial extension of the U.S. embargo of the island.

In mid-October 1962, a U-2 reconnaissance flight confirmed reports that the Soviet Union was building IRBM sites at several locations in Cuba. President Kennedy and his closest advisers—together known as the ExComm (Executive Committee of the National Security Council)—outlined three main possible courses of action: (1) openly approaching Castro, Khrushchev, and U.S. allies in a gambit to resolve the crisis diplomatically; (2) a declaration of open surveillance against the island combined with a "blockade against offensive weapons entering Cuba"; and (3) military action directed against Cuba, starting with an air attack against the missiles.[10] By October 22, President Kennedy announced a quarantine on all offensive military equipment under shipment to Cuba.[11]

Kennedy obtained OAS support for his action, and the United Nations was also involved in mediation. After several tense days of U.N. efforts, Kennedy and Khrushchev exchanged a series of letters that helped resolve the crisis. The essence of their agreement was that if the Soviets would withdraw their "offensive weapons" from Cuba under U.N. supervision, the United States would lift its naval blockade of the island and pledge not to invade.

Though the immediate tension dissipated with the October 28 agreement, the conflict was still far from over. Cuba refused to allow U.N. inspection and verification, and the United States and the Soviet Union differed on whether the IL-28 bombers were considered "offensive" weapons to be included in the dismantling. The formalization of the noninvasion pledge remained unresolved as well. By November 11, however, the Soviets agreed to remove the IL-28 bombers and convinced a reticent Castro to agree. The inspection issue, on the other hand, was more intractable, since Castro refused to permit on-site inspection. The crisis eased only after the Soviets agreed to allow U.S. ships and aircraft to photograph equipment on Soviet ships leaving Cuba, to verify that the missiles were being withdrawn.

Interestingly, Kennedy never finalized his agreement not to invade

Cuba. He had originally agreed to a noninvasion pledge in exchange for on-site inspection in Cuba. When on-site inspection was not granted, Kennedy retreated from finalizing his pledge. In fact, recently declassified documents indicate that Kennedy intentionally chose not to formalize the pledge because he wanted to leave U.S. options vis-à-vis Cuba open, and he used the inspection obstacle as an excuse. A November 7, 1962, State Department policy-planning strategy paper called for "a maximal U.S. strategy . . . directed at the elimination . . . of the Castro regime." In a November 17 analysis, Roger Hilsman noted that "a stalemate in the Cuban talks might actually be more beneficial to U.S. interests in Latin America [and] Cuba. . . than a settlement." Hence, when Khrushchev repeatedly pressed Kennedy to formalize the noninvasion pledge with the United Nations, Kennedy either ignored Khrushchev or deflected him on the grounds that the Soviets and Cubans had not met the on-site inspection promise.[12]

Legacies of the Cuban Missile Crisis

Some of the important retrospectives on the Cuban Missile Crisis show that the fiasco at the Bay of Pigs contributed to "the crisis to end all crises." Specifically, U.S. efforts to undermine Castro with Operation Mongoose may have contributed to the Cuban Missile Crisis. Peter Kornbluh notes that "the new information about the Missile Crisis may . . . lend credence to Khrushchev's claim that a primary motivation [for placing missiles in Cuba] was to deter a U.S. invasion of Cuba—a claim that U.S. analysts have always dismissed out of hand."[13] In fact, the "basic action plan" of Operation Mongoose, drafted in February 1962 by Lansdale, called for a series of covert operations inside Cuba that would culminate in an internal uprising in October 1962, supported by a U.S. invasion. Philip Brenner and Scott Armstrong also point to U.S. threat of force as a contributing factor to the Missile Crisis: "The new lessons of the Cuban Missile Crisis appear to be that no matter how brilliant, crisis managers cannot foresee all contingencies and know all the factors necessary to control events. More important, it was the U.S. threat of force before October and during the crucial 13 days that appears to have engendered and heightened the crisis."[14]

Thomas Paterson concludes that it was the U.S. use of force, and threat of force, that led to the Cuban Missile Crisis:

> Had there been no exile expedition at the Bay of Pigs, no destructive covert activities, no assassination plots, no military maneuvers and plans, and no economic and diplomatic steps to harass, isolate, and destroy the Castro government in Havana, there would not have been a Cuban Missile Crisis. The origins of the October 1962 crisis derived largely from the concerted U.S. campaign to quash the Cuban Revolution.[15]

The Cuban Missile Crisis also led to two important precedents that substantially defined future relations among Havana, Moscow, and Washington. First, it established the precedent of "linkage": as a result of the Missile Crisis, all major issues of disagreement between Washington and Havana would henceforth be linked to relations between Washington and Moscow. Second, the Missile Crisis established the U.S. "no-invasion pledge."[16] Whether formalized or not, however, the pledge did not mean that Washington was willing to tolerate the Castro regime. During the next ten years, the U.S. government continued to use every means available short of direct military intervention to overthrow the Castro government. The economic embargo became the primary tool of this policy.

Brenner characterizes the remainder of the decade as "a period of cold war between the two countries."[17] "In effect," he writes, "there were three major objectives of U.S. policy toward Cuba from 1959 to 1971: (1) to overthrow the Cuban government; (2) to isolate and 'contain' Cuba; and (3) to reduce the Soviet presence in Cuba."[18]

Multilateralization of the Cuba Embargo, 1963

The principal weapon in Washington's arsenal to isolate, contain, and oust the Castro government became the trade embargo. After the Cuban Missile Crisis, the Kennedy administration's (and later the Johnson administration's) main diplomatic goal vis-à-vis Cuba was to expand the U.S. embargo by instituting a multilateral hemispheric embargo, which would involve European nations as well.

U.S. efforts to internationalize the embargo rested on a two-track strategy: moral suasion and legislation. When U.S. diplomatic efforts to persuade other nations to stop trading with Cuba failed, the U.S. government could turn to increasingly stringent embargo legislation as a means of achieving its goals. While the State Department preferred to use diplomacy to dissuade allies from trading with Cuba, Congress, and occasionally the White House, preferred to rely on legislation to make the embargo multilateral.

Embargo legislation during 1963 focused on two principal areas: limiting shipping to Cuba, and prohibiting subsidiaries of U.S. corporations from engaging in trade with Cuba.

Cuban Shipping Targeted

To further intensify pressure on third countries to isolate Cuba economically, the White House approved National Security Action Memorandum No. 220 (NSAM 220), which denied U.S. government-financed cargoes to all merchant vessels engaged in the Cuba trade. This was significantly more rigorous than the Battle Act of 1962, which had only denied U.S. port access to vessels trading with Cuba. The Department of State protested NSAM 220, fearing it would be forced to take concrete action against foreign vessels before trying diplomatic methods to curtail foreign-vessel trading. In response, several exceptions were made in the law, enabling the Department of State to use a policy of moral suasion with back-up punitive measures when necessary.[19]

By April 1963, efforts to reduce allied shipping to Cuba had been fairly successful. The governments of Liberia, Turkey, Honduras, and Panama had officially barred their ships from Cuba trade; West Germany had issued a decree prohibiting ships under its registry from participating in trade between the Soviet bloc and Cuba; the Greek government had ordered Greek ships not under charter to the Soviet bloc to desist from carrying cargoes to Cuba; and the Lebanese government had promised to revise its shipping laws to accommodate U.S. policy objectives. Additionally, the governments of Norway, Denmark, and the Netherlands "informally cautioned" their shipowners not to act in a fashion that might "disturb" bilateral relations.[20] In all, nine hundred ships were affected by the order, 45 percent of which were U.S.-owned. U.S. efforts were by no means completely successful, however. Italy, Spain, and Britain remained intractable. The British, for example, insisted that no legal basis existed for preventing shipping to Cuba.[21]

As a result, Rusk made several proposals. First, he advised that the United States, through its ambassadors, should seek further cooperation from the offending nations, "pointing out the necessity of further U.S. action unless a prompt reduction in shipping to Cuba was attained."[22] If this action by the ambassadors failed, Rusk proposed that the United States should prepare to extend the provisions of NSAM 220 to all ships owned or controlled by persons engaged in the Cuba trade.[23]

During the first quarter of 1963, the policy of moral suasion coupled with the legislative "stick"—when necessary to reinforce voluntary efforts—appeared to be successful. Only fifty-nine "free world" ships called at Cuban ports compared with 352 for the same period the previous year. Between June 1962 and June 1963 there was a 60 percent decline in the number of vessels from capitalist countries engaged in the Cuba trade, from 932 in 1962 to 359 in 1963.[24]

Prohibitions on Subsidiary Trade, 1963

In mid-1963 the Kennedy administration acted to further internationalize the embargo. The White House believed that the statutory basis for the Cuban Import Regulations—the main tool of the trade embargo—was too narrow. The Cuban Import Regulations were limited to trade between the United States and Cuba, and therefore did not deal specifically with third-country imports of Cuban goods or goods that contained Cuban materials from third countries. Nor did the regulations specifically prevent U.S. citizens or U.S.-owned subsidiaries in third countries from trading with Cuba.

To address these limitations, the Cuban Assets Control Regulations (CACR) were issued on June 3, 1963. They revoked the Cuban Import Regulations and became the essential and lasting feature of the U.S. embargo against Cuba.[25] The new regulations specifically excluded third-country subsidiaries of U.S. corporations from engaging in unlicensed transactions with Cuba.[26] The CACR (1) prohibited all transactions carried out by the Cuban government, its representatives or citizens and U.S.-based entities; (2) blocked any individual, partnership, or other group of individuals from making transfers of payment or credit, conducting foreign exchange transactions, and importing or exporting money, gold, silver, or any other precious metals between the United States and Cuba; (3) prohibited persons subject to U.S. jurisdiction from engaging in unlicensed financial or commercial transactions of any kind with Cuba or nationals thereof; (4) blocked all assets in the United States belonging to Cuba or Cuban nationals; (5) prevented travel to, from, and within Cuba except where specific licenses were granted; and (6) prohibited imports of Cuban goods.

According to a Treasury Department official, the new regulations were far more stringent than they appeared. Most subsidiaries had U.S. citizens on their boards, which precluded the entire company from trading with Cuba.[27] Morley notes that Canadian trade with Cuba was significantly impacted by the CACR:

> Subsequent Treasury and State pressures on the parent companies to adhere to these new regulations were a powerful deterrent to the expansion of Canadian-Cuban trade. The willingness of U.S. corporations to comply with government policy was not lost on Canadian firms with export markets in the United States. Irrespective of minority or majority U.S. stock ownership, they began to terminate trade with Cuba that would threaten their American market.[28]

To avoid conflict over the new extraterritorial measures, the Treasury Department continued to use "moral suasion" to discourage U.S. parent companies from permitting their foreign subsidiaries to trade with Cuba.[29] This policy produced some desired changes in NATO; sales from Western European sources of "quasi-strategic" goods declined, and Cuban military purchases from Western Europe virtually ceased.

Hence, by mid-1963, the United States had invoked powerful legislation aimed both at curtailing shipping to Cuba and preventing subsidiary trade with the island. When diplomatic efforts to limit trade with the island failed, the United States could fall back on its rigorous extraterritorial anti-Cuba laws.

Other U.S. Efforts to Strengthen Embargo, 1963

In October 1963, Assistant Secretary of State for Inter-American Affairs Edwin Martin initiated a series of exchanges with England, Canada, Mexico, and Spain to create an "unrelenting squeeze" on airline links to Havana. Though few airline carriers still serviced Cuba, the United States wanted to sever all ties. This goal was only partially achieved. England refused to ban flights from Cuba to Grand Cayman but did agree to increase the monitoring of transients. Canada refused to halt its air ties but acceded to searching Cuban planes that made fuel stopovers in Canada en route between Havana and Prague. Mexico quietly agreed to postpone Cuban landing rights within its borders but continued its national airline's weekly flights to Havana. Spain posted no new travel bans and even increased the frequency of its flights to Havana.[30]

Because trade with Cuba continued despite U.S. efforts, in December of 1963 Congress amended the Foreign Assistance Act to further reduce international trade with Cuba. The amendment directed the president to curtail or eliminate economic and military assistance to countries that failed to take "appropriate steps" to withdraw their cargo-carrying ships and airplanes from the Cuba trade by February 14, 1964. The only exception to this legislative mandate was a presidential waiver on "national security grounds."

This amendment produced tension between Congress and the White House. The administration was opposed to the amendment because they saw it as limiting Washington's flexibility in amicably resolving the embargo issue with allied governments. The specific cut-off date was viewed as particularly restrictive.[31]

In accordance with the amendment, however, the United States terminated small amounts of military assistance (about $100 million each) to England, Yugoslavia, and France on the grounds that these countries had not taken "appropriate steps" to terminate Cuba trade. It also announced its intention to halt aid commitments to Spain ($30 million) and Morocco (over $20 million) until they accommodated the Foreign Assistance Act.[32]

Spain was the only country that maintained regularly scheduled air flights to Cuba; it also still had five Spanish-owned or registered vessels under charter to Cuba. As a result, Ex-Im Bank loans, surplus agricultural commodities, and direct U.S. economic aid to Spain virtually ceased. However, U.S. bilateral military aid to Spain was not interrupted.

In another effort to curb shipping to Cuba, in December 1963 the new Johnson administration revised regulations on allied shipping engaged in trade with Cuba. According to the new rules, ships would be removed from the U.S. Maritime Association's "blacklist" if offending shipowners agreed to take all of their other vessels out of Cuba trade as charters expired. Additionally, they could not sign any new charters to trade with Cuba. If shipowners failed to do this, their entire fleets, including vessels that had never entered Cuban ports, would be blacklisted.[33] As a result, Western shipping to Cuba was substantially reduced. For example, the number of trips made by British vessels declined from 180 in 1964 to 62 in 1967, and Greek and Lebanese ships visiting Cuban ports declined from 163 in 1963 to 23 in 1968.[34] It is estimated that Cuban shipping costs tripled after 1959 due to Cuba's increasing dependence on distant suppliers. In 1963 alone, Cuba was forced to divert $50 million from other areas to pay for extra shipping charges.[35]

Regionalization of the Embargo, 1964

By 1964, though most of the embargo legislation was in place, the new Johnson administration sought to close any remaining loopholes. Hence, three policy changes of consequence occurred that year. In May 1964, the Commerce Department revoked the general license permitting the sale of foodstuffs and medicines to Cuba. Henceforth, the Commerce Department permitted only limited humanitarian donations.[36] Cuba is thus the only country since World War II to face an embargo that has precluded the sale of foodstuffs and medicines. Even Vietnam and Iraq were allowed to buy foods and medicines from U.S. sources during wartime.[37]

In February 1964, additionally, a minor amendment to the embargo laws specified that all Cuban nationals who work at the Guantánamo naval base (a total of about 2,500) would be discharged unless they agreed to become permanent residents of the base or spend all their U.S. dollar earnings there. If their jobs were terminated, or if they spent all their earnings on the base, the result would be a $5 million hard currency loss to Cuba.[38]

The other legal change in 1964 came in October when the Commerce Department further strengthened its attempts to prevent foreign vessels from trading with Cuba. It amended the regulations to prohibit foreign ships calling in U.S. ports from obtaining bunker fuel if they intended subsequently to call at a Cuban port, or if they had called at a Cuban port any time after January 1, 1963.[39]

OAS Embargoes Cuba

The most significant event for the U.S. trade embargo during 1964 occurred in July when, under U.S. leadership, the OAS imposed an embargo on Cuba, condemning Castro for aggression and intervention in Venezuela. A cache of arms shipped from Cuba for use by Venezuelan guerrillas had been found in Venezuelan territory in late 1962; in late 1963, an OAS investigation team confirmed the Cuban origin of the arms. Caracas called for hemispheric sanctions against Cuba, and a foreign ministers' meeting of the OAS was convened in July 1964 to deal expressly with the problem. U.S. Secretary of State Dean Rusk addressed the delegates, calling for regional sanctions against Cuba. Though initial response to the U.S. sanctions proposal was mixed, U.S. arm twisting succeeded in obtaining a regional embargo of Cuba.[40] OAS member states voted that they should (1) have no diplomatic and consular relations with Cuba and (2) suspend all trade and sea transportation, with certain exceptions for humanitarian reasons, until the Permanent Council of the OAS determined by two-thirds vote that Cuba had ceased to pose a danger to the peace and security of the hemisphere. At that meeting Rusk stated, "It is the present Cuban Government's affiliation with the Sino-Soviet bloc and its vow to extend Communist power throughout the hemisphere that is incompatible with the purposes and principles of the Inter-American system."[41] The United States had finally won a major victory for its international embargo.

Attempts to Gain Allies' Compliance

Aside from the legislative strengthening of the embargo and the historic OAS decision, the United States continued to rely on diplomatic "moral suasion" to curtail trade with Cuba. 1964 is marked by efforts—both successful and failed—on the part of the United States to convince allies to abandon the Cuba trade. Japan, Canada, and Britain were the main capitalist nations that continued a substantial exchange with the island. An examination of some of those efforts and their outcomes follows.

Britain. Britain most flagrantly challenged the U.S. extraterritorial laws, and was subjected to a new U.S. tactic: covert operations against allies to prevent trade. In January 1964 the British Leyland Motor Corporation signed a contract to supply the Cubans with 450 buses for an estimated $11.2 million and at least $1 million worth of spare parts.[42] A five-year credit extension was guaranteed by the British government's Export Credits Guarantee Department. In the U.S. Congress, liberals and conservatives alike strongly condemned the deal. The following month, when President Johnson met with British Prime Minister Douglas-Home, their talks resulted in agreement on nearly all bilateral issues and a "complete disagreement on the issue of British trade with Cuba." Faced with a possible U.S. decision to terminate its $100,000 military-aid grant to England, Douglas-Home nevertheless publicly maintained that British trade excluded strategic items and did not involve loans or aid for general purposes. However, shortly after the meeting, the British informally discouraged local merchant shipping from carrying British goods, principally Leyland buses, to Cuba. Leyland used an East German vessel instead. Frustrated with Britain's refusal to heed the embargo, in April 1964 the United States appealed to

NATO. At a secret NATO session in Paris, Undersecretary of State Ball denounced Britain: "Is it . . . the intention of the members that a single nation should be able to frustrate a serious policy affecting the defense of the free world interests in a vital area of the world?" The British insisted that their trade with Cuba was "purely commercial." The NATO council voted 15 to 1 in opposition to British trade with Cuba.[43]

The following month, *The London Times* reported that the British government, in "a fraternal half-measure believed to be acceptable to the [Johnson] administration," had agreed to discourage trade with Cuba. Such action that might be taken, however, would not be enforced by legislative or judicial fiat, nor was it a "departure from the traditional British position of untrammeled trade in non-strategic goods."[44]

In October 1964, the United States remained frustrated by its inability to interrupt the Leyland bus contract. There is some evidence to indicate that at this point the CIA became involved. A Japanese cargo ship, the *Yamashiro Maru,* apparently cooperating with the CIA, rammed an East German freighter, the *Magdeberg,* as it left port in London carrying Cuba-bound Leyland buses. The *Magdeberg* sank and its cargo was ruined, though the crew was rescued.[45] Though there is no concrete evidence to link the sinking of the East German freighter with the CIA, Morley believes that the Japanese ship knew exactly what it was doing because British intelligence had informed Washington, D.C., of the Cuban-bound ships' schedules—information obtained through a wiretap in the Cuban embassy.[46] Despite these efforts, Leyland continued to honor its Cuban contract and sell buses to the island.

Japan. The State Department was also "extremely concerned" over the expansion of Japanese-Cuban trade. Tokyo was the largest capitalist buyer of Cuban sugar, with imports tripling from 161,000 tons in 1963 to 542,000 by 1967. U.S. embassy officials in Tokyo were instructed to "discourage [any] long-term [Japanese] commitments" to Cuban sugar purchases and to persuade Japan to look for alternative sugar sources. The director of the Economic Affairs Bureau in the Japanese Ministry of Foreign Affairs told U.S. Economic Counselor Arthur Gardner that foreign trade was the preserve of private capitalists and that, short of "administrative guidance," the government was powerless. Given the importance of harmonious relations with Japan, U.S. pressures over this issue were almost exclusively diplomatic. Though Japan did reduce its bilateral trade with Cuba from $87.9 million in 1964 to $33 million in 1968, desire to cooperate with the United States was only partially responsible for this change. Havana's balance of payments difficulties also contributed to diminishing Japanese-Cuban trade.[47]

Spain. Spain also proved to be a thorny issue for U.S. policymakers. In

January 1964, the State Department sent a cable to the Madrid embassy, stating that it welcomed recent actions by the Liberian, Panamanian, Italian, and West German governments to "restrict or prevent their shipping from calling at Cuba." Spain was described as "standing out among free-world countries" in that, according to current data, all indices of economic ties, except shipping, had actually expanded between 1962 and 1963.[48] Spain, however, had little choice in maintaining strong economic ties with Cuba. Its postwar economic industrialization had reached a point where exports were more important to economic growth than agricultural production. Because Spain remained outside the European Common Market, it was forced to look for alternative trade outlets.[49]

In late January 1964, in reaction to Spain's projected $50 million shipbuilding agreement with Cuba, CIA Director John McCone went to speak with General Franco in order to talk Spain out of the Cuba trade. By the end of February, Spain bowed under U.S. pressure and informed the United States that it was prepared to cooperate, but needed time to figure out how.[50] By the following month, Spain also agreed to stop transporting commercial cargo on Iberia Airlines passenger flights to Havana, and agreed not to renew charters on vessels engaged in the Cuba trade once they expired. The State Department described these actions as "appropriate."[51]

The United States was forced to move beyond the moral suasion policy on two occasions in 1964 that deserve mention here. In May of 1964 the French government and French locomotive company Brissoneau et Lotz sold twenty diesel locomotives to Cuba in a $4 million contract. The three-year credit term was shorter than usual for sales of this nature; the French government asserted, moreover, that the locomotives were nonstrategic and important to the depressed French manufacturing sector. Nonetheless, the U.S. government terminated its small amounts of military assistance to France on the grounds that France had not taken "appropriate steps" to halt Cuba trade. The United States also terminated military assistance to England, Yugoslavia, Spain, and Morocco until they accommodated the Foreign Assistance Act.[52]

Finally, in late 1964, the Soviet Union concluded a large grain agreement with the Canadian Wheat Board for purchase of 860,000 tons each of wheat and wheat flour during 1965–1966. The proposed Cuban allocation was considerably larger than past agreements, and the United States invoked the CACR to prohibit U.S. milling subsidiaries in Canada from processing any part of the shipment for delivery to Cuba.

Until mid-1964, Washington preferred to use private, informal pressures on domestic and foreign companies to coax them out of the Cuba trade. Secretary Rusk described the response of the targeted companies as "generally [one of] matter-of-fact acceptance." But the tremendous growth in Cuba's imports from capitalist countries during 1964 (about 80 percent over 1963 to $225 million) led Rusk to acknowledge that "diplomatic persuasion, reinforced in some cases by direct approaches to companies involved," had not entirely worked.

1965–1970: Refining the Machine

The years from 1965 through 1970 are marked by minor legislative changes in the embargo. Most of the changes were invoked to close loopholes that developed over time. This period is also noted for continued U.S. efforts to pressure its allies to stay away from the Cuba trade. Though the United States was successful in persuading many of its allies to avoid Cuba much of the time, there were cases when the offending country simply ignored U.S. protests. Sometimes these countries suffered the political and economic consequences of disregarding U.S. interests, but on other occasions the United States chose to look the other way. U.S. efforts to close trade with Cuba were also dogged by the fact that during this period, Cuba's creditworthiness was considered exemplary. There were several cases when the United States decided that maintaining good bilateral relations with a particular ally was more important than incurring the diplomatic costs associated with pressuring friends into action.

By the end of the period, the multilateral embargo had all but collapsed. As Cuba proved its creditworthiness, and the price of sugar continued to rise, nations that had heeded U.S. pressures in the 1960s began to discuss trade issues and conduct trade with Cuba in the early 1970s. Ultimately, even the United States began to reconsider its policy. The following pages review the final years of the period in closer detail.

Legislative Aspects of the Embargo, 1965–1973

Two substantive additions to the embargo were made during the 1965–1973 period: Food for Peace and Cuba's Country Group Z designation.

Food for Peace

In a further effort to make the embargo multinational, in May 1966 the House Agricultural Committee voted for a $3.3 billion "Food for Freedom" bill that included a prohibition on food aid to any country engaged in trade with Cuba or North Vietnam. It appeared that India, Pakistan, Yugoslavia, Poland, Morocco, and a number of Latin American countries would no longer be eligible for food aid. The Johnson administration, however, opposed limitations on the executive branch's ability to use food aid as a policy lever, and hence pressured for modifications. The outcome was a bill

(PL 480) closely resembling the original: the Food for Peace program banned all food shipments to any country engaged in selling or shipping strategic or nonstrategic goods to Cuba, with a proviso that the president could, in specific situations, waive the ban on transactions involving medical supplies and nonstrategic items.

India became the first country forced to test the law. Between 1965 and 1966, India sold $4 million worth of jute to Cuba. Experiencing a two-year drought at the time and threat of a large-scale famine, India was also expecting to receive 11 million tons of U.S. grain over the next year. In January 1967, Undersecretary of State for Political Affairs Eugene Rostow visited India. In exchange for a promise from the Indian government not to expand or vary its trade with Cuba, the United States agreed to a two-million-ton grain allocation to India, with three million more tons to be made available through the U.S. Commodity Credit Corporation, on the understanding that it would be matched by allied countries.[53] India and the United States thus reached a compromise under which both countries could save face, and the United States did not have to resort to invoking penalties against India.

Country Group Z

Legislation in 1965 amended the Commerce Department's "country group" designation system. Countries were divided into six groups, Country Groups T, V, W, X, Y, and Z. Cuba was placed in Country Group Z category, which is the most restrictive.[54] In practical terms, this new categorization meant closing one more loophole of the embargo: the re-export by third countries of U.S.-origin technical data and the *products* of U.S.-origin technical data were prohibited.[55]

Other minor amendments to the embargo legislation made during this period are summarized below, in chronological order.

In October 1965, the Office of Foreign Assets Control (OFAC) announced that it was prepared to issue licenses unblocking frozen accounts of U.S. citizens' assets in Cuban corporations wholly or substantially owned by U.S. citizens on or before July 8, 1963. The intention of the change was to prevent U.S. citizens from suffering as a result of the Cuba embargo.

In 1967, the Cuban Assets Control Regulations were amended to authorize payments or transfers of credit or securities from any blocked account to another blocked account under certain conditions. The regulations were also revised to make it clear that a decision by OFAC constituted final agency action under the regulations.

That same year, the State Department issued a new public notice proclaiming that "travel to, in, or through Cuba is restricted" and stating that such travel "would seriously impair the conduct of U.S. foreign affairs."

The notice provided that U.S. passports were not valid for travel to Cuba unless specifically endorsed by the State Department.

Finally, in 1969, the Commerce Department amended its export regulations to state expressly that all applications to export commodities and technical data to Cuba would be denied except for "certain humanitarian transactions."

OAS Tightens Embargo, 1967

One of the larger public victories for the United States in its battle to isolate Cuba came in September 1967 when the OAS approved more stringent economic sanctions against Cuba. Facing growing Cuban-inspired and armed revolutionary movements in the hemisphere, Latin American governments proved more willing than they had been in 1964 to tighten the screws on the Cuban government.

Though this OAS decision to tighten the embargo provided important rhetorical ammunition for U.S. policymakers, its particulars still fell short of U.S. hopes. Secretary Rusk successfully called on OAS members to refuse bunkering facilities as well as government-financed cargoes to ships trading with Cuba. In effect, this extended the U.S. shipping blacklist to Latin America. But the United States was unable to win approval for a resolution blacklisting foreign firms trading with Cuba. Even the shipping resolution was considered ineffective since the non-Communist countries trading with Cuba—Britain, France, West Germany, Spain, Canada, and Japan—generally arranged for their trade to be carried in ships bearing Communist countries' flags.[56] Nonetheless, the OAS vote was seen as a symbolic U.S. victory in its efforts to further squeeze the Castro government.

Soviet-Cuban Relations, Mid-1960s

While the United States was tightening the economic embargo on Cuba in the mid-1960s, Soviet-Cuban relations were simultaneously going through a particularly stressful period.[57] As early as 1962, following the Cuban Missile Crisis, the Soviet Union began to exercise caution vis-à-vis its Cuban partner.[58] Aside from the direct confrontation between Cuba and the Soviet Union related to differences over removal of Soviet missiles from Cuba, the Missile Crisis led the Soviets to reevaluate their goals in Latin America, return to a belief in geographic determinism, and recognize U.S. dominance in the hemisphere.

The Missile Crisis revealed that the Soviet Union was not interested in direct confrontation with the United States over Latin America. Soviet interest in the region centered on exploiting situations where the United States had lost ground and on expanding Soviet positions in those cases. In fact, the Soviets were primarily interested in developing economic and trade relations with Latin America, and less concerned with spreading communism in the United States' backyard.[59] At the same time, the Cubans learned from the Missile Crisis that they could not depend exclusively on the Soviet Union and were therefore spurred in their quest to create new revolutionary governments in Latin America. Hence, while Soviet policy toward Latin America following the Missile Crisis leaned toward supporting normal state-to-state relations with nations of the region regardless of their ideological belief, Cuba was further inspired by the crisis to support revolutionary movements. Between 1962 and 1968, the Cubans struggled with the Soviets over foreign policy matters.[60]

Three particularly important conferences hosted by the Cubans contributed to shaping the antagonistic relationship between the two allies during these years. In 1964, Castro hosted a pro-Moscow Latin American Communist Party conference. He compromised with the Soviets at the conference by agreeing that there were two acceptable ways to achieve socialism in the hemisphere: armed struggle (which Castro preferred) and peaceful coexistence (the Soviet position).

In 1966 the Tri-Continental Conference was held in Havana, principally because the Soviets were trying to outmaneuver the Chinese. By 1966, the Soviets had retreated from their 1964 position of limited commitment to revolutionary movements. Soviet theorists no longer thought that the Third World was ripe for revolution. The Chinese, however, took the opposite position, rejecting all possibility of accommodation with even liberal regimes, and arguing that armed struggle was the *only* strategy. The Soviets thought that by holding the conference in a friendly nation, Cuba, they would be able to gain the upper hand over the Chinese. The Cubans, however, had other ideas. They seized the opportunity provided by the conference and promoted revolutionary struggle—a position more closely allied with China than with the Soviet Union. When the Latin American governments subsequently questioned the Soviets about their participation in the conference, the Soviets pointed out that only a low-level Soviet delegation had attended, and that Soviet policy of pursuing normal state-to-state relations remained in effect. The Cubans were furious that the Soviets disavowed the conference.

The following year, the LASO (Latin American Solidarity Organization) conference was held in Cuba. Castro invited representatives from a number of Latin American revolutionary movements, making it clear that his allegiance was with these emerging movements rather than with the established Communist parties. Castro's efforts to assert his independence from Moscow culminated in January 1968 with the "Escalante Affair," in which he purged a group of Moscow-leaning members from the Cuban

Communist Party.[61] Until 1968, the Soviet Union displayed a remarkable amount of patience as they let the Cubans play out their radical strategy. They first attempted to restrain the Cubans through ideological criticism, but when this failed to yield desired results, they exerted economic pressure. In 1968 the Soviets threatened to cut off economic support to the island unless the Castro government stopped publicly attacking Soviet policies and abandoned its efforts to export violent revolution to Latin America. The Soviets backed their threats by slowing oil deliveries to Cuba and for several weeks suspended shipments of critical industrial goods.[62] Responding to Soviet sanctions, the Cuban government agreed to stop publicly criticizing the Soviet Union and Latin American Communist parties. The Soviets, in return, restored previous aid and increased their technical assistance to Cuba.[63] In the summer of 1968, Havana proved its allegiance to Moscow by endorsing the controversial Soviet invasion of Czechoslovakia.

Diplomatic Pressure, 1965–1970

During this period, the United States continued to rely heavily upon diplomatic pressure to curtail trade with Cuba.[64] In 1966, U.S. attempts to ban the Cuba trade met with measured success. In the summer of 1966, for example, the United States successfully blocked a French government sale of heavy equipment to Cuba, which would have involved $35 million in long-term government-guaranteed credit. In November of that year, the United States cautioned Greece that all U.S. military and economic assistance to that country could be terminated if the Greek government did not act to prevent Greek shipping to Cuba. Greece then moved to enforce the existing ban prohibiting Greek vessels from carrying cargoes to and from Cuba. Defiant shipowners were threatened with legal sanctions: up to six months' imprisonment, substantial monetary fines, or the revocation of the ship's masters license for up to two years.[65]

That same year, in an effort not to antagonize an important trade partner, the United States overlooked Canadian-based U.S. subsidiary trade when U.S. parts formed a minimal percentage of the overall order. For example, Cuba ordered five refrigerator trucks built on a chassis manufactured in Canada by a U.S. subsidiary. The chassis contained 55 percent U.S.-origin parts, but these constituted only 18 percent of the total value of the trucks. The Canadian government labeled them "Canadian products" without consulting Washington. The U.S. authorities let it go.[66]

Britain, however, continued to directly thwart Washington's efforts at closing Cuba trade. In early 1967, a British firm, Simon-Carves, signed a multimillion-dollar contract with Cuba for a fertilizer complex. The loan was underwritten by the British Export Credits Guarantee Department

(ECGD), which noted that Cuba had been "meticulous" in meeting payments on earlier trade deals, including the Leyland bus loan. Despite U.S. pressure, the British government insisted on treating trade with Cuba like that with any other Communist country; the ECGD's willingness to grant the five-year loan was thus to be determined exclusively by considerations of Cuba's creditworthiness.[67]

In response to the move, senior White House official Walt W. Rostow met with British Prime Minister Harold Wilson to make it clear that "public and Congressional opposition to such [government guaranteed credit] deals is intense," and that such deals would make it difficult for Washington to support British policy in Rhodesia.[68] The British went ahead with their plans, nevertheless. It was later reported that the deal did not impact Simon-Carves exports to the United States. A Simon-Carves spokesperson said that the deal with Cuba had "no effect whatever" on U.S. operations.[69]

How Did Cuba Survive a Multinational Embargo?

Between 1960 and 1964 the Cuba sanctions were made nearly airtight. They prohibited all imports, exports, and financial transactions between Cuba and the United States; virtually no trade took place between the two nations during the early 1960s. Moreover, the OAS, under U.S. leadership, expelled Cuba from the organization, broke diplomatic relations with the island, and adopted economic sanctions as well. U.S. efforts to expand the embargo to include Europe also met with measured success. Using moral suasion when possible, and economic retaliation when necessary, the United States was able to gain compliance for its Cuba embargo from many of its allies and trading partners. Nevertheless, Britain, Canada, Mexico, Spain, and Japan maintained some trade with Cuba throughout this period.

Why, then, despite this apparent success of achieving strong international compliance with the embargo policy, did the United States fail to realize its major goal of destabilizing the Castro government? A few explanations are considered in the following pages.

Cuba's Trade Patterns Adapt

In 1959 about 69 percent of all Cuban trade was with the United States. By 1962 with the imposition of the embargo, U.S. trade with Cuba had been reduced to 0.1 percent of total Cuban trade.[70] U.S. trade was kept at this level through the 1963–1973 period.

Between 1964 and 1966, Havana's trade with Western countries dropped from 36.9 percent to 19.6 percent of its total, reflecting Washington's efforts to confine Cuba's trade with the West to barter or cash sales.[71] By the latter part of the decade, nonsocialist countries conducted an average of 27 percent of Cuba's total trade. Japan took the largest share; Spain came in second; the United Kingdom was third; and France, Italy, Canada, West Germany, Holland, and Sweden each conducted between 1 and 2 percent of total Cuban trade.[72]

Cuba was able to circumvent the embargo by seeking out new trade partners, primarily among the United States' major ideological adversaries, but among U.S. allies as well. The socialist bloc substituted for previous U.S. trade, accounting for an average of 73 percent of Cuba's total trade during the 1961–1973 period. The Soviet Union was Cuba's main trade partner, accounting for an average of 48 percent of Cuban trade. China's share of Cuba's total trade averaged 9 percent; Czechoslovakia and East Germany constituted about 4 percent each; and Bulgaria, Poland, Rumania, and Hungary each accounted for between 1 and 2 percent.[73]

History has shown that target nations may turn sanctions to their economic advantage if they are able to find new, strong, and reliable trade partners.[74] Cuba was able to do so. In 1972, Cuba was admitted into full membership in the Council for Mutual Economic Assistance (CMEA), making Cuba the only member of the nine-nation group not geographically contiguous to the rest of the group.[75] In joining the group, Cuba further institutionalized its ties to the socialist bloc, and secured a number of bilateral economic agreements, including a restructuring of Cuba's debt, a line of credit, long-term trade agreements, and a new price for Cuban sugar exports of 12 cents per pound—substantially higher than the 7.4 cents on the world market.[76] Hence, the U.S. embargo forced Cuba to find new trade partners who became, in some arenas, more lucrative for the Cuban economy than the United States had been.

U.S. benevolence probably would not have matched that of the Soviets had the United States and Cuba maintained close relations during this period. In simple numerical terms, Cuba received more than $40 billion in aid from its Soviet patron between 1961 and 1985, a full one-quarter of all Soviet aid distributed. By contrast, Israel, the top-ranking recipient of U.S. aid, received $45.3 billion during the same period of time. On a per capita basis, this is three times more than Cuba received from the Soviet Union. Egypt, the second-ranking recipient of U.S. aid, received about $19 billion between 1961 and 1985.[77] Hence, only if Cuban aid from the United States had matched U.S. aid to Israel—a most improbable event—would Cuba have fared better, in the assistance sphere, without the embargo.

This is not to say that the embargo has not been costly to Cuba. Economic disruption resulting from the embargo has included a change in Cuba's principal trade partners, lack of spare parts for heavy machinery and other goods, and the closing of alternative nonsocialist markets when the embargo became multilateral. These forms of disruption amounted to a loss to the Cuban economy despite the aid Cuba received from its new patron.

Multilateral Embargoes: Low Success Rate

Though it may seem counterintuitive, sanctions theory holds that multilateral embargoes have low success rates. This is due in part to the fact that nations cannot agree on what constitutes sanctionable behavior. In addition, allied nations sometimes gain by trading with the target nation since the absence of competition from the sender's market may allow more favorable prices. Furthermore, sanctions imposed by multilateral fora generally take longer to invoke because of the bureaucratic decision-making procedures involved. The lengthier build-up time provides the target with an opportunity to find ways to circumvent the proposed sanctions.

In the Cuba case, the United States had difficulty obtaining consensus in both regional and international organizations. Though the OAS eventually complied with U.S. demands and invoked a regional embargo of Cuba, it was not without conflict. In August 1960, for example, as we have seen, U.S. Secretary of State Christian Herter failed to get the OAS to condemn Castro or Cuba, and only received a mildly worded resolution that condemned all intervention in the hemisphere. The OAS embargo on Cuba (with the exception of Mexico) was invoked from 1964 to 1974, but throughout the regional embargo, different OAS member countries have questioned the efficacy of the policy and have refused to participate.

Moreover, sanctions theory suggests that regional sanctions policies have more success than international sanctions because of the proximity factor: it is more costly for a target nation to trade with distant partners. This is not true in the Cuba case. Because Latin America accounted for a fairly small fraction of Cuban trade prior to the Cuban revolution, OAS participation in the embargo had little impact on the outcome of the sanctions policy. The United States viewed OAS participation primarily as a tool it could use to convince NATO to cease involvement in the Cuba trade. In February 1962, for example, State Department Counselor Walt W. Rostow asked the North Atlantic Council to take the OAS decision to exclude Cuba from the inter-American system into account when formulating policies toward Cuba.

U.S. efforts to expand the embargo to include NATO allies met with varied response. From the beginning, some U.S. allies both publicly condemned U.S. efforts to globalize the embargo and refused to comply. Canada and Britain, for example, have been particularly outspoken critics of U.S. efforts to make the embargo multilateral. In fact, several U.S. allies found that Cuba was an inviting market precisely because they no longer faced competition from U.S. sources.

The United States has had little success gaining compliance for its Cuba sanctions policy in the United Nations. On the contrary, the United Nations has condemned the U.S. embargo. Aside from the OAS embargo and various Latin American organizations' adoption of similar (though repetitive) measures, no other multilateral organization has adopted sanctions against Cuba. In sum, the United States has had difficulty obtaining consensus on the Cuba embargo in both regional and global fora. When such consensus is lacking, the moral basis for the policy is lost.

Domestic Bureaucratic Squabbles

The embargo was also undermined during this early period—and throughout its duration—by interagency conflict within U.S. decision-making circles. The Cuba embargo has been stretched and pulled in different directions according to the differing agendas of the various policymakers involved. Presidential election campaigns and interagency conflicts that have included, at various times, the executive branch, the legislative branch, the Treasury Department, the State Department, and the National Security Council have all served to shape the Cuba embargo. Several of these bureaucratic conflicts affected the sanctions policy right from the start.

Presidential campaigns as an architect of Cuba policy. Presidential campaigns have shaped U.S. policy toward Cuba since the Nixon-Kennedy campaign of 1960. Almost every election since 1960 (except perhaps the 1972 campaign) ensured a clamping down on U.S. policy toward Cuba as each candidate strived to appear the most anti-Communist.

As the presidential campaign of 1960 drew to a close, the Kennedy staff lit upon a recently published report blaming the Eisenhower administration for "losing Cuba." In the heated exchange that followed, both candidates pushed themselves into corners on the Cuba issue. As we have seen, Kennedy then had to live up to his campaign promises to support armed intervention on the island, probably against his better judgment. Subsequent chapters will demonstrate time and again that the Cuba case is an excellent example of the sacrifice of "good" foreign policy decisions on the mantle of domestic political posturing.

White House vs. Congress on Cuba policy. As in other areas of policy formulation, the White House has a long history of attempting to keep foreign policy toward Cuba in its private domain. When changes to embargo laws have been discussed, the White House has often taken the position that it wants flexibility in its range of actions against Cuba, and that it does not want to be boxed into a corner by U.S. law. For example, Secretary of State Dean Rusk told a closed congressional hearing on Cuba in 1962 that the administration hesitated to enact more stringent measures to force compliance with the embargo "because that would create some very sharp issues with friendly governments who at the moment lack the legal resources to move promptly to comply."[78] He assured the senators that the administration was working "behind the scenes" to reduce their shipping in the Cuban trade.[79]

Likewise, in December 1963, Congress amended the Foreign Assistance Act to direct the president to curtail or eliminate economic and military assistance to countries that failed to take "appropriate steps" to withdraw their vessels and airplanes from the Cuba trade. The White House objected to the amendment on the grounds that it limited Washington's flexibility in resolving the embargo issue amicably with allied governments.[80] As discussed earlier, the 1966 disagreement over food aid as a category of the embargo or a flexible policy lever available to the administration provides another example of intragovernmental conflict impeding smooth implementation of the embargo.[81]

Treasury Department and its influence on Cuba policy formulation. The Treasury Department and the State Department have also collided over Cuba policy. The Treasury Department, entrusted to implement main components of the embargo, has had its own ideas about embargo policy. Throughout 1961, for example, when the embargo was first fully invoked, the Treasury Department advocated placing the embargo under the TWEA in order to avoid litigation and to close potential loopholes. The State Department repeatedly resisted invoking TWEA because it feared that calling Cuba an "enemy" would cause political disturbances in Latin America. By 1962, Treasury prevailed on the grounds that litigation problems and "loopholes" would abound, hampering Treasury's ability to administer the embargo, if TWEA were not invoked.[82]

Conclusions

Differing forces with disparate goals have influenced the shape of the U.S. embargo. When presidential candidates shaped future Cuba policy from the campaign stump, their interests were centered less on the impact of the embargo on Cuba and more on parochial issues such as attracting votes. Similarly, the Treasury Department's impact on the embargo had less to do with concern for effecting change in Cuba than with retaining power in a large bureaucracy. The executive and legislative branches also had differing policy goals as well as goals that changed over time. Congressional members used the embargo in part as a symbolic measure to appease certain constituent concerns. The White House was also aware of public opinion but at more of a distance than Congress. Hence, it was able to focus on the foreign policy goals of the embargo in a more pragmatic and unfettered manner.

In this chapter, we have seen how the United States carefully constructed a nearly airtight domestic embargo against Cuba. We have also seen how the United States attempted to gain international support for its Cuba embargo using both moral suasion and, when necessary, legislation. Several U.S. allies were penalized financially for trading with Cuba, and others were denounced in international fora. Despite the occasional wayward ally, during this period the United States enjoyed the highest level of international complicity with its sanctions policy during the entire thirty-eight-year course of the embargo. Nevertheless, as this chapter explains, despite the high level of international support, the embargo policy still failed to achieve its major goals. First, Cuba was able to turn to other trade partners to circumvent the embargo. The Eastern Bloc, primarily the Soviet Union, came to Cuba's aid. A number of capitalist-oriented countries also maintained limited though important trade with the island. Second, though the United States was successful in eventually obtaining a regional embargo of Cuba, it served little purpose because Latin American trade with the island was insubstantial before the regional sanctions were invoked. Finally, in this chapter we have seen how domestic political disputes also undermined the effort to find an effective U.S. policy toward Cuba.

By the end of the period, the embargo policy had been in effect for over a decade with little to show for it. Castro was still in power, and Cuba was firmly entrenched in the Soviet trade and assistance sphere. Cuba's growing economy served to make the island an increasingly interesting place for foreign investment. Nonsocialist countries were tired of an embargo policy that failed to show results. Most U.S. allies had never fully embraced the sanctions but abided by them mostly to placate the United States. Several U.S. allies and regional powers began to move back into the Cuba market, and the decade-old, carefully constructed U.S. multilateral embargo showed signs of serious decay.

Notes

1. Morley, *Imperial State and Revolution,* pp. 155–158.

2. "Chronology of Important Events in U.S.-Cuban Relations, 1957–1962," p. 17.

3. Cable from Mexico City to the Secretary of State, September 4, 1962, National Security Archive, Cuban Missile Crisis Document Set, Document Number 00345. The conference adopted Resolution 36, which barred admission of any country with an incompatible economic system. Resolution 37 named Cuba as such a country.

4. Chang, *Chronology of the Cuban Missile Crisis,* p. 38.

5. *New York Times,* September 8, 1962.

6. *New York Times,* September 24, 1962.

7. "Chronology on Cuba," *Congressional Record,* January 31, 1963.

8. *New York Times,* September 28, 1962.

9. For excellent information on the Cuban Missile Crisis, see Blight and Welch, *On the Brink;* Nathan, *Cuban Missile Crisis Revisited;* Allison, *Essence of Decision;* Chang and Kornbluh, *The Cuban Missile Crisis;* Garthoff, *Intelligence*

Assessment and Policymaking; Garthoff, *Reflections on the Cuban Missile Crisis;* Kennedy, *Thirteen Days;* and Larson, *The Cuban Crisis of 1962*.

10. Chang, *Chronology of the Cuban Missile Crisis,* p. 119.

11. Kennedy also called for: (1) continued and increased surveillance of Cuba; (2) full retaliation by the United States against the Soviet Union if any missile were launched from Cuba against any nation in the Western Hemisphere; (3) reinforcement of the U.S. naval base at Guantánamo; (4) a call for an immediate meeting of the OAS; (5) a call for an emergency meeting of the United Nations Security Council; and (6) a halt by Khrushchev of the Soviets' "clandestine, reckless, and provocative threat to world peace and to stable relations between our two nations." See Chang, *Chronology of the Cuban Missile Crisis,* p. 159.

12. Chang and Kornbluh, *The Cuban Missile Crisis,* p. 236.

13. Kornbluh and Walter, "History Held Hostage," *Washington Post,* October 11, 1992, p. C2.

14. Scott Armstrong and Philip Brenner, "Putting Cuba and Crisis Back in the Cuban Missile Crisis," *Los Angeles Times,* November 1, 1987, Part V, p. 3.

15. Paterson, *Contesting Castro,* p. 260.

16. Robbins, *The Cuban Threat,* pp. 113–115. Brenner points out that Kissinger established the basis for the pledge in 1970. See Brenner, "Thirteen Months," in Nathan, *The Cuban Missile Crisis Revisited,* p. 283.

17. Brenner, *From Confrontation to Negotiation,* p. 16.

18. Ibid., p. 17.

19. National Security Action Memorandum No. 220, February 5, 1963.

20. Morley, *Imperial State and Revolution,* p. 227.

21. Rusk, "Memorandum for President Kennedy," April 17, 1963, National Security Archive, Cuban Missile Crisis Document Set.

22. Ibid.

23. Ibid. Rusk also suggested that the U.S. government request U.S.-owned and -controlled oil companies to refrain voluntarily from bunkering vessels known to be engaged in the Cuba trade, and that the United States seek cooperation of the United Kingdom in the application of a similar policy by British oil companies.

24. Morley, *Imperial State and Revolution,* p. 202.

25. Krinsky and Golove, *Economic Measures Against Cuba,* p. 112.

26. Morley, *Imperial State and Revolution,* p. 195.

27. Sommerfield, "Treasury Regulations Affecting Trade with the Sino-Soviet Bloc and Cuba," pp. 861, 868.

28. Morley, *Imperial State and Revolution,* p. 195.

29. Krinsky and Golove, *Economic Measures Against Cuba,* p. 114.

30. Morley, *Imperial State and Revolution,* p. 203.

31. "U.S. Studies Policy on Cuban Traders," *Washington Post,* February 13, 1964, pp. 1–2. Morley, *Imperial State and Revolution,* p. 216.

32. Tad Szulc, "U.S. Curtails Aid to Five Countries that Sell to Cuba," *New York Times,* February 19, 1964, pp. 1, 2. Morley, *Imperial State and Revolution,* p. 216.

33. Rich, "The U.S. Embargo Against Cuba," chronology.

34. Morley, *Imperial State and Revolution,* p. 208.

35. Ibid., p. 370.

36. Krinsky and Golove, *Economic Measures Against Cuba,* p. 114.

37. Clara David, U.S. Treasury Department, interview, January 23, 1995.

38. "Cuba and Guantanamo," *New York Times,* February 13, 1964.

39. Krinsky and Golove, *Economic Measures Against Cuba,* p. 115.

40. Morley, *Imperial State and Revolution,* pp. 158–161.

41. *CubaINFO,* Vol. 6, No. 2, January 28, 1994, p. 1. The vote was 15 to 4 (Chile, Bolivia, Uruguay, and Mexico) with one abstention. The reason cited for the resolution was Cuba's support for revolutionary movements in Venezuela. See Krinsky and Golove, *Economic Measures Against Cuba,* pp. 114–115; "OAS: Tightening the Noose Round Cuba," in *Latin American Newsletters,* August 11, 1967, p. 120. The decision was reaffirmed by the OAS in September 1967. See U.S. State Department, "Background Notes," distributed to Latin American embassies, in U.S. Congress, *U.S. Trade Embargo of Cuba,* p. 20.

42. For more information, see Hennessy and Lambie, *The Fractured Blockade.*

43. Morley, *Imperial State and Revolution,* p. 223.

44. "British Concessions to U.S. on Cuba Trade," *London Times,* May 12, 1964, p. 10; Morley, *Imperial State and Revolution,* p. 233.

45. George Lambie, "Anglo-Cuban commercial relations in the 1960s: A case study of the Leyland Motor company contracts with Cuba," in Hennessy and Lambie, *The Fractured Blockade,* pp. 180–184. See also Jack Anderson and Les Whitten, "CIA Accused in '64 Thames Collision," *Washington Post,* February 14, 1975; and Morley, *Imperial State and Revolution,* p. 327.

46. Morley, *Imperial State and Revolution,* p. 236.

47. Ibid., p. 223.

48. Ibid., p. 225.

49. Ibid., pp. 207, 225.

50. Ibid., p. 226.

51. Ibid., p. 227.

52. Morley, *Imperial State and Revolution,* p. 216; Rich, "The U.S. Embargo Against Cuba," chronology.

53. "India Agrees to Provision of U.S. Food for Peace Act," *The Economic Times* (Bombay), January 27, 1967, p. 1; Morley, *Imperial State and Revolution,* p. 217.

54. In 1995, only two countries remained in Country Group Z designation: North Korea and Cuba. Clara David, U.S. Treasury Department, interview, January 23, 1995.

55. Krinsky and Golove, *U.S. Economic Measures Against Cuba,* p. 115. Membership in "Country Group Z" category has varied over the years. In 1988, for example, the countries included in this group were Cambodia, Cuba, Nicaragua, North Korea, and Vietnam.

56. "OAS: No Unanimity About Castro," *Latin American Newsletters,* September 29, 1967, p. 176. It is interesting to note that Mexico, Chile, Colombia, Uruguay, and Ecuador abstained from the key clause Dean Rusk supported.

57. For more information on Soviet-Cuban relations see Duncan, *The Soviet Union in Latin America;* Dinerstein, "Moscow and the Third World"; Levesque, *The USSR and the Cuban Revolution;* and Blasier, *The Giant's Rival.*

58. See Wayne Smith, "Castro's Cuba: Soviet Partner or Non-aligned?"

59. Cole Blasier, "The Soviet Union and the Cuban-American Conflict," in Blasier and Mesa-Lago, *Cuba in the World.*

60. See Valdés, "Revolutionary Solidarity in Angola," pp. 88–89.

61. See Halperin, *The Taming of Fidel Castro,* p. 272.

62. See Smith, "Castro's Cuba: Soviet Partner or Nonaligned?" See also "Communist Threat to the United States through the Caribbean, Testimony of Orlando Castro Hidalgo," Hearings before Internal Security Subcommittee, Senate Committee on the Judiciary, October 16, 1969; and LeoGrande, "Cuban Dependency," p. 26.

63. Robbins, *The Cuban Threat,* p. 163.
64. Brenner, *From Confrontation to Negotiation,* p. 17.
65. Morley, *Imperial State and Revolution,* p. 218.
66. Ibid., p. 221.
67. "Cuba: More Contracts?" *Latin American Newsletters,* April 28, 1967, p. 4.
68. Morley, *Imperial State and Revolution,* p. 235.
69. "Cuba, More Contracts?" *Latin American Newsletters,* p. 4.
70. Mesa-Lago, "The Economy and International Economic Relations," p. 185; Downey, testimony, U.S. Congress, *U.S. Trade Embargo of Cuba,* p. 165. Mesa-Lago notes that there was some trade in 1963—U.S. export of goods to Cuba in exchange for prisoners taken during the Bay of Pigs invasion. In 1971–1975, the United States sent close to $20 million to Cuba in bulk gift parcels and medicines, but this accounted for only 0.1 percent of Cuba's trade volume.
71. *Morley, Imperial State and Revolution,* p. 219.
72. Mesa-Lago, "The Economy of International Economic Relations," p. 186.
73. Ibid., p. 186.
74. Gregory Nokes, "Embargoes Imposed for Lots of Reasons; Don't Always Work," AP News Analysis, May 2, 1985. See also George Gedda, "The Nicaragua Embargo and the Parallels with Cuba," AP News Analysis, May 2, 1985; and Joel Brinkley, "Cuba Case Said to Cast Doubt on Embargo," *New York Times,* May 2, 1985, p. A10.
75. For more information on Cuba and CMEA, see Pamela Falk, "The Cost of Cuba's Trade with Socialist Countries," in Brenner et al., *The Cuba Reader,* pp. 307–315.
76. Downey, testimony, U.S. Congress, *U.S. Trade Embargo of Cuba,* p. 166.
77. The aid numbers for Israel and Egypt come from Clyde R. Mark, Congressional Research Service, Issue Brief 85066, June 29, 1994, p. 14; and Congressional Research Service, Issue Brief 93087, June 29, 1994, p. 14. Soviet researcher Andrei Kortunov of the Institute of the U.S.A. and Canada noted that the Soviet Union's total foreign aid budget was almost six times greater on a per capita basis than that of the United States. See Purcell, "Cuba's Cloudy Future," p. 116.
78. U.S. Congress, Senate, Committee on Foreign Relations, Briefing on Cuban Developments, January 25, 1962, in Morley, *Imperial State and Revolution,* p. 201.
79. Ibid., p. 201.
80. "U.S. Studies Policy on Cuba Traders," *Washington Post,* February 13, 1963, pp. 1–2.
81. Kaplowitz and Kaplowitz, "New Opportunities for U.S. Cuban Trade," p. 59.
82. Morley, *Imperial State and Revolution,* pp. 120–122 and 187–189.

5

U.S. Policy Reconsidered: 1971–1980

During the tail end of the 1960s, Latin American countries and other U.S. allies began contemplating trade with Cuba once again. The gradual unraveling of the embargo was not unnoticed in Washington. In 1972, Henry Kissinger reportedly said that if President Nixon was reelected in November, then normalization of relations with Cuba would be "on the agenda."[1] This, in fact, was not a surprising statement because by the early 1970s, the level of tension between the United States and Cuba had diminished. A number of factors coalesced at this time to contribute to the atmosphere of amity.

When President Richard Nixon took office in 1969, although he vowed, "There'll be no change toward that bastard [Castro] while I'm President," the Nixon-Kissinger White House actually faced a more complex situation.[2] It was the Nixon administration that ushered in detente and sought accommodation with the Soviet Union and China, thus contributing to a decline in anti-Communist sentiment in the United States. On another front, difficulties in waging the Vietnam War led to disagreements within the U.S. government over the proper role for the United States in the Third World.

Cuba had curtailed its support for revolutionary movements by 1968 and had begun to develop correct relations with several Latin American governments.[3] This shift was partly in response to Soviet entreaties and partly because of a leftward swing in Latin America, especially in Peru (1968) and Chile (1970).

After Nixon was reelected in 1972, the momentum to improve U.S.-Cuban relations continued unabated. By 1973, a movement within the U.S. Congress to relax tensions between the United States and Cuba had gained momentum; during 1973 and 1974, individual members of Congress stated their opposition to the State Department's intransigent Cuba policy.[4] In January 1973, for example, a group of Republican congressmen issued a report urging the Nixon administration to consider normalizing relations with Castro.[5] The State Department publicly maintained that Havana was still "a threat to the peace and security of the hemisphere," and therefore, "there are no grounds for seeking accommodation with an openly hostile nation." Nevertheless, that same year, the U.S. government signed an anti-hijacking agreement with Cuba. Under the agreement, both sides agreed to prosecute hijackers, or return them to the other country for prosecution. This was the first time the United States and Cuba sat down together to resolve a conflict in over a decade.

Momentum continued in 1974, when Senators Claiborne Pell (D-R.I.) and Jacob Javits (R-N.Y.) traveled to Cuba and subsequently introduced legislation asking President Ford to take steps to improve bilateral relations.[6] Earlier that spring, the Senate Foreign Relations Committee had approved, 12 to 0, a nonbinding resolution to end the trade embargo and restore relations with Havana.[7]

At about the same time, in August 1974, U.S. Secretary of State Henry Kissinger appointed William Rogers as assistant secretary of state for inter-American affairs. Rogers had previously served as a member of the Linowitz Commission, a private influential group of business leaders and former government officials, which advocated normalizing relations with Cuba. Hence, by the mid-1970s, it clearly looked as though the United States was easing its Cuba policy.[8]

Latin America Helps Break the Embargo

Perhaps the most important impetus for change in the U.S. trade embargo of Cuba came not as a result of internal U.S. policy discussions but from Latin America. Latin American leaders began to take more independent policies vis-à-vis Cuba for several reasons. First, as previously mentioned, Castro himself had removed the major stumbling block, by turning away from openly supporting guerrilla movements. Second, Cuba was "good business." Cuba appeared on its way to solving many of its most troublesome economic difficulties, and other Latin American nations wanted a piece of the action. Moreover, with a global economic recession looming, competition for markets became intense, and Washington did not seem to be in a position to apply sanctions to embargo busters. Furthermore, the anachronistic, anomalous nature of U.S. policy toward Cuba became increasingly obvious as the United States befriended China and the Soviet Union. Finally, trading with Cuba provided a cheap but significant way for Latin American leaders to demonstrate independence from Washington.[9]

By the early 1970s a growing number of Latin American countries were trading with Cuba and calling for the OAS to lift the trade sanctions. In February 1970, for example, at a conference of the Inter-American Economic and Social Council in Caracas, President Rafael Caldera of

Venezuela and Prime Minister Eric Williams of Trinidad and Tobago called for the resumption of diplomatic and trade relations with the Castro government. Though the resolution was defeated, it put the Cuba issue back on the agenda of hemispheric politics.[10]

Fidel Castro was also interested in ending Cuba's hemispheric isolation; he made substantial headway in the early 1970s. In 1970 Chile's Allende government renounced the OAS sanctions and established relations with his government. The following year, both Ecuador and Peru made diplomatic overtures to the Castro regime. In the spring of 1972, Peru introduced a bill in the OAS to lift the ban on trade with Cuba and to permit member states to re-establish diplomatic relations with the island. Though the bill was defeated, the divided vote reflected Latin America's renewed interest in Cuba.[11]

The warming trend between Cuba and Latin America continued. In December of 1972, four of Cuba's Caribbean neighbors—Barbados, Guyana, Jamaica, and Trinidad and Tobago—established diplomatic and trade relations with Cuba, and the following year, Argentina as well renewed trade relations.[12] Argentina extended Cuba a credit line for $200 million a year over a six-year period at 6 percent annual interest. Cuba immediately purchased 170,000 tons of wheat and maize, and expressed interest in future purchases of large-scale manufactured products such as tractors, railway equipment, and food processing equipment.[13] Even more dramatic, in the following year Argentina announced that subsidiaries of U.S.-owned corporations based in Argentina would be *required* to sell to Cuba. Under strong pressure from Argentina, the U.S. Treasury Department granted Chrysler, General Motors, and Ford a special release from the embargo on Cuban trade in April 1974.[14] Robbins notes, "The hated embargo was finally breached—and a Latin American state had forced Washington to do it."[15]

Cuba: A Reliable Trade Partner, 1974–1975

By 1974, Cuba had established itself as a reliable trade partner and had succeeded in diversifying its trade portfolio beyond the socialist bloc. That year, 45 percent of Cuba's exports were sold to Western governments, up from 24 percent in 1970.[16] The average price of sugar skyrocketed to 60 cents a pound on the world market in 1975, from 7.4 cents in 1972.[17] Sugar prices combined with profitable nickel and seafood to make Cuba an attractive borrowing nation.[18] Between 1974 and 1975, Cuba received a $900 million trade credit from the Spanish government, $350 million from France, $155 million from Canada, and $596 million from England.[19] At the same time, the Cuban economy performed very well. Average yearly rates of growth in the early 1970s were 13.0 percent in Gross Social

Product (GSP). In per capita terms, rates were 11.3 percent in GSP.[20] The value of Cuba's total trade increased from $3 billion in 1973 to $5.2 billion in 1974, an increase of 68 percent. Dollar value of total exports nearly doubled to about $2.7 billion, as a result of the tripling of world sugar prices. Cuba's import capacity increased commensurately, and total imports rose by 42 percent.[21] In 1974, in fact, Cuba had a $200 million trade surplus.[22] The Cuban economy had reached record heights in 1975.[23]

By 1975 it was thus apparent that the original Western Hemispheric consensus to isolate Cuba had eroded. Ten of Latin America's twenty-two nations had reestablished relations with Cuba, and the United States was under increasing pressure from its allies to lift the extraterritorial aspects of the embargo.[24] Cuba also became active in a number of subregional economic organizations, including the Latin American Energy Organization, the Organization of Sugar Export Countries, the Caribbean Multinational Shipping Company, and the Sistema Económico Latinoamericano (SELA). In 1975, Cuba was accorded observer status in CARICOM, the common market of the Caribbean's English-speaking countries.[25] As we have seen, Cuban trade with Western industrialized countries also climbed during the early 1970s. Cuban exports to Japan and Western Europe jumped from $218 million in 1970 to $860 million in 1974, and imports from these countries rose as well.[26] Canada increased trade with the island precipitously in the mid-1970s. In April 1975, the Canadian minister of industry, trade and commerce, Alastair Gillespie, led a business delegation to Havana and came away with $25 million worth of contracts, and plans for $400 million more over the next few years. Talks about establishing airlinks between the two countries were under way, as were joint venture talks in the tourism sector.[27] In 1975, Japan continued to be Cuba's largest nonsocialist trading partner. Two-way trade totaled $600 million, with Cuba racking up a $200 million trade surplus.[28]

Tensions Ease, 1974–1975

Washington's obsession with isolating Cuba had also cooled off by the mid-1970s. For some time during the Nixon administration, Kissinger had expressed his interest in reevaluating U.S. policy toward Cuba, but his actions were stymied by Nixon's personal animosity toward Castro.[29] With President Gerald Ford in the White House, Kissinger was free to act more pragmatically. In the fall of 1974, he decided that the time was ripe to enter into discussions with the Castro government. Assistant Secretary of State Rogers was authorized to begin a series of clandestine meetings with Cuban diplomats to discuss terms for reestablishing relations.[30] Discussions concentrated on the trade embargo, compensation for the $1.8 billion in U.S. claims against Cuba, release of $30 million in Cuban assets frozen by the United States, release of political prisoners in Cuba, reunion of Cuban families, and the status of the Guantánamo Bay naval base.[31] Though discussions were abandoned within the year, when Cuban troops entered into the Angolan civil war, the talks helped usher in a series of regulatory changes to the U.S. embargo of Cuba.[32]

In the summer of 1974 the Treasury Department added a number of provisions liberalizing the CACR. The import prohibitions were eased in four respects: (1) the importation of gifts of small value directly from Cuba was permitted; (2) the importation of Cuban books, publications, films, phonograph records, and other research materials by scholars returning from Cuba was permitted; (3) the above items were also permitted for commercial purposes as long as the payment for the materials was placed in a blocked account and not sent to Cuba; and (4) journalists were permitted to import newspapers, magazines, photographs, films, tapes, and other news materials.[33]

Travel restrictions were slightly eased as well. Special licenses were issued to scholars, journalists, and news correspondents for payment of expenses for travel, research, news gathering, and transmitting to the United States.

A number of new provisions to the regulations benefited Cuban émigrés. They principally provided for the issuance of licenses unblocking certain assets that were frozen under the previous regulations. The unblocked assets included proportionate shares of joint bank accounts held by an émigré and a Cuban national, shares of proceeds of insurance policies, shares of assets of Cuban partnerships, and sole proprietorships where an émigré was an owner, despite the fact that other owners were blocked Cuban nationals.[34]

Extraterritorial Laws Under Attack, 1974

The 1974 liberalization did not affect the extraterritorial aspects of the embargo. From 1963 through 1974, subsidiaries of U.S. corporations located in third countries were, for all practical purposes, excluded from the Cuba trade.[35] The sole exceptions to this restriction came in April 1974 when the State Department permitted U.S. auto subsidiaries located in Argentina to sell automobiles to Cuba, and in the following March, when Mexican subsidiaries of U.S. automotive firms were also authorized to trade with the island.[36]

In March of 1974 the extraterritorial aspect of the embargo came under intense scrutiny when MLW-Worthington, the Canadian subsidiary of Studebaker-Worthington, announced plans to sell $18 million worth of railroad locomotives to Cuba.[37] U.S. efforts to stop the sale caused considerable friction with Canada as the Canadian Parliament voiced demands that the deal be allowed to go through.[38] The extraterritorial aspect of the embargo drew intense attention in the U.S. press when both the *New York Times* and the *Wall Street Journal* carried editorials supporting the deal.[39] The issue was settled when J. P. Grandy, Canadian deputy minister of industry and commerce, traveled to Havana to confirm the deal, while two U.S. directors resigned from the Canadian company.[40] U.S. Secretary of Treasury George Shultz announced that the extraterritorial problem "was under study in Washington."[41] In the next year, the extraterritorial aspect of the embargo would be dismantled.

1975: U.S. Secretly Talks to Cuba, OAS Lifts Embargo

1975 proved to be the most dramatic year yet for the U.S. embargo of Cuba. Two major things happened that changed the embargo law for the next eighteen years: The OAS lifted official sanctions against Cuba, making the embargo a strictly bilateral affair for the first time since 1964; and the United States lifted restrictions on subsidiary trade with Cuba. These events were related.

Within the U.S. government and business sectors, momentum for a change in U.S. policy toward Cuba had been building; Congress particularly had been pressuring for change for several years.[42] In May 1975, Senator George McGovern traveled to Cuba, and upon his return advocated that the embargo be lifted.[43] That same month, a group of forty U.S. businessmen who worked in Latin America warned that renewal of trade between Latin American states and Cuba could cause new problems for U.S. business unless the United States eased its embargo. They warned that continued adherence to a tough policy could lead to confrontations with Latin American governments over whether U.S. companies in Latin America should trade with Cuba.[44] At this juncture, a consulting firm called Alamar Associates was created in Washington, devoted entirely to introducing U.S. businesspeople to the Cuban market.[45] And the U.S. Commerce Department reported that it had received more than one hundred inquiries from U.S. companies about prospects for trade with Cuba.[46]

U.S. public opinion also swayed toward normalizing relations with Cuba: a Harris survey conducted in May 1975 showed that more than 50 percent of the public at large and more than 80 percent of national leadership favored "full bilateral normalization with Cuba."[47]

The administration was also in certain quarters cautiously voicing the need for change. In a major policy speech in Houston in March 1975, Kissinger stated that the United States was willing to move in a new direction if Cuba would meet us halfway. He said that the U.S. government saw no virtue in "perpetual antagonism" between the two countries, noting further that the United States would "consider changes in its bilateral relations with Cuba" if the OAS lifted its "diplomatic and commercial embargo of the island."[48] Kissinger's message was probably intended more for other Latin American nations than Cuba: the new Cuba policy was part of his more general strategy to develop a "new dialogue" with other Latin American states.[49] In this regard, one U.S. official explained, "The Cuba question has been a nuisance. No matter what we would try to discuss with Latin countries, Cuba kept coming up. With Cuba out of the way, it may be possible for the OAS to concentrate on other hemispheric business."[50] Hence, while the U.S. mood did not signal a sudden warming in relations between Washington and Havana, it reflected the changing political realities of Latin America.

Kissinger privately recommended lifting the sanctions on U.S. subsidiaries. In a secret memo to President Ford, he wrote, "These steps will be recognized as constructive ones by Castro, and will put the onus on him to take the next conciliatory gestures towards us."[51] Despite Kissinger's optimistic assessment, other members of the Ford administration remained subdued, at least publicly. In testimony before Congress, Assistant Secretary Rogers opposed a bill that called on the Ford administration to lift the embargo.[52] Similarly, President Ford himself said he saw no prospect for any normalization of U.S. relations with Cuba. He further remarked that even if the OAS decided to lift the trade embargo, the U.S. government would continue its sanctions "until there is some change in policy by Cuba toward the United States."[53] No doubt looming U.S. presidential elections helped shape the more reticent public position of the administration. Ronald Reagan was challenging Ford for the Republican nomination and attacking the Ford-Kissinger policy of detente.

By mid-summer 1975, Cuba's efforts to improve bilateral relations in Latin America, coupled with the economic strength it had gained from the high price of sugar on the international market, paid off. At a July meeting of the OAS in San Jose, Costa Rica, 16 of 21 voting OAS members—including the United States—voted to terminate the OAS trade embargo against Cuba and to allow each nation to determine its own policy.[54] Though the lifting of the regional embargo was not expected to alter Cuba's trade appreciably, it was an important political victory for the Castro government.

Subsidiary Trade Permitted, 1975

Less than a month after the OAS vote, the United States lifted its ban on subsidiary trade with Cuba. A State Department official said the move was a logical result of the OAS vote to remove sanctions against Cuba, and not a conciliatory gesture aimed at improving relations with the Castro government.[55]

Specific changes in the U.S. embargo included the following:

(1) Licenses would be granted to permit "transactions between U.S. subsidiaries and Cuba for trade in foreign-made goods when those subsidiaries are operating in countries where local law or policy favors trade with Cuba." A Treasury Department license to export goods from a third country to Cuba was still required, and licenses would only be issued if the goods were produced in the third country and consisted of no more than 20 percent of materials originating in the United States. The goods had to be nonstrategic in nature; and no technical data of U.S. origin, other than service and operation data, could be transferred. Furthermore, the export transactions could not involve any U.S. dollar accounts, or financing provided by a U.S.-owned or -controlled firm, except for normal short-term financing.[56] Though the regulations applied to "any person subject to the jurisdiction of the United States," U.S. nationals who were directors of a subsidiary were precluded from dealing with Cuba, even though the subsidiary itself was free to do so.[57] This constituted a significant liberalization of the embargo, which had previously precluded the entire firm from trading with Cuba if one board member were subject to U.S. jurisdiction.[58]

(2) The Commerce Department revised the bunkering regulations to permit third-country ships engaged in the Cuba trade to dock at U.S. ports.[59] This revision effectively repealed the blacklists that had plagued vessels in the Cuba trade, denying them access to U.S. ports for over a decade.[60]

(3) The Ford administration modified the regulations preventing refueling in the United States by foreign merchant vessels engaged in trade with Cuba.

(4) The Ford administration asked Congress to change legislation prohibiting nations that traded with Cuba from receiving U.S. food aid under PL 480.[61]

These changes were applauded by a broad spectrum of U.S. and international society. The *New York Times* carried an editorial hailing the partial lifting of the embargo.[62] The Commerce Department released a study saying that the trade embargo "is becoming more costly for U.S. [businesses] and its effectiveness has been dwindling, primarily because increased sugar prices have given Cuba more money to spend."[63] Within a day of the announcement, thirty U.S. companies sought information on trade possibilities with Cuba.[64] Dupont, Monsanto, and Rohm and Haas, all U.S. chemical processing firms, immediately asked "all subsidiaries to take a fresh look at Cuba."[65] Even Cuban exiles interviewed by the *New York Times* expressed acceptance of the rapprochement between the United States and Cuba.[66]

Normalization Sputters, 1975

Almost as soon as liberalization of the embargo was announced, it became apparent that normalization of relations, which many had hoped would follow in due course, would not quickly materialize. The first signs came from Havana: President Castro welcomed the U.S. decision to lift parts of the economic sanctions against Cuba, but said that the trade embargo must be lifted *entirely* before serious negotiations over the establishment of normal diplomatic relations between the two countries could occur.[67] That was a heavy precondition.

In Washington, the Ford administration remained cool toward Cuba, though a steady stream of senators and representatives planned trips to the island in the months following the liberalization. The 1976 election was approaching, effectively restraining any further White House action on Cuba; few believed President Ford would risk his chances the following year by seeming to appease the Communists just to the south.[68]

Legal hurdles and controversial issues further dogged opportunities for warmer relations. On the U.S. side, the chief difficulties to be resolved were compensation for expropriated property, continued Washington allegations that Cuba was "exporting revolution," Cuban ties to the Soviet Union, and family reunification. Cuba had equally thorny issues: the Guantánamo naval base, compensation for economic damage caused by U.S. sanctions, and military damage caused by the Bay of Pigs invasion and covert operations. Hence, even at the time of liberalization of the embargo, analysts cautioned not to count on a quick, easy improvement in relations between Washington and Havana.[69]

Cuba further inflamed U.S. sensitivities when it hosted the Puerto Rican Independence Solidarity Conference within a month after liberalization was announced. Kissinger made it clear following the Puerto Rican conference that the U.S. government regarded Cuba with extreme suspicion. And in Havana, Castro's anti-U.S. rhetoric continued unabated when he remarked, "The United States is maintaining the economic blockade with all its strength."[70]

As the year drew to an end, opportunities for improved relations between the two countries continued to deteriorate. Cuban troops began entering the Angolan conflict in November 1975, causing furor in Washington. The Ford administration portrayed the intervention as a criminal act and demanded that Cuba withdraw from Angola.[71] Castro refused, saying, "At that price, there shall never be any relations with the United States."[72] It is probable that Castro made a shrewd calculation: he knew U.S. policy toward Cuba would toughen during an election year, and he likely calculated that he had more to gain from entering Angola than he had to lose in Washington.[73]

1976: A Year of Contradictions

The year 1976 proved to be something of a contradictory year in which official antagonism between the United States and Cuba remained elevated, yet simultaneously U.S. businesses began vigorously exploring possibilities of future trade with the island. Not only did the private sector continue to press its interests in the Cuba market with the State Department, but in a blatant move at the height of the Angola conflict in February 1976, some fifty companies gathered in Havana for a seminar on trade possibilities.[74] At that time, official Washington looked the other way. Later that year, however, conflict between government and business sectors mounted. In September, the first private charter between the United States and Cuba carried four U.S. businessmen to the island. Upon return, the plane was seized by Miami customs officers and impounded under orders from the Commerce Department. Kirby Jones of Alamar Associates, the business consulting firm that sponsored the trip, was ordered to furnish information under oath to the Treasury Department, which then accused Alamar of violating the TWEA.[75]

Ironically, while the Treasury Department was harassing Jones for his involvement with Cuba, Henry Kissinger was using Jones as a "special channel" to carry messages to Castro. Between November 1975 and January 1976, Jones carried a series of messages between Castro and the U.S. government related to Cuba's willingness to permit family visits.

As was described in Chapter 4, this type of schizophrenic behavior is not uncommon in a bureaucracy fraught with multiple players and competing interests. The conflicting messages it sends out, however, undermine policy, and no doubt Havana interpreted the contradictory actions to mean that the U.S. administration was indecisive about its goals in relation to Cuba. Most probably Castro took into account Washington's lack of commitment to a real change in U.S. policy when he calculated the costs and benefits of Cuba's continued intervention in Angola.

1976 ended on a low note when, on October 6, a bomb exploded on a *Cubana Airlines* plane after take-off from Barbados, killing all seventy-three people aboard. A Cuban exile and former CIA employee, Luis Posada Carriles, was arrested in Venezuela and charged with responsibility for the act. In retaliation, Cuba suspended its 1973 antihijacking agreement with the United States.[76]

Of major significance for Cuba in 1976 was the slump in world sugar prices to less than eight cents a pound, down from its high of more than 60 cents in 1975. The Cuban government responded by cutting imports and delaying new investments involving spending in nonsocialist countries. By the mid-1970s, sugar still accounted for more than 80 percent of the island's exports.[77] Cuba's economy at this juncture was still characterized by the traditional vulnerability of a developing country heavily dependent on a single agricultural export. Nevertheless, Cuba was considered better equipped than most to face setbacks: a guaranteed Soviet-bloc market, a good international credit rating, and a disciplined and highly motivated work force helped offset some of the worst effects of the sugar price recession.[78]

The election of Jimmy Carter to the White House in November 1976 brought a few glimmers of hope for reconciliation with the United States. The Commission on U.S.–Latin American Relations, for example, influential in the Carter campaign, recommended that the embargo be lifted.[79] In addition, one Carter aide commented, "If we are out to improve and strengthen our relations generally with the countries of Latin America and their 300 million people, Cuba would be a natural place to start."[80]

1977–1980: The Carter Administration and Cuba Policy Revisited

The Carter years are illustrative of three important aspects of economic sanctions. First, the Carter administration is a case study in the consequences of disagreement among domestic actors over foreign policy. Clashes between the State Department and the National Security Council over U.S. objectives in Cuba remained unresolved during this period, and the resulting ambiguous policy contributed to both the Mariel boatlift and the Soviet Brigade crisis. Both crises in turn may have contributed to Carter's failure to gain reelection. On the other hand, Carter administration efforts demonstrate that minor goals may be obtainable through a sanctions policy even when major foreign policy objectives are not. Shifting away from the major objective of ousting Castro, the Carter White House introduced the goal of improving human rights as a significant part of the U.S. agenda in Cuba. In this regard U.S. policymakers were finally able to achieve some success.

Finally, certain Carter initiatives show that at times easing a sanctions policy can be more productive than pursuing a course of unremitting hostility. Carter oversaw the dismantling of specific aspects of the embargo, and there is no doubt that these moves contributed to Castro's decision to release political prisoners in Cuba.

From the beginning, the Carter team was of mixed minds on Cuba. Cyrus Vance, Carter's secretary of state, tended to favor a slow process of normalization of relations, while Zbigniew Brzezinski, Carter's national security adviser, saw little reason to alter the status quo.[81] While still on the campaign trail, Vance wrote to Carter: "The time has come to move away from our past policy of isolation [toward Cuba]. Our boycott has proved ineffective, and there has been a decline of Cuba's export of revolution in the region."[82] At his Senate confirmation hearing on January 10, 1977, he stated publicly his view that the embargo had been ineffective and that the time to begin normalizing relations had arrived.[83] During the first month of the Carter administration, Secretary of State Vance also indicated that the withdrawal of Cuban troops from Angola was *not* a precondition for bilateral talks and improving relations. Several weeks later, U.S. spy flights over Cuba—an irritant in U.S.-Cuban relations since the 1962 missile crisis—were terminated.

Carter's National Security Adviser Zbigniew Brzezinski, however, raised objections to improved relations with Cuba from the start, arguing that nothing was to be gained from normalizing ties. As Wayne Smith notes, Brzezinski contended that there was "no cohesive body of public opinion which favored such a move. In contrast, there was a strong body of opinion against it."[84] Brzezinski also argued that Cuba was simply a puppet of the Soviet Union, and that gestures toward Havana might be interpreted in Moscow as a sign of weakness. He saw most political and military events under an East-West prism, interpreting even local conflicts as efforts by the Soviets to expand their empire. For example, as we shall see, Brzezinski believed that Soviet-Cuban activity in Angola and the rest of southern Africa was the source of most of the problems in that region, and that any U.S. initiative toward the island should be predicated on substantial Cuban withdrawal from the area.[85] At times, Brzezinski went as far as to take U.S. policy toward Cuba into his own hands without consultations with the State Department or even the president.[86]

Carter appeared to appease Brzezinski[87] when, on February 16, 1977, he said that Cuba must withdraw its troops from Angola, cease its interference in "this hemisphere," and respect human rights within its own borders before the United States would consider normalization.[88] Castro took offense at Carter's preconditions for normalization of relations between the two countries.[89] He stated his own precondition, moreover, that the embargo be lifted before negotiations could start.[90]

As we have seen, however, these hard-line stances do not tell the whole story. Improving the human rights situation in Cuba became a key U.S. goal during Carter's early days. President Carter consistently stated that relations between the two countries would improve if Castro would simply ensure the human rights of the Cuban people. The release of political prisoners (both U.S. and Cuban nationals) was central to U.S. concerns on this matter.[91]

Another important goal for the embargo during Carter's tenure was compensation for nationalized U.S. properties. Discussions about lifting the embargo in its entirety would necessarily also entail an agreement on the compensation issue. Parts of the embargo, nonetheless, could be lifted unilaterally, such as the ban on sales of medicines to Cuba.[92]

The contradictory positions of Vance, Brzezinski, and Carter reflected the continuing struggle for control of Washington's policy toward Latin

America.[93] Despite this dissension, from the beginning of the Carter administration until Cuban troops intervened in the conflict in the Horn of Africa in 1978, relations between Washington and Havana steadily improved. Even with the renewed hostility after that date, several minor changes were made in the CACR that relaxed the trade embargo. The following section details the most important legislative changes to occur in those years.

Legislative Changes to the Embargo, 1977

With the possible exception of the Ford-Kissinger decision to lift the embargo on certain subsidiary trade with Cuba, the Carter administration did more to dismantle the embargo than any other administration. Within two months of the Carter inauguration, U.S. policy on travel to Cuba was dramatically altered: the State Department, under direction from the White House, permitted passport restrictions on travel to Cuba to lapse. For its part, on March 21, 1977, the Treasury Department promulgated a general license permitting all economic transactions related to travel to Cuba. Under the new section, persons who visited Cuba were authorized to pay for their transportation and maintenance expenditures (meals, hotel bills, taxis, etc.) and were allowed to purchase up to $100 worth of Cuban goods for personal use or resale, which could be brought back with the visitor to the United States.[94] According to attorneys Michael Krinsky and David Golove, "This amounted to approval of U.S. tourist travel to Cuba."[95]

Several new sections to the CACR were added early in Carter's administration: (1) U.S.-owned or -controlled foreign firms could reimburse foreign national employees for expenditures incidental to travel to Cuba;[96] (2) U.S.-owned or -controlled foreign firms were authorized to bunker and supply Cuban vessels and aircraft; (3) Cuban Americans residing in the United States were allowed to send a maximum of $500 for any three-month period to close relatives in Cuba, and additional $500 remittances were permitted for the purpose of allowing relatives to emigrate; (4) under certain conditions, Cuban nationals holding U.S. visas could travel to and within the United States; and (5) an interest payment on certain frozen accounts of Cuban nationals was imposed. This provision was designed to forestall the diminution in value of blocked assets through inflation.

The Carter White House made several other moves to improve relations with Cuba during its first year in office. In February 1977, Fred Brown, a State Department spokesman, publicly acknowledged and accepted a Cuban proposal to begin bilateral talks on maritime boundaries and fishing rights;[97] in April 1977, the two countries announced the signing of agreements in these areas.[98] Soon after, in June, the U.S. National Security Council decided to end the practice of "blacklisting" foreign ships that called at Cuban ports.[99] Formerly, such vessels were forbidden to haul U.S.

government-generated cargo or to refuel in U.S. ports. The longest-lasting change came with the establishment of diplomatic "Interests Sections" in Washington and Havana, in June 1977. Until 1977, U.S. interests in Cuba had been represented by the Swiss government, and Cuban interests in the U.S. were represented by the Czech government. After the June agreement, small groups of diplomats were permitted to occupy their former embassies in one another's capitals.[100]

Why the Changes?

Congress

The congressional initiative toward repealing the Cuba embargo that began in the early 1970s gained a modicum of momentum after President Carter came to office. A number of congresspeople and senators visited Cuba in 1977–1978, who then kept the issue alive both on Capitol Hill and with direct appeals to the White House. Legislators advocating a "new Cuba policy" argued that the embargo had "long outlived its usefulness as a weapon against the Cuban government. It serves no U.S. purpose."[101] They also argued for a change on business grounds, noting that the longer the embargo remained in force, the more difficult it would be for U.S. multinationals to enter the Cuban market.[102] It was also suggested that the existence of the embargo remained the main impediment to resolving other issues of bilateral concern, such as the outstanding claims issue, the removal of Cuban troops from Africa, and the release of political prisoners.

A variety of new Cuba policies were debated. Rep. Jonathan Bingham (D-N.Y.) advocated lifting the trade embargo on Cuba without preconditions.[103] Sen. Hubert Humphrey (D-Minn.) similarly called for an end to the embargo, pointing out that it cost U.S. businesses up to $650 million in lost trade annually.[104] Senators George McGovern and James Abourezk, both South Dakota Democrats, advocated a partial lifting of the embargo to allow Havana to import food and medicine. In pressing his point, McGovern argued, "The embargo never did make any sense. It only made Cuba more dependent on the Soviet Union and eliminated any influence we might have."[105] The following month, the Senate Foreign Relations Committee voted 10 to 7 in support of McGovern's proposal to permit Cuba to buy U.S. medicines, agricultural supplies, and foodstuffs.[106] The House of Representatives, however, voted against all trade with Cuba, and later the full Senate also decided against recommending a partial lifting of the trade embargo.[107]

Antinormalization sentiment remained strong in Congress. Rep. John Ashbrook (R-Ohio) spearheaded the coalition against the McGovern proposal to sell foods and medicines to Cuba, while Sen. Bob Dole (R-Kans.)

actively campaigned in the Senate against normalization.[108] In June 1978, Sen. Dewey Bartlett, on behalf of thirty colleagues, introduced a resolution requesting the White House to close the Interests Sections in Washington and Havana, deny all applications for commercial trade licenses, stop the normalization process, and link any future openings to Cuba's military withdrawal from Africa.

In the end, despite momentum generated in the opposite direction, Congress failed to achieve major changes in U.S. policy toward Cuba during this period. There were simply no payoffs for departing from parochialism and advocating a change in policy. The legislature's historic deference to the executive branch also limited its willingness to act.[109]

Although Congress was not successful in overhauling U.S. policy toward Cuba, congressional action on Cuba in the mid-1970s did accomplish several things. Congress put pressure on the executive for change; it served to legitimate a new policy by advocating it in a number of fora, including speeches, the introduction of "sense of the Congress" resolutions, congressional hearings, and trips to Cuba; it sent signals to Cuba that the United States was considering a change of policy; and finally, congressional debates served to test the waters for those within the executive branch who were internally advocating a new Cuba policy.[110]

U.S. Business Interests Climb

Despite the precipitous decline in the price of sugar on the world market, U.S. businesspeople continued to express their interest in trade with Cuba. Responding in part to Washington's positive signals toward Havana in early 1977, a group of more than fifty U.S. businesspeople traveled to Havana in April of that year and held a series of discussions with Cuban trade officials.[111] The group also met with Castro several times. In Washington, the White House had cleared the trip in advance and expressed interest in the group's findings.[112] Cuban Foreign Trade Minister Antonio Villaverde reportedly told the visitors that the United States could capture up to 40 percent of Cuba's total trade. Total Cuban trade in 1976 amounted to $7.2 billion, of which 60 percent was with Communist nations.[113] In June, another group—representing forty U.S. corporations—visited the island.[114] U.S. corporations that independently sent representatives included PepsiCo, Xerox, McDonnell Douglas, and Boeing.[115]

Cuba greeted its U.S. corporate guests with enthusiasm. The visiting business groups were wined and dined by Cuban officials, and President Castro usually met with them as well. Castro's message to the visiting entrepreneurs: "Lift the embargo and solutions to all other outstanding problems between the U.S. and Cuba may follow."[116] Cuban trade officials indicated they wanted to trade with the United States, and that they were in need especially of U.S. foodstuffs, followed in importance by industrial equipment and technology. They said Cuba could sell sugar, tobacco, nickel, and fishery products to the United States.[117]

Cuban Foreign Trade Minister Marcelo Fernandez Font visited Washington in October to press for a lifting of the economic embargo. The first cabinet level minister to visit Washington from Cuba in seventeen years, he met with legislators, businesspeople, and others, citing a long shopping list of items that could be exchanged if the embargo were lifted.[118]

Business interests have historically played a role in advancing or deterring embargo policy.[119] If, for example, the business community actively opposes an embargo policy, it can use its substantial power to get the policy reversed. In the Cuba case, however, business interests have usually played second fiddle to U.S. government goals in determining the shape of U.S. policy. Even during the early days after the Cuban revolution, U.S. business interests followed the government's lead rather than initiating their own response to changes in Cuba. The oil companies' 1960 decision to refuse to refine Soviet oil, for example, originated with the U.S. government and not with the business community. The oil companies complied with official government suggestions.

By the early 1970s, however, it was clear that the embargo policy had neither achieved Castro's overthrow nor ensured that former U.S. investors in Cuba would be compensated for claims. Moreover, the Cuban economy was booming. Hence, it is not surprising that during this period, the U.S. business community was most openly interested in trade with Cuba. Yet despite the fact that U.S. companies flocked to Havana, little of this interest transformed itself into political action. Business leaders hesitated to take a prominent anti-embargo position partly to avoid being targeted by the vocal conservative element of the Cuban exile community and partly because the Cuba market simply was not large enough to warrant taking on the U.S. government.[120] *Business Week* writer Gail DeGeorge commented: "Most businesses remain loath to speak out against the embargo for fear of angering some faction of the Cuban-American community. . . . For most companies, Cuba is simply too small and too poor a market to risk political exposure until the end of the embargo is nearly certain."[121]

As we have seen, in 1975 U.S. businesses were emboldened by the government's decision to dismantle the subsidiary trade aspect of the embargo. U.S. companies began arriving in Havana then to stake their claim for future trade opportunities once the embargo was lifted—something they viewed as imminent. However, once the White House reversed its Cuba policy, the U.S. business community eventually followed suit and began to retreat.

At no point in the almost forty-year history of U.S. sanctions against Cuba has the U.S. business community formed or organized a substantial lobby to further its interests on the island. In fact, several efforts made by

Washington lobbyists to organize the business community into a unified force against the embargo were rebuffed.[122] Hence, despite the activity of the business community during the 1970s, this interest did not translate itself into unified action to modify the Cuba embargo policy.

1978–1980 and the Decline of the Anti-Embargo Lobby

The Africa Imbroglio

Early 1978 found Cuban troops moving into the Horn of Africa and new conflict brewing within U.S. governing circles over Cuba policy. As the year progressed, all hope for the easing of sanctions faded.

Beginning in November 1977, Cuban troops had arrived in Ethiopia to defend government forces against Somali incursions. Conflict erupted in the White House between Vance, who recommended cooperation with European allies and African states to negotiate a regional solution, and Brzezinski, who saw the intervention as part of an aggressive Soviet policy and recommended sending a carrier task force to waters off Ethiopia. Although the carrier task force was ruled out, Brzezinski's East-West prism was superimposed on this regional conflict, leading eventually to a complete freeze in the normalization process with Cuba. His perspective also damaged U.S.-Soviet detente; Brzezinski remarked, "SALT lies buried in the sands of Ogaden."[123] This, however, was his wishful thinking, and a bit premature.

Following through on his word, President Carter opened up bilateral talks with the Castro government without requiring as a precondition that it withdraw the Cuban presence in Angola. Yet disagreements within the Carter administration soon plagued U.S. policy toward Africa as well as toward Cuba. Government indecision culminated in the Shaba II incident in May 1978, when the White House falsely accused Cuba of backing irredentist forces that had invaded the Shaba province of Zaire. Enterprising reporters and wary congressional offices quickly exposed the administration's accusations as fictitious. In fact, it emerged that President Castro had actively tried to *prevent* the incursion and had even approached the United States to cooperate in defusing the situation.[124] Forced to retreat from his allegations, Carter had marred his domestic image and permanently sown mistrust and confusion in Havana.

Opinion Moves Against Normalization

The Cuban presence in Africa prompted a major White House policy review. In November 1978, a State Department official noted that "the mood on Cuba [is] anti-improvement in the White House and the National

Security Council."[125] Moreover, U.S. public sentiment had begun to sway against normalization of relations. A poll by the Associated Press and NBC News revealed that 54 percent of respondents opposed restoration of normal relations with Cuba; only 48 percent had been opposed in 1977.[126]

In response to Cuba's moves and U.S. public opinion, the Carter administration briefly considered reestablishing the ban on U.S. travel to Cuba. In addition, a study jointly prepared by the State Department and the National Security Council suggested that U.S. "allies could be asked to reduce their trade with Cuba, halt aid programs and limit technology transfers."[127] In November 1978, U.S. surveillance flights over Cuba were resumed for at least one flight, and they were repeated in October 1979, following the Soviet Brigade episode.[128] Finally, in November 1980, without warning, the U.S. banned the import of a number of special steels from the French Creusot-Loire Company because they contained Cuban nickel.[129]

Some Contact Continues

Despite movement in much of the administration to back away from Cuba, contact continued between the two nations on a variety of levels, and U.S. business interest remained elevated. In May 1978, Lawrence Theriot became the first Commerce Department official to visit Cuba in seventeen years. Theriot interviewed twenty-two Cuban officials in five days and returned indicating that the potential Cuban market could be "very important to companies in certain sectors."[130] In January 1979, a group of U.S. congresspeople again visited Cuba. Castro reportedly held to his previous position and said that if the United States wanted to improve relations with Cuba, it should lift its trade embargo of the island, at least partially.[131] And in October 1979, Sen. Lowell Weicker (R-Conn.) advocated resumption of trade and diplomatic relations with Cuba; he told the U.S. Senate, "I believe the time to reach out to Castro and to our historical friends in Cuba is now."[132]

Official contacts between the two governments also led to Cuba's authorization to permit the emigration of hundreds of Cubans with either family or citizenship ties to the United States, and some Cuban-Americans were permitted to visit relatives in Cuba. Moreover, charter flights between Miami and Havana resumed on a limited basis, carrying business representatives, academicians, and tourists to the island.[133]

By 1979 representatives of 450 U.S. companies had visited Cuba.[134] Kirby Jones continued to encourage trade discussions, reportedly making about forty trips to Cuba with U.S. businesses between 1977 and 1979.[135]

At the end of 1979, a group of Cuban exiles named the Committee of 75 publicized an agreement with President Castro authorizing the release of five thousand political prisoners and an increase in the number of Cuban-

Americans permitted to return every month to visit families on the island.[136] In fact, the U.S. government had negotiated the agreement with the Cuban government earlier in the year but had refused to take public credit for the action, for fear that acknowledgment of talks with the Cubans might send the wrong signals to countries whose cooperation the U.S. sought in opposing Cuban activities in Africa. Hence, despite the achievement of a major goal in Carter's Cuba policy, it appeared for all intents and purposes that the Cuban-American community had achieved what the administration could not.[137] Both the exiles and Castro applauded the U.S. Justice Department's decision to quickly screen and admit the newly released prisoners to the United States in groups of up to four hundred per month. They criticized, however, U.S. reluctance to similarly expedite the admission of ex-prisoners, some of whom had been free for years, and had expressed interest in emigrating to the United States.[138]

The emigration accord, family visits, and the release of thousands of political prisoners—all major foreign policy successes—were achieved by the Carter administration for two primary reasons. First, unlike previous administrations that had set their sights on all-encompassing changes such as altering Cuba's foreign policy or ousting Castro, the Carter White House focused on goals that are more easily attainable through a sanctions policy.[139] Second, Carter was successful because rather than tightening the embargo, he eased it. On occasions when the United States initiated a softer approach toward Cuba, first under Kissinger's leadership and later under Carter's, the Cuban government generally responded favorably; official contacts between the two governments led to the resolution of several issues that were deemed important by the United States. Wayne Smith, who participated in the initial bilateral dialogues during the 1970s rapprochement, writes: "The premise underlying the new approach was that we were likely to accomplish relatively more by trying to negotiate our disagreements than by pushing them to confrontations, and more by reducing tension than by increasing it."[140] Smith argues that the ultimate failure of the Carter administration rapprochement was not due to flawed diplomacy and negotiation efforts, but to a National Security Council that undermined those efforts at every bend in the road.[141]

Soviet Brigade

Despite distinct successes on specific issues, U.S. relations with Cuba took a turn for the worse, and not surprisingly, it was during the U.S. presidential election year. Any remaining hopes among advocates of normal relations with Cuba were crushed in August 1979, when Democratic Sen. Frank Church (formerly an opponent of the embargo) announced in a press conference during a tough reelection campaign that a new Soviet combat brigade had been discovered in Cuba.[142] Later evidence would prove that the brigade was not a *combat* brigade but a *training* brigade, and that it was not *new* but had been in Cuba since the Cuban Missile Crisis of 1962.[143] In the interim, however, the Carter administration so seriously mishandled its response to Church's accusations that, as leading analysts have suggested, the brigade issue dealt a mortal blow to both detente and SALT II. The Cubans, moreover, interpreted the sudden flare-up and subsequent response to the brigade issue as clear evidence of bad faith on the U.S. side.[144] They had even less incentive than before to kowtow to U.S. government interests, since lifting the embargo appeared, once again, to be a pipe dream.

Mariel

In April of 1980, relations dipped to their lowest point during Carter's tenure when four hundred Cubans waiting in line for visas entered the U.S. mission in Havana and refused to leave. In what has come to be known as the "Mariel boat lift," over 120,000 Cubans, including some 2,000 mental patients and prisoners, entered the United States in the spring and summer of 1980.[145] The Mariel episode demonstrates how both sides seriously misunderstood one another. At the height of the episode, for example, Castro demanded that the U.S. government begin talks on normalizing relations in order to resolve the conflict. His demands indicated not only his keen interest in normalization but also his perception that Mariel had put the United States in a position of vulnerability. Certainly the last thing President Carter could do, however, in the midst of Mariel was initiate talks aimed at normalizing relations with Cuba. Had the United States all along maintained an open dialogue with Cuba, Mariel may have been avoided. Castro's attempt, though, to force the United States to the negotiating table in this fashion simply indicates how little he understood U.S. foreign policy.

Western Trade with Cuba Grows, 1979

Despite intensification of U.S. conflict with Cuba and Cuba's increasing hard currency debt, other Western nations maintained trade relations and continued to extend credit to the island. For example, in January 1979, Spain renewed a five-year trade agreement through which it would receive Cuban coffee, tobacco, nickel, and seafood and in return finance exports of capital goods, ships, and machinery to the island.[146] Furthermore, in April 1979, less than a year after French troops fought Cuban-trained rebels in Zaire's Shaba province, the French bank Credit Lyonnais put together a banking syndicate in Europe that would lend Cuba 200 million German marks for seven years at 1 percent over the London interbank rate. Despite active U.S. opposition to the loan, the deal went through.[147] Canadian, Japanese, and British banks also made loans to Cuba at that time;[148] all maintained vigorous trade relations with the island. In 1979, Japan remained Cuba's number one trading partner in the capitalist world; trade between the two island nations topped $300 million in 1978.[149] Canada was Cuba's second most important Western trade partner. In fact, Japan, Spain, and Canada together purchased 50 percent of all Cuban exports destined for the capitalist market and sold 56 percent of Cuba's imports.[150]

In Latin America, Mexican President José Lopez Portillo took a particularly active position against the U.S. trade embargo. In a May 1979 public communiqué, after Castro visited Mexico, Portillo called on the United States to end its fifteen-year economic "blockade" of Cuba and to remove its military base on the island.[151]

By 1978, Cuba had reduced its trade deficit with Western countries to $500 million from $900 million in 1977. This was achieved by reducing imports from the West to $1.27 billion in 1978, down from $1.6 billion the previous year. Cuba's imports from capitalist countries fell from 40 percent of total Cuban trade in 1975 to 17 percent in 1979.[152] During the same time period, Cuban exports to the West rose from $725 million to $780 million.[153] Western nations still accounted for 25 to 30 percent of Cuba's total trade turnover at the end of the 1970s.

Eastern Bloc Trade Grows

Cuban trade with Communist countries rose during this period. Imports jumped 25 percent from $2.8 billion in 1977 to $3.5 billion in 1978, and Cuban exports rose from $2.9 billion in 1978 to $3.8 billion in 1979, an increase of 30 percent.[154] The Soviet Union continued to be Cuba's main trade partner during the later 1970s; in 1978, trade between Cuba and the Soviet Union was worth a record 4 billion rubles (.66 ruble = $1).[155] By 1979, Soviet aid to Cuba had reached about $3.3 billion a year.[156]

Cuban Economy, 1979

Cuba's economy underwent a sharp decline in 1979, when its growth rate fell to 4.3 percent from 9.4 percent in the previous year. In per capita terms, the rate of growth fell from 8.2 percent in 1978 to 3.1 percent in 1979, and was projected to fall to 1.8 percent in 1980. In a candid speech to the National People's Government Assembly in December 1979, Castro explained the sharp economic downturn, blaming commodity shortages and the high cost of energy; he made references as well to the difficulty of receiving goods from the Soviet Union and other socialist countries.[157] Castro predicted that economic hardship would continue for some time into the future, calling attention to additional problems that plagued the economy:[158] sugar rust disease had cut into sugar production; blue mold disease had wiped out the tobacco crop, costing $75 million in hard currency sales and forcing shutdowns in tobacco factories; and a 200-mile fishing rights limit pushed Cuba's fleet from the best waters, forcing the catch down 25 percent.[159]

U.S. Presidential Election, 1980

As we have seen, the possibility for improved relations declined further with the U.S. presidential electoral campaign. Presidential candidate Ronald Reagan attacked Carter for his Cuba policy, criticizing the administration for "inconsistencies in dealing with foreign nations that violate human rights" and pointing to Cuba as an example.[160] Even Castro entered the U.S. domestic political arena, stating that he would welcome Carter's reelection as "the only president in the last 20 years to have made some positive gestures toward us."[161] In an apparent effort to aid the Carter campaign, Castro, unsolicited, announced a general pardon for all U.S. citizens held in Cuban prisons. Further conciliatory gestures on his part at the time included the return of two Cuban hijackers to the United States for prosecution, the decision not to punish four hundred Cubans who had sought refuge in the U.S. Interests Section, and termination of the Mariel boatlift.[162] Castro was undoubtedly the last lobbyist Carter needed on his side. Carter lost his reelection bid, and Cuba faced a new era in its relations with the United States.

Conclusions

U.S. policymakers during the Carter administration hoped the embargo would push Castro to improve human rights in Cuba. In fact, dialogue between the two countries proved more fruitful than the embargo had been in this respect. In negotiations with U.S. officials, Castro agreed to release five thousand political prisoners, a decision suggesting that the Cuban government was more responsive to diplomatic negotiation than to pressure.

The embargo also served to demonstrate to Cuba and the world that the United States did not approve of Cuba's African adventures. U.S. policymakers chose not to lift the embargo while Cuba continued to send troops to Africa, thus clearly indicating condemnation of the intervention.

Resolving the claims issue was another goal of the embargo during the Carter years. U.S. officials believed that lifting the embargo would be appropriate reciprocity for settling the outstanding issue of compensation. Because the claims issue was unresolved, the embargo remained in place.

Finally, U.S. policymakers maintained the embargo to appease the conservative Cuban American community. There was simply not enough political capital to be gained by lifting the sanctions. U.S. presidential election politics dealt a final defeat to the anti-embargo lobby during this period. Candidate Ronald Reagan's anti-Cuba rhetoric, coupled with the untimely Mariel debacle, erased any hope for normal trade relations between the two neighbors, at least for the medium term.

Notes

1. "Cuba: Lure of the Market," *Latin American Newsletters,* October 20, 1972, p. 329.

2. Morley, *Imperial State and Revolution,* p. 247. It is also interesting to note that on a personal level, President Nixon was committed to maintaining a policy of isolation: his friends Charles (Bebe) Rebozo and Robert Abplanalp had close links with the Cuban exile community in Miami. See "Cuba, Mountain or Molehill?" *Latin American Newsletters,* March 8, 1974, p. 76.

3. Morley, *Imperial State and Revolution,* p. 249; Smith, "Cuba: Soviet Partner or Nonaligned?"

4. Senator Gale McGee (D-Wyo.), testimony, U.S. Congress, *Nomination of Henry A. Kissinger Part I,* p. 144; Morley, *Imperial State and Revolution,* p. 282. Sen. John J. Sparkman (D-Ala.), chairman of the Senate Foreign Relations Committee, said that "our policy of isolating Cuba has been a failure, and it is time to re-examine that policy with a view toward ending the futile economic boycott and restoring normal relations." McGee, chairman of the Senate Subcommittee on Western Hemisphere Affairs, said "this isolationist policy is a luxury we cannot afford, especially at a time when our relations with the rest of the hemisphere are subjected to serious problems over economic matters." See *Facts on File,* March 8, 1975, p. 146 E1.

5. The report was entitled "A Detente with Cuba." See Kornbluh and Blight, "Dialogue with Castro: a Hidden History," p. 45.

6. *New York Times,* March 5, 1975; see also Brenner, *From Confrontation to Negotiation,* pp. 17–18; Smith, *The Closest of Enemies,* p. 92.

7. "Senate Unit Backs Trade with Cuba," *Washington Post,* April 24, 1974, p. A1.

Senator Edward Kennedy (D-Mass.) introduced legislation in the Senate on March 4, 1974 to end the U.S. trade embargo on Cuba, and to end punitive measures against third countries and shipping companies that dealt with the island. Congressman Jonathan Bingham (D-N.Y.) introduced a bill in the House of Representatives to end the trade embargo, matching Kennedy's bill. See *Facts on File,* March 8, 1975, p. 146 E1; *Facts on File,* May 17, 1975, p. 346 B2.

8. Brenner, *From Confrontation to Negotiation,* p. 18; *New York Times,* August 31, 1974, p. 8.

9. "Cuba: Mountain or Molehill?" *Latin American Newsletters,* March 8, 1974, p. 76.

10. Robbins, *The Cuban Threat,* pp. 190–191. The fact that Venezuela sponsored the resolution is significant because Venezuela sponsored the 1962 OAS resolution to suspend Cuba's membership.

11. "OAS: Pyrrhic Defeat," *Latin American Newsletters,* November 15, 1974, p. 353.

12. Robbins, *The Cuban Threat,* pp. 190–191.

13. "Argentine Export Possibilities," *Latin American Newsletters,* December 14, 1973, p. 31; see also Morley, *Imperial State and Revolution,* p. 251.

14. *Journal of Commerce,* April 22, 1974, p. 1; "Cuba: Mountain or Molehill?" p. 76; Downey, testimony, U.S. Congress, *U.S. Trade Embargo of Cuba,* p. 170.

15. Robbins, *The Cuban Threat,* p. 192. See also *New York Times,* March 6, 1974, p. 55.

16. Lawrence Theriot and Linda Droker, "Cuban Trade with the Industrialized West, 1974–1979," East West Trade Policy Staff Paper, Project D-76 (Department of Commerce, 1981). See also Theriot, "Cuba Faces the Economic Realities of the 1980s" (Government Report), p. 8; Mesa-Lago, "The Economy and International Economic Relations," pp. 184–185.

17. It is important to note that despite the high price of sugar on the world market, the Soviet Union continued to pay for Cuban sugar according to its long-term sugar agreement of 30 cents per pound. Hence, Cuba sold its 4 million tons of sugar to the Soviet Union at below world market prices when prices were at their height. See *Latin American Newsletters,* January 20, 1978, p. 20; *U.S. News and World Report,* June 26, 1978, p. 39.

18. Mesa-Lago, "The Economy and International Economic Relations," p. 179.

19. Downey, testimony, U.S. Congress, *U.S. Trade Embargo of Cuba,* p. 168; *New York Times,* January 26, 1975, p. 69. See also Mesa-Lago, "The Economy and International Relations," p. 210.

20. Mesa-Lago, "The Economy and International Economic Relations," p. 171. Mesa-Lago notes that U.S. intelligence sources calculated that in GNP terms, the absolute rates of growth were probably 2.7 percent. Nevertheless, the 1970–1975 period saw a record growth rate for the revolution, ranking among the highest in Latin America during these years. See also *Latin American Newsletters,* January 20, 1978, p. 20.

21. Downey, testimony, U.S. Congress, *U.S. Trade Embargo of Cuba,* p. 167.

22. *Business Week,* May 12, 1975, p. 22.

23. Mesa-Lago, "The Economy and International Economic Relations," p. 179.

24. *Business Week,* May 12, 1975, p. 22; *U.S. News and World Report,* May 19, 1975, p. 38.

25. "Small New Countries in the Caribbean Are Starting to Follow Cuba's Example," *New York Times,* July 26, 1976, p. 3.

26. *The Economist,* August 9, 1975, p. 63.

27. *Business Week,* May 12, 1975, p. 22.

28. *Business Week,* May 12, 1975, p. 22. For information on Cuba's trade with other Western nations, see *Latin American Newsletters,* July 18, 1975, p. 110.

29. Kornbluh and Blight, "Dialogue with Castro," p. 46; Robbins, *The Cuban Threat,* p. 198.

30. Smith, *The Closest of Enemies,* p. 93; Brenner, *From Confrontation to Negotiation,* p. 18. For greater detail, see Kornbluh and Blight, "Dialogue with Castro," pp. 45–49; Robbins, *The Cuban Threat,* pp. 192, 197–198.

31. *New York Times,* March 29, 1977.

32. For a thorough discussion of Cuba's Africa policy, see LeoGrande, *Cuba's Policy in Africa, 1959–1980;* Valdés, "Revolutionary Solidarity in Angola," pp. 87–118; Márquez, "Operation Carlotta," pp. 101–102; Marcum, *The Angolan Revolution: Exile Politics and Guerrilla Warfare, 1962–1976;* and Marshall, "Cuba's Relations with Africa: The End of an Era," pp. 47–68.

33. *Federal Register,* July 9, 1974; Krinsky and Golove, *Economic Measures Against Cuba,* pp. 116–117.

34. *Federal Register,* July 9, 1974; Krinsky and Golove, *Economic Measures Against Cuba,* p. 117.

35. Richard R. Albrecht, General Counsel, Department of Treasury, explained in testimony that the U.S. regulations did not specifically deny subsidiaries the right to trade with Cuba: "The Treasury regulations do not require that a license be obtained for transactions with Cuba by American subsidiaries abroad . . . . The regulations do, however, apply to American citizens who are officers or directors . . . of such subsidiaries. Such citizens are required not to authorize or allow the subsidiaries in question to trade with Cuba. The absence of a license requirement is an attempt to minimize questions of so-called extraterritorial application of U.S. regulations to corporations in foreign jurisdictions." See Albrecht, testimony, U.S. Congress, *U.S. Trade Embargo of Cuba,* p. 189.

36. Downey, testimony, U.S. Congress, *U.S. Trade Embargo of Cuba,* p. 170.

37. *New York Times,* March 6, 1974, p. 55.

38. The Canadian government applied intense pressure on the U.S. government over this matter. Canadian embassy official Vernon Turner told Deputy Assistant Secretary for Canadian Affairs Richard Vine that his government considered a change in U.S. policy on this issue "to be a matter of highest importance in U.S.-Canadian relations." Kornbluh and Blight, "Dialogue with Castro," p. 46. For more information on Canadian trade with Cuba, see *U.S. News and World Report,* April 28, 1975, p. 47.

39. *Wall Street Journal,* March 21, 1974, p. 12; *New York Times,* March 21, 1974, p. 41. The *New York Times* continued to support the lifting of the embargo. See *New York Times,* March 4, 1975, p. 32.

40. *Wall Street Journal,* March 19, 1974, p. 14.

41. *Latin American Newsletters,* March 29, 1974.

42. See Philip Brenner, *The Limits and Possibilities of Congress* (New York: St. Martin's Press, 1983), pp. 40–63.

43. *New York Times,* May 8, 1975, p. 11; *Facts on File,* May 17, 1975, p. 346 B2. During McGovern's trip, President Castro asked the United States to end its commercial embargo of Cuba. He said, "We wish friendship. We belong to two different worlds, but we are neighbors. One way or another we owe it to ourselves to live in peace." *U.S. News and World Report,* May 19, 1975, p. 38; *Newsweek,* May 19, 1975, p. 39.

44. *Journal of Commerce,* May 6, 1975, p. 1.

45. *Journal of Commerce,* July 30, 1975, p. 1; Washington lawyer and businessman Martin Klingenberg, who helped reopen trade with China, traveled to Cuba to learn about the potential for U.S.-Cuban trade. He noted, "My impression is that the Cubans are interested in the possibilities of resuming economic contacts with the U.S." See *Journal of Commerce,* May 12, 1975, p. 22.

46. Downey, testimony, U.S. Congress, *U.S. Trade Embargo of Cuba,* pp. 159–187. See also *Latin American Newsletters,* July 18, 1975, p. 110; *U.S. News and World Report,* August 4, 1975, p. 63.

47. Kornbluh and Blight, "Dialogue with Castro," p. 47.

48. *New York Times,* March 5, 1975, p. 13; see also Smith, *The Closest of Enemies,* p. 93; U.S. Congress, *Toward Improved United States-Cuba Relations,* p. 71; *Facts on File,* March 8, 1975, p. 146 E1; *U.S. News and World Report,* March 17, 1975, p. 35. For a detailed review of Kissinger's approach, including information on Kissinger's efforts at clandestine talks with Havana prior to the OAS vote, see Kornbluh and Blight, "Dialogue with Castro," p. 47.

49. Kissinger's speech was broadcast to Latin America five times in three

languages, reaching an estimated audience of 70 million. *U.S. News and World Report,* March 17, 1975, p. 35.

50. *U.S. News and World Report,* August 4, 1975, p. 44.

51. Kissinger to the president, "Third Country Sanctions against Cuba," August 19, 1975, reprinted in Kornbluh and Blight, "Dialogue with Castro," p. 48.

52. *New York Times,* June 12, 1975, p. 40; Hon. William D. Rogers, Assistant Secretary of State for Inter-American Affairs, testimony, U.S. Congress, *U.S. Trade Embargo of Cuba,* pp. 151–158.

53. *New York Times,* June 15, 1975, p. 22.

54. *New York Times,* July 30, 1975, p. 1; *U.S. News and World Report,* July 28, 1975, p. 11; *The Economist,* August 9, 1975, p. 63.

55. *New York Times,* August 22, 1975, p. 1. "U.S. officials repeated on numerous occasions that the changes to the embargo did not really relate to bilateral relations with Cuba, and that improving relations with Havana depended on Cuba's attitude, including its policy toward claims by Washington on U.S. property and assets nationalized by the Cuban government." See, for example, *Facts on File,* August 30, 1975, p. 636 D1.

56. Interview with Catherine Mann, Treasury Department official, July 19, 1988.

57. *Federal Register,* October 8, 1975.

58. Stanley Sommerfield, "Treasury Regulations of Foreign Assets and Trade," p. 277.

59. Bunkers, however, were denied to vessels registered in, owned or controlled by, or under charter lease to Cuba or a Cuban national.

60. Export Administration Bulletin, Number 145, August 29, 1975.

61. Krinsky and Golove, *Economic Measures Against Cuba,* pp. 117–118; *Facts on File,* August 30, 1975, p. 636 D1.

62. *New York Times,* August 22, 1975, p. 30.

63. *New York Times,* October 19, 1975, p. 16.

64. *New York Times,* August 23, 1975, p. 30.

65. *Chemical Week,* September 3, 1975, p. 14.

66. *New York Times,* August 31, 1975, p. 44.

67. *New York Times,* August 22, 1975, p. 1; *Facts on File,* August 30, 1975, p. 636 D1.

68. *U.S. News and World Report,* September 8, 1976, p. 17.

69. *U.S. News and World Report,* September 8, 1975, p. 17.

70. "Cuba Still Cool on U.S. Link," *Latin American Newsletters,* September 26, 1975, p. 152.

71. Kissinger told Kornbluh and Blight that Castro's intervention in Angola revealed basic lack of interest on Cuba's part in fundamentally improving bilateral relations. "There was absolutely no possibility that we would tolerate the Cubans moving into a new theater, become a strategic base in the cold war, and still improve relations." See Kornbluh and Blight, "Dialogue with Castro," p. 48.

72. *New York Times,* March 29, 1977; *Washington Post,* March 30, 1977, p. A11; Smith, *The Closest of Enemies,* p. 94; Robbins, *The Cuban Threat,* p. 198. Kornbluh and Blight conclude that from Castro's perspective, Cuba gained more from its involvement in Angola than it lost from failing to improve ties with Washington. Cuba gained stature in the Third World, a sense of mission at home, and improved political and economic relations with the Soviet Union as a result of its Angola venture. See Kornbluh and Blight, "Dialogue with Castro," p. 49.

73. Kornbluh and Blight, "Dialogue with Castro," p. 49.

74. Among the companies were RCA, Dupont, Borden, John Deere, Coca

Cola, General Motors, Singer, Monsanto, Rockwell International, American Can, and U.S. Steel. See *Latin American Newsletters,* October 22, 1976, p. 163; *Newsweek,* February 16, 1976, p. 15.

75. Correspondence provided this author among Kirby Jones of Alamar Associates, his attorney Donald Rehm, and the Treasury Department. See also Rich, "U.S. Embargo Against Cuba: Its Evolution and Enforcement," chronology.

Despite the conflict, the Treasury Department, under the 1975 liberalization of the embargo, licensed $293 million in goods to Cuba during the first nine months of 1976. According to Commerce Department figures, only Japan and the Soviet Union exported goods worth more than $300 million to Cuba in 1975. See *Washington Post,* January 11, 1977, p. A14.

76. For more information on the antihijacking agreement, see *Aviation Week and Space Technology,* October 25, 1976, p. 30.

77. *Business Week,* April 18, 1977, p. 134. See also Alvarez, "Cuba's Sugar Industry in the 1990s," p. 1; Jane Bussey, "Dependency on Sugar Haunts Cuba," *Miami Herald,* February 14, 1992, p. A1.

78. *Latin American Newsletters,* November 26, 1976, p. 182. For more information on Cuba's 1976 trade, see *Miami Herald,* December 3, 1976, p. 34; *Latin American Newsletters,* December 24, 1976, p. 199; *Facts on File,* February 21, 1976, p. 138 D2.

79. *Washington Post,* January 11, 1977, p. A14.

80. *Associated Press,* January 12, 1977.

81. Much literature has addressed the Cuba case during the Carter years. See, for example, Brzezinski, *Power and Principle;* Lake, *Somoza Falling;* Vance, *Hard Choices;* Hargrove, *Jimmy Carter as President;* Gaddis Smith, *Morality, Reason and Power;* Hoffman, "The Hell of Good Intentions"; and Wayne Smith, *The Closest of Enemies.*

82. Vance, *Hard Choices,* pp. 452–53. The memo was dated October 1976.

83. *Latin American Newsletters,* February 25, 1977, p. 62.

84. Smith, *The Closest of Enemies,* p. 100.

85. Morley, *Imperial State and Revolution,* p. 257.

86. For example, in November 1977 Brzezinski gave a background briefing stating that a steady Cuban military buildup in Angola and Ethiopia was making normalization of relations with Cuba "impossible." *New York Times,* November 17, 1977, p. 1; see also Smith, *The Closest of Enemies,* pp. 122–123. Brzezinski also publicly linked the Soviet-Cuban position in the Horn of Africa to SALT, a position that the administration unanimously opposed. Smith, *The Closest of Enemies,* p. 135; Brzezinski, *Power and Principle,* pp. 184–185.

87. *The Washington Post,* March 5, 1977, p. A1.

88. *Latin American Newsletters,* February 25, 1977, p. 62.

89. *Facts on File,* March 12, 1977, p. 180 A2.

90. *The Economist,* March 5, 1977, p. 50; *The Washington Post,* March 6, 1977, p. C1.

91. Jimmy Carter, statement at a press conference in Plains, Georgia, February 13, 1977, and March 11, 1977. See Smith, *The Closest of Enemies,* p. 102.

92. Smith, *The Closest of Enemies,* p. 104.

93. *Newsweek,* March 14, 1977, p. 33.

94. Treasury Department chronology, in Rich, "The U.S. Embargo Against Cuba," chronology.

95. Krinsky and Golove, *Economic Measures Against Cuba,* p. 118.

96. *Federal Register,* November 3, 1977.

97. *Associated Press,* February 4, 1977.

98. *Washington Post,* April 29, 1977, p. A1; *Business Week,* April 18, 1977, p. 132.

99. *Facts on File,* October 15, 1977, p. 781 A2. Though the NSC made this decision on June 10, it was not announced by the Maritime Administration until September 7, 1977.

100. *Washington Post,* June 4, 1977, p. A1; *Newsweek,* June 13, 1977, p. 47; *Facts on File,* June 18, 1977, p. 455 F2, and September 10, 1977, p. 685 A3; *Associated Press,* August 20, 1977, and September 1, 1977. For a good description of the events leading to this decision, see Smith, *The Closest of Enemies.*

101. U.S. Congress, *Toward Improved United States–Cuba Relations,* p. 21.

102. Morley, *Imperial State and Revolution,* p. 285.

103. *U.S. News and World Report,* March 7, 1977, p. 73; *Facts on File,* March 12, 1977, p. 180 A2. Other congressmen to visit the island included Rep. Ron Dellums (D-Calif.) and Sen. Frank Church (D-Idaho). Church secured freedom to emigrate for the Cuban relatives of U.S. citizens residing in Havana. Previously, U.S. citizens had been free to leave the island but without their Cuban relatives. See *Facts on File,* October 15, 1977, p. 781 A2.

104. *Associated Press,* April 18, 1977. Other figures vary. Some say the embargo cost U.S. businesses up to $750 million annually. Lawrence Theriot, the Cuban desk officer in the Commerce Department's Bureau of East-West Trade, estimated that U.S.-Cuba trade could reach $300 million a year in each direction. *Business Week,* April 18, 1977, p. 134.

105. *The Washington Post,* April 12, 1977, p. A2; *Associated Press,* April 19, 1977. In response to McGovern's suggestion of "basketball diplomacy," the U.S. Treasury Department authorized a group of South Dakota university students to travel to Cuba to play the Cuban national team in April 1977. It was the first visit to Cuba by a U.S. sports team since 1961.

106. *New York Times,* May 11, 1977, p. 3; *Washington Post,* May 11, 1977, p. A1. The committee rejected McGovern's original proposal to open U.S. markets to Cuban exports of sugar and other agricultural products. See also *Associated Press,* May 10, 1977; *Facts on File,* May 21, 1977, p. 389 C3.

107. *Washington Post,* May 13, 1977, p. A1; *New York Times,* May 13, 1977, p. 5; *Associated Press,* May 12, 1977; *Latin American Newsletters,* June 24, 1977, p. 93. The vote was 288 to 119 to prohibit such trade. The following month, the Senate rejected attempts to impose tough preconditions on normalization of relations between the United States and Cuba, and voted 54 to 37 to recommend a set of general goals to be pursued in any negotiations between the U.S. and Cuban governments. See *Washington Post,* June 17, 1977, p. A6; *New York Times,* June 17, 1977, p. 9; *Associated Press,* June 16, 1977.

108. *Associated Press,* May 12, 1977; *Washington Post,* June 4, 1977, p. A1.

109. *Congressional Record,* 95th Congress, 2nd Session, June 28, 1978, Daily Digest, pp. S10025–S10031, June 28, 1978. See also Brenner, *The Limits and Possibilities of Congress,* pp. 88–90; Morley, *Imperial State and Revolution,* p. 287.

110. See Brenner, *The Limits and Possibilities of Congress,* pp. 93–94.

111. The group consisted of notable firms such as General Mills, Pillsbury, Control Data, Honeywell, and 3M. Of the forty-eight different firms represented, twenty-four of them were in agricultural and food services, seven in banking and financial concerns, and the rest were involved in industrial goods, chemicals, and publishing. *Business Week,* April 18, 1977, p. 132; *Associated Press,* April 18, 1977.

112. *Associated Press,* April 23, 1977; *Washington Post,* April 20, 1977, p. A17.

113. *New York Times,* April 21, 1977, Section 4, p. 1; *Washington Post,* May 21, 1977, p. D9. This number varies. Evelio Lastra Ramos, director of Western trade of the Cuban Foreign Trade Ministry, reportedly told the group that the United States could capture 50 percent of Cuba's trade, while another (unnamed) Cuban trade official put the figure at 20 percent. According to a *New York Times* article, Cuban trade officials told U.S. government officials that the United States could command 30 percent of total Cuban trade, or about $300 million. *New York Times,* December 18, 1977, Section 3, p. 9. The U.S. Agriculture Department estimated that the United States could capture at least 33 percent of Cuba's food imports. See *New York Times,* May 16, 1977, p. 16; *Associated Press,* April 20 and 23, 1977, and May 16, 1977.

114. *New York Times,* June 23, 1977, Sec. 4, p. 3; *Newsweek,* July 4, 1977, p. 66. See also *Associated Press,* July 4, 1977.

115. *Business Week,* April 18, 1977, p. 132. In October, a large delegation of Massachusetts business executives traveled to Cuba to discuss trade opportunities with Cuban counterparts, and in November, a group of twenty-three Florida agricultural experts arrived in Cuba to assess the potential impact of Cuban agriculture on the U.S. industry. See *Facts on File,* November 26, 1977, p. 896 C1; *Associated Press,* November 30, 1977.

116. *Associated Press,* April 23, 1977.

117. Ibid.

118. *New York Times,* October 4, 1977, p. 10; *Washington Post,* October 4, 1977, p. A18.

119. Renwick, "Economic Sanctions," pp. 79, 82.

120. Gail DeGeorge, "Almost Tasting Trade," *Business Week,* September 19, 1994, p. 32; Alligood, "U.S. Subsidiary Trade to End?" p. 1.

121. DeGeorge, ibid.; Alligood, ibid.

122. Arlene Alligood, Washington editor of *Cuba Business,* tried persistently but unsuccessfully during the late 1980s and early 1990s to unify the business community. During the 1970s, Kirby Jones's efforts to unify the community had met with a similar demise. Similarly, when Johns Hopkins University attempted to establish a network of businesses interested in potential trade with Cuba in the late 1980s, it was also unsuccessful. The author was involved with the Hopkins effort and had various conversations with Alligood and Jones about their experiences.

123. William J. Lanouette, "The Senate's SALT II Debate Hinges on 'Extraneous' Issues," *National Journal,* Vol. 11, No. 38, September 22, 1979, p. 1564.

124. *Newsweek,* June 5, 1978, p. 48.

125. *New York Times,* November 12, 1978, p. 17.

126. *Associated Press,* August 28, 1978. It was reported that 31 percent of those polled in 1978 favored diplomatic relations with Cuba, but in 1977, 38 percent were in favor.

127. *Newsweek,* June 5, 1978, p. 48; *Washington Post,* May 25, 1978, p. A3.

128. *Washington Post,* May 8, 1980, p. A1.

129. Morley, *Imperial State and Revolution,* p. 278.

130. *The Washington Post,* May 15, 1978, p. D10.

131. *Facts on File,* January 19, 1979, p. 40 E3.

132. *Reuters,* October 4, 1979. Weicker traveled to Cuba in October 1980 and advocated resuming trade in "medicine, feed grain and goods not related to weaponry." See *New York Times,* October 19, 1980, p. 21.

133. *Associated Press,* August 28, 1978.

134. *Washington Post,* May 15, 1978, p. D10.

135. *New York Times,* January 28, 1979, Section 7, p. 1. See also *Washington Post,* July 18, 1978, p. B1.

136. *Washington Post,* December 10, 1978, p. A33; Smith, *The Closest of Enemies,* p. 158.

137. See Smith, *The Closest of Enemies,* pp. 148–163.

138. *Washington Post,* December 10, 1978, p. A33.

139. Hufbauer, Schott, and Elliott, *Economic Sanctions Reconsidered,* Second Edition, p. 59.

140. Smith, *The Closest of Enemies,* p. 117.

141. Ibid., p. 285.

142. It is interesting to note that Sen. Church lost his reelection bid in spite of his move to the right on the Cuba issue.

143. *British Broadcasting Corporation,* May 9, 1980, part 1.

144. For more information on the Soviet Brigade issue, see Newsom, *The Soviet Brigade in Cuba;* and Duffy, "Crisis Mangling and the Cuban Brigade," pp. 67–87.

145. *Washington Post,* May 8, 1980, p. A1; *Washington Post,* May 9, 1980, p. A22; *U.S. News and World Report,* May 19, 1980, p. 8. For more information on Mariel, see Smith, *The Closest of Enemies;* Sklar, U.S. Congress, *The Political Economy of the Western Hemisphere: Selected Issues for U.S. Policy,* pp. 100–116.

146. *British Broadcasting Corporation,* January 25, 1979; Morley, *Imperial State and Revolution,* p. 270.

147. *Business Week,* April 23, 1979, p. 39. See also *Facts on File,* April 4, 1980, p. 253 F2; *Latin American Newsletters,* March 20, 1981, p. 1; Morley, *Imperial State and Revolution,* p. 278.

148. *Business Week,* April 23, 1979, p. 39; *Christian Science Monitor,* July 3, 1980, p. 11. By the end of 1979, Canadian exports to Cuba represented 22 percent of Cuban imports from non-Communist nations.

149. *British Broadcasting Corporation,* October 30, 1979. See also *Latin American Newsletters,* November 23, 1979, p. 5.

150. Morley, *Imperial State and Revolution,* p. 269. For a chart of Cuba's international financing, see Morley, p. 271.

151. Cuban trade with Mexico fluctuated. In 1977, Cuba conducted over $36 million worth of trade with Mexico. In 1978 and 1979 this number dropped to $24.3 million and $12 million, respectively, and then recovered to $33 million in 1980. See the *Washington Post,* May 18, 1979, p. A31; *Latin American Newsletters,* August 8, 1980, p. 10.

152. Morley, *Imperial State and Revolution,* p. 269.

153. *Facts on File,* November 16, 1979, p. 872 B2.

154. Ibid.

155. *Latin American Newsletters,* March 16, 1979, p. 82; *Latin American Newsletters,* February 8, 1980, p. 3; *British Broadcasting Corporation,* April 18, 1980.

156. *U.S. News and World Report,* October 1, 1979, p. 24. Much of the Soviet aid came in the form of sugar and oil subsidies. In 1978, Cuban sugar deliveries were priced at about 40 cents per pound, but the world price for sugar that year was about 8 cents per pound. At the same time, Cuba purchased 9.2 million tons of oil at $7.40 a barrel, compared with the world market price of $12.50. Soviet aid to Cuba between 1960 and 1978 was estimated to be $13 billion. Forty percent of that was in interest-free loans, and 60 percent consisted of nonrepayable subsidies—artificial prices for sugar, oil, nickel, and other goods. See *The Economist,* November 3, 1979, p. 69.

157. Castro specifically referred to a lumber shortage because "the Russians are failing to meet their delivery schedules." See *Forbes,* May 12, 1980, p. 49.

158. Castro said, "Some have said that we are experiencing difficulties. This gives the impression that we are crossing a current, a river. It would be better to say that we are sailing in a sea of difficulties. We have been in this sea for some time and we will continue in this sea. The problem can last 20 more years." See *Forbes,* May 12, 1980, p. 49.

159. *Forbes,* May 12, 1980, p. 49.

160. *Associated Press,* April 19, 1980; William Lanouette, "The Senate's SALT II Debate Hinges on 'Extraneous" Issues,'" p. 1564.

161. *Associated Press,* June 18 and 27, 1978.

162. *The Economist,* October 18, 1980, p. 40; *Washington Post,* October 14, 1980, p. A1.

6

The Reagan Years and the Rebuilding of the Embargo: 1981–1989

When Carter left office in early 1981, he handed the incoming Reagan administration a Cuba policy that held less hope for reconciliation than the one he had inherited four years earlier. Nevertheless, important changes had been made to the embargo policy during the Carter years, significantly liberalizing the sanctions. The following twelve years of Republican Reagan-Bush administrations systematically dismantled Carter's changes, so that by the eve of Bush's exit from the White House, the U.S. embargo against Cuba was just about airtight. This chapter briefly reviews Cuba's economic situation in the 1980s and examines in detail President Reagan's embargo policy. Chapter 7 looks at the Bush administration policy toward Cuba.

The Situation in Cuba, 1980s

During the 1980s, the Cuban economy turned from bad to worse. The price of sugar on the world market declined from a high of 25 cents per pound in 1980 to 7 cents a pound in 1983 and 3 cents per pound in 1985.[1] The drop in world oil prices also damaged the Cuban economy because by the middle of the decade, Cuba's hard currency export earnings from the re-export of Soviet oil topped its sugar earnings.[2] Natural disasters such as hurricane and drought also hindered sugar production, and hence export earnings.[3] The sustained decline of the dollar during the Reagan years combined with higher loan interest rates further wounded the ailing Cuban economy. The devaluation of the dollar caused two problems. First, purchasing power of Cuban exports declined. Second, the foreign debt contracted in other currencies increased with U.S. dollar devaluation.[4] Cuba's debt soared from $1.2 billion in 1981 to over $5.5 billion by the end of the Reagan era.[5] Cuba's mounting debt crisis coupled with its other economic difficulties forced the country to sharply reduce hard currency imports. Cuban imports from Western sources declined from a high in 1978 of 40 percent of the island's total to less than 15 percent in the mid-1980s.[6]

The U.S. trade embargo of Cuba also continued to damage the Cuban economy. José Luis Rodriguez, at the time deputy director of the Center for the Study of the World Economy, reported in 1986 that the U.S. embargo was costing Cuba $400 million per year, mostly in added freight and storage charges and in lost markets in the United States.[7] A 1988 study by the Cuban National Bank found that the U.S. embargo had cost Cuba a total of $12 billion.[8] Several Cuban studies in the early 1990s put the cost of the embargo to Cuba at $40 billion.[9]

Cuba responded to the declining economic situation by taking a variety of belt-tightening and alternative measures, such as expanding tourism and nonsugar exports such as nickel, playing with market-style incentives including private or "parallel" markets, and conserving oil consumption.[10] In 1986 Cuba also initiated a "rectification campaign" that asked Cubans to work harder for less.[11]

Cuban Trade with Non-Communist Countries

In an effort to attract badly needed foreign currency, the Cuban government began taking major steps to improve its economic ties with Western nations. Most significantly, the Cuban government opened the way for joint ventures with foreign corporations in 1982.[12] The law allowed Western companies a 49 percent share in joint ventures with Cuban state companies, with promises that the Cuban government would not interfere in pricing, production, or labor.[13] Foreign partners could choose their own managers and directors. Particular attention was given to the tourist sector. In the early 1980s Cuba also opened a commercial trading company that was engaged in buying and selling products on the free market.[14]

In 1987, more than 370 firms from twenty-three European, Latin American, and Asian countries participated in Cuba's largest-ever annual trade fair. By that year, Spain had overtaken Japan as Cuba's leading trade partner in the West.[15] British interest in the Cuba trade also continued apace. As noted previously, by reducing competition, sanctions can make the target nation more attractive to other trade partners, and this has been true in Cuba's case. More than one hundred British companies visited the island through trade missions between 1985 and 1987. One of the factors stimulating British trade with Cuba, according to a 1987 report in the *Financial Times,* was "the attraction of doing business in America's back garden without having to compete with U.S. companies."[16] Canada also continued to do substantial trade with the island, and the balance of trade shifted to favor Cuba in the late 1980s. The Canadian trade attaché in Havana noted in 1988 that he might as well pack his bags and go home if the United States were to reopen trade with Cuba.

Cuban Trade with Socialist Countries

As Cuba's debt crisis mounted and credits from Western sources dried up, Cuba returned to its most reliable trade partner, the Soviet Union. By 1984, 86 percent of Cuba's trade was tied up with Comecon nations. The centerpiece of this trade was Cuba's sale of sugar to Comecon at prices six to seven times above those of the low world market value, and the Soviet guarantee to meet Cuba's energy needs.[17] In an effort to meet export quotas to the Soviet Union of about half the sugar produced on the island, Cuba began purchasing sugar at the low world market prices in 1984 and 1985 and then selling it to the Soviet Union at the subsidized price. In 1985, for example, Cuba spent $100 million for foreign sugar and then sold it to the Soviets for more than $1 billion. With its sugar proceeds, Cuba bought an excess of Soviet oil and sold the surplus to the West, earning about $400 million in hard currency.[18]

By 1986, the re-export of Soviet oil became Cuba's biggest export earner.[19] Cuba was receiving an estimated $4–5 billion a year in subsidies from the Soviet Union by the late 1980s;[20] Soviet aid between 1961 and 1985 totaled about $40 billion.[21] Moreover, the Soviet Union increased its five-year trade and aid package to Cuba by 50 percent in 1986. The Soviet action was due in part to increased U.S. commitments in Central America and in part to the weakness of the Cuban economy.[22]

At nearly every opportunity, however, President Castro made it clear that he hoped to switch trade orientation when possible. Castro wanted to increase economic ties with the West to at least 20 percent of Cuba's overall trade, with a focus on expanding exports to existing Western markets in the European Community, Canada, and Japan.[23]

Castro also made numerous overtures to Washington, a number of which this chapter describes in detail. For example, in May 1982 Cuba announced it was ready for "wide-ranging talks" and a "relative accommodation" with the United States. [24] Although the United States rebuffed early initiatives such as this, Cuba continued to send signals of interest in dialogue. In 1985 Castro expressed willingness to take back some of the more than one thousand criminals who had arrived in the United States as part of the 1980 Mariel boatlift;[25] then, following through on this offer, in November 1987, he agreed to the return of a total of about 2,700 Cubans who were ineligible to remain in the United States. Cuba also indicated its willingness to withdraw from Angola, and signed an agreement brokered by the United States to do so in 1988. Furthermore, Cuba allowed the State Department to send supplies to the U.S. Interests Section by way of charter flights from Miami, and in 1988 lifted some restrictions on visits by Cuban-Americans.[26] Finally, Cuba permitted a U.S. human rights delegation to visit a group of long-term political prisoners on the island.[27]

On the other hand, Cuban policy toward the United States was not totally accommodating. Cuba reacted strongly to the 1985 initiation of Radio Martí by suspending the 1984 immigration agreement and by denying visas to Cuban-Americans to visit family on the island. Moreover, in 1987 Cuba broadcast a seven-part series on Cuban television demonstrating espionage activities by U.S. officials at the U.S. Interests Section in Havana.[28] The U.S. responded by expelling two Cuban diplomats stationed at the Cuban Interests Section in Washington, D.C.

Despite these setbacks, Havana's Washington policy during the Reagan years was by and large conciliatory. Cuban overtures probably stemmed from a variety of sources. First, President Castro continued efforts to improve relations with Latin America during the decade of the 1980s; his conciliatory approach toward Washington most likely constituted one aspect of Cuba's effort generally to adopt a more conventional international policy. Second, Cuba probably saw itself as laying the groundwork for more favorable relations with a post-Reagan United States. Third, Soviet Premier Mikhail Gorbachev had improved relations with the United States and probably let Havana know that it expected an effort on its part to do the same. Finally, economic troubles besetting the island played no small role in Cuba's overtures; the Cuban government probably believed that concessionary moves on its part would lead the United States to reconsider the embargo.[29] They did not.

Reagan Administration Tactics: A Preliminary Overview

Even before President Ronald Reagan took office in January 1981, it was clear that U.S. policy toward Cuba would change. In the summer of 1980, a group called the Committee of Santa Fe wrote a position paper outlining a new U.S. policy for Latin America, calling for a set of hostile actions toward Cuba that later formed the basis of Reagan administration policy. The paper proposed expulsion of Cuban diplomats from the United States, resumption of aerial surveillance of Cuba, a travel ban, reconsideration of the 1977 U.S.-Cuba fishing agreement, and the establishment of "radio free Cuba." Moreover, if the radio propaganda war failed, the report advocated a "war of national liberation against Castro."[30] Another influential conservative lobby, the Heritage Foundation, released a policy paper called "Mandate for Leadership" that said Washington should "denounce repeatedly in the United Nations and other international forums, Cuba's disruptive international and oppressive domestic policies."[31] Nearly every one of the suggestions from both of these groups was implemented. Key members of the Santa Fe group, furthermore, obtained positions in the Reagan administration.

U.S. Links Central America and Cuba

In February 1981, one month after President Reagan took office, Secretary of State Alexander Haig introduced a new framework for U.S. policy toward Cuba. He said that the United States must "deal with the immediate source of the problem in El Salvador—and that is Cuba."[32] In that same month, the U.S. State Department issued a "White Paper" that blamed the civil war raging in El Salvador on "indirect armed aggression by Communist power through Cuba."[33] Throughout the subsequent eight years, Central American civil wars were consistently blamed on Cuba's "export of revolution."[34] In fact, conflict in Central America became the focal point of U.S. policy toward Cuba. Reagan administration officials consistently charged that Cuba was serving as "a proxy for the Soviet Union" in the Western hemisphere, and threatened to "go to the source" of the Central American troubles: Cuba.

What were the Soviets and Cubans really doing in the region? There is no doubt that the Sandinista revolution in Nicaragua in 1979 led Havana and Moscow to reevaluate possibilities for revolution in the hemisphere. In the wake of the Nicaraguan revolution, leftist parties in Guatemala and El Salvador endorsed armed struggle and began searching for assistance. In response, Cuba and the Soviet Union did provide minimal material assistance to the Farabundo Marti National Liberation (FMLN) guerrillas in El Salvador in 1980–1981. Cuba's main efforts in Central America, however, concentrated on unifying each nation's various popular-front organizations.[35]

After the defeat of the Salvadoran rebel "final offensive" in January 1981, and the apparent fact that revolutionary victory in Guatemala was an elusive goal, Soviets and Cubans retreated from advocating armed struggle. By the mid-1980s, Havana changed its approach to Central America and began focusing on correct state-to-state relations; Cuba also actively supported various peace processes in the region. The principal reasons for changing its Central America policy in the late 1980s were twofold. First, Cuba's earlier, more militant policy had not yielded substantive results. Second, Havana viewed the liberalizing changes in the Soviet Union with caution, concluding that Cuba needed to expand and diversify its economic relations so as to compensate for the potential loss of its special ties to the socialist bloc. A more normal relationship with Central America would help Cuba improve relations with other Latin American and European nations as well.[36]

While the Cuban government repeatedly advocated a negotiated settlement to the Central American conflict, the Reagan administration continued to portray Moscow and Havana as the aggressors and refused to meet them at the negotiating table. In fact, the Reagan White House regularly refused to acknowledge Soviet and Cuban overtures toward a negotiated solution.[37]

In this way it was able to portray Cuba as an uncompromising aggressor and therefore an issue of concern to U.S. national security.

U.S. Goals in Cuba

During the Reagan administration's eight years in office, a political, economic, and military offensive was mounted against the Cuban government under the auspices of protecting U.S. national security.[38] The principal goals of the White House policy, according to Secretary of State George Schultz, were to disrupt and destabilize the island economy, terminate the Cuban-Soviet alliance, end Cuba's internationalism, and finally "reinsert Cuba within the Capitalist political-economic orbit."[39] Ultimately, the Reagan White House sought an end to the Castro government.

In an effort to achieve these goals, the Reagan administration concentrated on tightening the economic embargo of the island. The strategy had two main components: (1) reinstate a global economic embargo by closing loopholes for Cuban "front" companies,[40] banning importation of goods containing Cuban parts, especially nickel, and making it difficult for Cuba to renegotiate its Western debt; and (2) reinstate the travel ban. The White House reasoned that Cubans' interest in consumer goods was a source of weakness for the Cuban state, and that exacerbating that weakness through a tightened embargo would produce social unrest in Cuba, leading eventually to systemic collapse. On the other hand, if the embargo failed to achieve collapse, at least it would demonstrate the level of U.S. antipathy toward the Castro government. As one U.S. official said, "The embargo is primarily political—not economic. It is not intended to bring down the Cuban government. All it is intended to do is to increase the difficulties for Cuba and signal our repudiation for its interventionist policies."[41] The ultimate goals of the embargo, then, were twofold. At best, the Reagan administration hoped that it would bring about the end of the Castro government. At least it would demonstrate U.S. opposition to Cuba's objectionable foreign policy.

Other efforts undertaken by the Reagan administration to achieve its policy goals in Cuba included the initiation of "Radio Martí," aimed at broadcasting information to Cuba;[42] repeated denial of visas to Cuban officials who wished to travel to the United States for conferences and other professional activities;[43] a full-scale diplomatic attack on the status of human rights in Cuba;[44] and major military exercises off Cuban coasts and at the Guantánamo naval base, intended to harass the Cuban government. With respect to the latter, repeated threats of military force against Cuba were used to inflame Cuban sensitivities.[45] In May 1982, for example, the United States launched a giant naval exercise off the coast of Cuba; a flotilla of sixty ships and forty-five thousand troops participated, making it the largest maneuver ever carried out in the area. The command center was the old naval base at Key West (ninety miles from Cuba), which had been abandoned by the Defense Department in 1974, but was reestablished for use by all four services under the Reagan administration. The maneuver's explicit purpose was "to show Cuba that the U.S. has the military power to protect its Caribbean interests."[46] In addition, in December 1986, a U.S. SR71 spy plane flew the length of the island, rattling windows. Surveillance planes usually skirted the island, but this flight was billed "deliberately provocative" by Cuban Foreign Ministry official Ricardo Alarcón.[47]

Some Issues Resolved

Despite the increase in much publicized hostility toward the island, in the waning days of President Reagan's tenure, a slight warming trend in relations between the two countries was evident. The biggest indication of improvement in relations came in November 1987 with the reinstatement of a 1984 immigration agreement allowing twenty thousand Cubans to emigrate to the United States each year. (Cuba had abrogated the agreement in 1985 when the United States began broadcasting Radio Martí to the island.) Hence, in reinstituting the agreement, Cuba acquiesced to U.S. intransigence over the use of radio propaganda. It was also about this time that Castro agreed to take back hundreds of the Mariel boatlift criminals.

In another major foreign policy change, Havana agreed to discuss withdrawing its troops from Angola, and accordingly, in December 1988, the United States brokered a tripartite agreement among Angola, South Africa, and Cuba.[48] This was the pinnacle of Reagan administration efforts in southern Africa and a high point in U.S.-Cuban relations as well.

Other developments had accompanied this achievement. For example, the Cubans began to demonstrate flexibility on the domestic front: the International Red Cross and the U.N. Commission on Human Rights were allowed to visit Cuban prisons, and twenty foreign Catholic priests were allowed to work on the island. By the summer of 1988 the Reagan White House had even muted its longstanding complaints that Cuba was the source of hemispheric trouble.[49] Relations between the United States and Cuba hadn't been better since the early Carter years.

Amendments to the Cuba Embargo, 1981–1988

In April of 1982, the general travel authorization issued under President Carter was revoked. Travel to Cuba was limited only to official government exchanges, visits to close relatives by Cuban exiles, and travel related to news gathering, professional research, or similar activities. Specific travel licenses could be granted in appropriate cases for humanitarian reasons or for purposes of public performances in Cuba in connection with cultural or athletic activities.[50] Though the travel ban was challenged in court, the Supreme Court ruled in favor of the ban in 1984.[51]

In the spring of 1982, U.S.-Cuban relations were again set back when the Reagan administration announced that the 1977 fishing agreement would be allowed to lapse.[52] This was an important symbolic action because the fishing agreement had been the first accord signed between the two countries after the long freeze in diplomatic relations. In addition, in July of 1982, the CACR was amended to curtail the import of goods containing Cuban nickel.[53] The section of this chapter entitled "Efforts to Globalize Embargo" discusses this amendment in detail.

In 1986, OFAC published for the first time a partial listing of persons and firms specially designated as nationals under the Treasury Department's Foreign Assets Control Regulations. This list was produced to curtail trade between individuals or firms who were acting as "front" organizations for the countries under the embargo. The Cuban government sometimes evaded the embargo by obtaining U.S. goods through companies controlled by the Cubans, but located in foreign countries.[54] The list contained 118 specially designated nationals of Cuba, one designated national of Cambodia, and no designated nationals of North Korea or Vietnam, clearly indicating that it was directed at preventing trade with Cuba.[55]

That same year, the Cuba embargo laws were changed to further restrict the flow of funds to Cuba through gifts and family remittances.[56] The regulations were also changed to make it more difficult for Cubans to enter the United States from third countries. This law was enacted to halt what the State Department called "Cuban trade in human beings." Administration officials said that would-be émigrés were charged more than $30,000 to leave Cuba.[57]

In 1988, OFAC launched a "major initiative" to "identify Cuban merchant shipping front companies throughout the world and to block vessels operated by them from access to U.S. port facilities."[58] In conjunction with this action, thirty-two Cuban shipping companies operating out of Panama, Cyprus, Malta, and Liberia were designated nationals of Cuba. That same year, OFAC expanded its enforcement capacities through the development of joint procedures with other federal agencies "for the early and continuous coordination of intelligence and investigative information, program development, technical assistance, case monitoring, effective prosecution and penalties for violations of controls."[59] Furthermore, in November 1988, OFAC established a licensing system for travel agents, air charterers, and others providing travel services or sending remittances to Cuba.[60]

Other minor changes included permitting individuals to import single copies of Cuban publications, unblocking the *pro rata* shares of individuals resident in the United States or the authorized trade territory in the nationalized assets of Cuban corporations, and removing OFAC's prior requirement that, to be eligible for a license to do business with Cuba, a foreign subsidiary of a U.S. corporation could have no more than a minority of U.S. nationals on its board of directors.[61]

Domestic Efforts to Tighten the Embargo, 1981–1988

Under the direction and supervision of the Reagan White House, the Treasury Department began scrupulously enforcing aspects of the embargo that had previously been ignored. Most of the Treasury actions were intended to harass individuals involved with Cuba, and to warn individuals contemplating involvement with the island against such action.

Within a month of assuming office, the Reagan administration expelled a Cuban diplomat on the grounds that he had attempted to circumvent the ban against U.S. trade with Cuba by setting up front companies. According to a *New York Times* report, the move was principally intended to "remind and warn U.S. businessmen that trade with Cuba is illegal."[62] In another action signaling the new mood of the administration, in May 1981, the Treasury Department required that U.S. subscribers to Cuban periodicals obtain federal licenses to receive the periodicals, noting that this was not a new law, but that the department was "simply enforcing long-standing but long-ignored rules" of the TWEA.[63] In October of the same year, a Florida charter airline was fined $4,000 for violating U.S. customs rules by transporting undeclared magazines to Havana.[64] In addition, that same month, a New York gallery was forced to cancel a major Cuban art exhibit and sale because U.S. officials said it violated the embargo.[65]

In August 1984, the Reagan administration began investigating trips to Cuba by scholars, journalists, lawyers, and other professionals to see if these visits violated restrictions on tourist and business travel to the island. Marazul Tours, the travel company involved, was subpoenaed and forced to turn over to the government thousands of records, including the names of more than thirteen thousand U.S. citizens who had visited Cuba since 1982. Marazul's lawyer, Harold Mayerson, called the government investigation an "outrageous intrusion," remarking, "The government is either trying to harass Marazul and force it to withdraw from arranging travel to Cuba or intends to remove the company's license to handle visits to Cuba. Either way, the goal appears to be to further limit travel to Havana."[66]

In February 1985, a Miami businessman and owner of American Airways Charters—a company that provided charter air service to Cuba—was convicted of conspiring to violate the U.S. trade embargo. The government argued that the charter flights contained goods ranging from soda machines to airplane parts and communications equipment.[67] In further action, in the final moments of the Reagan presidency, the government indicted a Texas bass fisherman on ten criminal charges under the TWEA for conspiring to take eight U.S. fishermen into Cuba.[68]

Efforts to Globalize Embargo

As in the 1960s and early 1970s, under the Reagan administration the U.S. government once again inaugurated a vigorous campaign to globalize the embargo. Basing its effort on Cuba's continued "aggression" in the hemisphere, in late 1981 the White House prepared a classified report entitled "Cuba's Covert Activities in Latin America," which charged Cuba with promoting terrorism and subversion in virtually every Latin American country. Copies of the report were sent to U.S. diplomatic posts in Latin America, NATO countries, and even the Vatican, and efforts to persuade the OAS to unite against Cuba followed.[69]

U.S. efforts to make the embargo multilateral in the 1980s met with partial success. This chapter reviews three important components of the Reagan administration's efforts to globalize the embargo policy: (1) preventing Cuban nickel from entering the United States; (2) preventing Cuba from refinancing its debt; and (3) keeping Cuba isolated in the hemisphere.

Closing the Nickel Trade

In a comprehensive effort to close loopholes in the embargo, the Reagan administration instituted a "certification process" whereby foreign companies wishing to export goods to the United States had to produce a certificate of non-Cuban origin in certain cases. The impressively expanding Cuban nickel industry was specifically targeted. On numerous occasions, OFAC posted notice that nickel-bearing materials from specific countries would be detained by customs until their release was authorized by the Foreign Assets Control Board. Information pertaining to questionable nickel usually arrived at the State Department through U.S. embassies abroad or through domestic companies.[70] In general, Cuban nickel issues were resolved by guarantees to the U.S. government from the government of the company in question. Often, for example, the foreign government involved issued certificates verifying the non-Cuban origin of nickel-bearing materials and articles that their companies could then present to U.S. customs officials.[71] By 1982, the CACR was amended to provide that certificates of non-Cuban origin were required in certain cases.[72]

Numerous countries complied with the U.S. legislation. In 1981, France began issuing "certificates of origin" to guarantee that its U.S. exports did not contain Cuban nickel, and in January 1982, Italy followed suit.[73] In a 1983 exchange of notes between the Netherlands and the United

States, the Dutch government verified that Dutch steel mills did not use Cuban nickel, and in 1984, West Germany as well formally complied with the U.S. certification process.[74]

Japan was, initially, less willing to comply with U.S. law. Japan imported small quantities of Cuban nickel but reacted strongly against U.S. pressure in 1983 to halt its Cuban imports. The Japan-Cuba Economic Conference, for example, noted that no Japanese law restricted trade with other countries, and the Japanese government confined itself at first to reporting U.S. threats to the Japanese firms at risk.[75] By 1984, however, the Japanese trade ministry had bowed under U.S. pressure, and began issuing certificates of origin for nickel used by Japanese steel corporations.[76]

Soviet nickel exports to the United States were also problematic. Until 1983, the Soviet Union imported about half of all Cuban nickel exports, and exported about $12 million worth of unwrought nickel to the United States. When the Soviet Union refused in 1983 to guarantee that its nickel-bearing products did not contain Cuban nickel, the United States banned all nickel imports from the Soviet Union.[77] The ban remained in effect until 1986, when it was partially lifted.[78] In June 1990, OFAC announced that the Soviet Union had agreed to certify that nickel and nickel-bearing products intended for export to the United States did not contain any Cuban-origin nickel; as a result, OFAC lifted the ban entirely.[79] Hence, the Reagan administration, and later the Bush administration, were able to obtain almost universal compliance in their efforts to prevent Cuban nickel from entering the United States.

Preventing Cuba from Rescheduling Its Debt

Interruption in commercial finance can exact high prices on targets and lead to successful sanctions episodes.[80] In an effort to interrupt Cuba's commercial finance, the Reagan administration launched an impressive campaign to prevent other nations from allowing Cuba to reschedule its debt.

When sugar prices reached a four-year low in September 1982, Cuba asked Western banks to reschedule payments on $1.2 billion of its $3.5 billion commercial debt.[81] In addition to the decline in sugar prices, soaring interest rates, the U.S. trade embargo, and an absence of new foreign credits had also damaged the Cuban economy. Cuba's main Western bank lenders were Japanese, French, and Canadian institutions. The Reagan administration exerted intense efforts to prevent Cuba from rescheduling debts and receiving new credits.[82] On one front, over the next year, U.S. officials attempted to prevent foreign bankers from responding to Cuba's request; in August 1982, Cuban Vice-president Carlos Rafael Rodríguez noted that U.S. efforts had complicated Cuba's ability to reach a successful outcome with its Western creditors.[83] In a further effort to hinder Cuba's attempts to renegotiate its debt, in October 1982 the U.S. State Department sent a memo to U.S. embassies in Paris, Rome, Tokyo, and other lender nations questioning the veracity of Cuba's National Bank report on the Cuban economy.[84] The following month, the Reagan administration threatened direct intervention in debt negotiations, arguing that it was so entitled because of outstanding loans made to prerevolutionary Cuban governments. If the threats were carried out, U.S. participation would have forced each creditor to negotiate individually with Cuba, and U.S. officials would have ensured that Cuba was accorded no special treatment.[85]

Despite U.S. pressure, by April 1983 Cuba had rescheduled 95 percent of the total due that year. Though less than what Cuba wanted, the new agreement was sufficient to provide Cuba the relief it needed.[86]

In 1984, Cuba was likewise successful at rescheduling $254 million in short-term loans to the Paris Club, largely because its economic performance during the preceding twelve months had been exemplary. Cuba had achieved all the economic targets established in its 1983 rescheduling agreement, and its economic growth rate that year (5.2 percent) exceeded lenders' expectations. Nonsugar exports increased, and total exports rose by 12 percent, while imports increased at about the same rate. Moreover, Cuba's total foreign debt had declined 6 percent since 1981, comparing favorably with other Latin American nations, which had experienced a debt increase of about 30 percent during the same time period.[87] Because of Cuba's impressive record, in 1984 the island showed a $195 million increase in new medium-term loans from foreign governments.[88]

By 1985, Cuba's debt to Western creditors amounted to $3.42 billion.[89] That year, Cuba was again able to reschedule much of its Western debt;[90] again, Cuba received new credit in 1985.[91]

The following year, however, found Cuba in sharp economic decline. A poor sugar harvest, low world sugar prices, a reduction in profits earned from the re-export of Soviet oil (which had accounted for 42 percent of Cuba's hard currency earnings in 1985), and the falling dollar left Cuba with a trade deficit of almost $300 million against an anticipated trade surplus of $260 million.[92] In May, Cuba proposed deferring interest payments on more than $1 billion of its debt owed to commercial banks in Western Europe, Japan, and Canada. By July, a hard-currency shortage forced Cuba to stop payment on both principal and interest for most of its (now) $4 billion debt. Very soon after, Cuba was able to reschedule 95 percent of the portion of its debts due in 1986. The terms of the new agreement, though short of Cuba's expectations, were nonetheless reasonable.[93] Though lenders rejected Cuba's request for $300 million in new funds, they offered Cuba an additional $85 million and an extension for another year on $600 million in trade credit lines.[94]

1987 also proved to be a difficult year for the Cuban economy. Cuban debt reached $5.24 billion as a result of hurricane, drought, low sugar prices, a falling dollar, and falling oil prices.[95] Moreover, for the first time in three decades, Soviet exports to Cuba decreased. The Cuban government sought Western creditor nations to reschedule its debt over fifteen years, including a five-year grace period.[96] In fact, Cuba registered a trade surplus with Western trading partners in 1987. The $34.2 million surplus, however, paled in relation to the $289.3 million deficit of the previous year; the improvement, moreover, was largely due to lower imports.[97]

The United States proved incapable of imposing a debt squeeze on the Cuban economy for several reasons. First, Cuba had an exceptional track record as a responsible debtor nation. Moreover, in comparison with other Latin American nations at the time, Cuba's debt was minimal. The lending banks were also influenced by the fact that COMECON continued to help Cuba with its debt problems, offering extremely favorable debt renegotiation terms. Finally, the United States simply did not have a weapon to force Western creditors into submission. The West Europeans and Japanese were sufficiently economically independent, and sufficiently dependent on trade, to place the growth of commercial relations above U.S. interests.[98] In sum, although the U.S. embargo did make it far more difficult for Cuba to obtain loans at favorable rates, it failed on two accounts: the United States was unable to obtain international cooperation generally for the policy, and more specifically, it could no longer gather enough support to even interrupt Cuba's commercial finance arrangements.

Isolating Cuba in the Americas

Embargoes are more effective when they have the support of regional actors;[99] the Reagan administration accordingly expended considerable effort to keep Cuba isolated in the hemisphere. White House pressure was aimed at preventing the establishment and development of bilateral relations between Cuba and other nations in Latin America, and at continuing to exclude Cuba from regional organizations, principally the OAS.

The administration met with moderate success early in the decade, but as regional pride grew, and as authoritarian regimes were replaced by democratic ones, White House efforts failed by and large to close the widening cracks in Cuba's regional isolation. Cuba's 1989 success in securing the Latin American seat in the UN Security Council is a prime example of its stronger regional ties and of waning U.S. influence in the hemisphere. Cuba had been denied the seat in 1980, partly because of its support for the Soviet invasion of Afghanistan, but also because the United States lobbied against its bid. By the end of the decade, however, all this had changed. The following section of this chapter highlights several of the most important changes in Cuba's relations with regional powers in Latin America during the 1980s: Mexico, Brazil, and Argentina.

Mexico: When the Reagan administration took office in 1981, Cuba was still considerably isolated in Latin America. Cuba's relations with Jamaica, Colombia, Panama, Peru, and Venezuela, once normal, had deteriorated in 1980–1981.[100] Seeking to capitalize on this trend, Secretary of State Haig addressed the OAS in December, goading the organization to take some form of collective action against Cuba on the grounds that Cuba was exporting revolution to Central America.[101] As in the past, Mexico proved to be the only Latin American nation willing to go out on a limb and deepen relations with its island neighbor. Even Mexico, however, was forced at times to bow to U.S. pressure early in the Reagan years. In January 1981, Mexican President Jose López Portillo had signed two major economic agreements with Cuba, despite U.S. efforts to prove Cuba's complicity in supporting El Salvador's guerrillas.[102] By August of that year, however, Mexico excluded Cuba from the North-South summit in Cancún in order to secure President Reagan's attendance.[103] Nevertheless, after that temporary setback, Mexican trade and diplomatic relations with Cuba subsequently showed continual improvement.[104] In 1988, for example, the conservative Mexican president, Miguel de la Madrid, met with President Fidel Castro in both Mexico and Cuba.

Brazil. In 1982 the Brazilian government of General Joao Figueiredo permitted the first Brazilian trade mission in two decades to visit Cuba, though formal relations were not established until after the 1985 election of Brazil's first civilian government in twenty years.[105] U.S. pressure, coupled with the Brazilian military's traditional antipathy to Cuba, postponed the restoration of relations between the two nations until 1986. Sérgio Danese, second secretary at the Brazilian embassy in Washington, noted in 1988 that "signals" from the United States suggested that it would be "disadvantageous and useless" for Brazil to restore relations with Cuba, and that Washington would be "disappointed" if Brazil did so.[106] Washington's ambassador to Brazil, Langhorne Motley, claimed, "The United States is not intent on pressuring friends. We are intent on speaking with friends in an effort to present our point of view. If they accept, fine. If they don't, then at least we've offered our perspective."[107]

In July 1986 Brazil and Cuba resumed diplomatic relations, and Brazilian exports to Cuba reached $40 million that year.[108] Trade between Cuba and Brazil grew rapidly, and by 1989, it reached $130 million.[109] With the reestablishment of relations between regional superpowers Brazil and Cuba, the United States received the most powerful blow to its efforts to prevent Cuba's reintegration into the hemisphere.

Argentina. The Malvinas conflict in 1982 was another turning point for Cuba in its relations with the hemisphere. The Cuban government was a strong supporter of the Argentine position, and in June 1982, Cuba took the lead in mobilizing pro-Argentine support at the Havana meeting of the nonaligned nations. Argentina's trade with Cuba had been growing since the mid-1970s, when Argentina was at the center of the U.S. subsidiary trade conflict. As an outgrowth of the Malvinas conflict, between 1982 and 1985 Argentina's trade and credit line to Cuba expanded considerably. By 1985, Argentina had surpassed Mexico as Cuba's most important trade partner.[110]

Other Latin American nations. Venezuela and Cuba improved trade relations with each other in the early 1980s. During those years as well, Colombian President Belisario Bentancur was building a personal relationship with President Castro, which culminated in Colombia's efforts to readmit Cuba to the OAS in 1985.[111] Uruguay's Julio Maria Sanguinetti and Ecuador's León Febres Cordero likewise made important steps toward improving commercial and diplomatic relations with the island in the mid-1980s.[112] Bolivia and the Dominican Republic also renewed relations with Cuba at the time.

The Cuban government capitalized on its new standing in Latin America when, in 1985, it organized a hemispheric conference on the Latin American debt. At the conference, Castro issued a declaration saying that the Latin American foreign debt of $360 billion was unpayable and must be canceled by the banks. Appealing to Latin America's sense of regionalism—and to traditional sentiment against the United States that was especially high during Reagan's "secret war" in Nicaragua—Castro argued that Latin American debtors ought to unite in a "debt cartel."

The Reagan administration received its final rebuff from the hemisphere when, despite personal notes and telephone calls from President Reagan himself, Latin American leaders voted against the U.S. motion to condemn Cuba for human rights violations in the March 1987 meeting of the UN's Human Rights Commission.[113]

Thus, despite extensive efforts on the part of the Reagan White House to isolate Cuba regionally, the Reagan administration in fact presided over an era of increased Cuban integration into the hemisphere. Newly democratic nations of Latin America were eager to demonstrate their independence from the United States, and Cuba became a perfect conduit. Morley concludes: "The relative decline in U.S. leverage with its southern neighbors on this issue must be linked to Washington's inability to wield the kinds of economic pressures (e.g., providing or withholding aid) against many hemispheric countries with the same efficiency and impact as it did in the 1960s."[114]

Congress Toes the Line

For most of the Reagan years, Congress took a complacent, if not supportive position vis-à-vis White House policy toward Cuba. In 1981, the Senate voted 84-0 to bar the expenditure of any government funds to promote trade with Cuba, tempering the vote, however, with a resolution asking President Reagan to "consider the full range of economic and diplomatic options" available to improve relations with the nations of the Caribbean, including Cuba.[115]

In 1982, Senator Steven Symms (R-Idaho) introduced an amendment to a 1982 supplemental appropriations bill that would (1) prevent Cuba, "by whatever means necessary, including the use of arms," from extending its "aggressive or subversive activities" to other countries in the hemisphere; (2) prevent the creation of a Cuban military capability that could threaten the security of the United States; and (3) establish cooperation with the OAS and "with freedom-loving Cubans to support the aspirations of the Cuban people for self-determination." Symms' objectives were similar to those of previous administrations: to destabilize the Cuban government and to isolate Cuba internationally.[116]

In 1983, the U.S. Congress approved the creation of Radio Martí, which began broadcasting on May 19, 1985. The Cuban-American community had long advocated a propaganda station and had also been a significant source of support for Ronald Reagan's presidential campaign. Cuba undoubtedly recognized that the radio station was probably little more than a symbolic reward for that support. Nevertheless, the Cubans predictably reacted immediately, and strongly. Within hours of the station's inauguration, Cuba suspended the 1984 immigration agreement and barred Cuban exiles from visiting the island.

This definitive response in all likelihood did not come as a surprise to the Reagan administration. The Castro government had demonstrated time and again that it would meet U.S. aggression with retaliation, not acquiescence. No doubt the Reagan administration had in fact anticipated Cuba's antagonistic response because it immediately issued a proclamation barring Cuban government or Cuban Communist party officials from traveling to the United States.[117] In actuality, the White House had been contemplating such a ban ever since the Santa Fe Committee had suggested it in their 1980 position paper. The Reagan administration was now able to implement the action, ostensibly as part of a response to Cuban hostility rather than as part of its own aggressive policy.

In further congressional action following approval of Radio Martí, in 1987, Rep. Claude Pepper (D-Fla.) introduced legislation to strengthen the trade embargo against Cuba and received overwhelming support. The bill authorized the U.S. trade representative to offer recommendations on more effective enforcement of the embargo, including the reestablishment of a ban on foreign ships that stopped in Cuba before docking in U.S. ports.[118] Sen. Lawton Chiles (D-Fla.) and Sen. Robert Dole introduced similar legislation on the Senate side, requiring, among other things, that the U.S. trade representative begin negotiations with U.S. allies to reduce their trade with Cuba.[119]

Despite the hard-line administration position on the Cuban embargo and general congressional support of the White House, a few legislators continued to advocate lifting the embargo. Congressman George Crockett (D-Mich.) and Congressman Ted Weiss (D-N.Y.) were among the most vocal. In March 1981, Crockett conceded that "pushing for an end to the embargo now would be very difficult politically, in view of the country's conservative mood and recent Reagan administration statements harshly criticizing Cuba. . . . However," Crockett said, "it is time to begin a meaningful dialogue" aimed toward eventually lifting the trade ban.[120] A few years later, in January 1985, Representative Weiss introduced legislation to end the Cuban embargo and to establish full diplomatic relations with the island. Weiss based his argument on Cuba's trade potential: "Our economic denial of Cuba has really amounted to self-denial, cutting off a major market for American manufactured goods."[121]

In 1987 and 1988, Representatives Bill Alexander (D-Ark.) and Doug Bereuter (R-Nebr.) introduced legislation that would ban food trade sanctions.[122] Alexander told Congress that he proposed the measure because trade embargoes "cost my constituents money" in lost exports: sanctions on trade with Cuba had resulted in a $450 million loss to rice farmers in his districts. Bereuter, on the other hand, favored the measure "because it's immoral to embargo food." Reagan administration officials testified that they did not believe that agricultural trade embargoes are effective foreign policy tools; they opposed the proposed legislation instead on the grounds that it would limit presidential discretion in relation to such sanctions.[123] Sen. Max Baucus (D-Mont.) introduced a similar bill on the Senate side that would have allowed some cash-only agricultural trade with Cuba on products widely available on the world market. The bill was defeated in a 71-25 vote.[124]

August 1988 brought a small victory for those in Congress who supported a more lenient policy toward Cuba. As part of a new trade bill, Congress enacted the "Berman Amendment" to the TWEA in regard to Cuba, denying the president authority to regulate or prohibit the import or export of any informational materials such as publications, films, posters, phonograph records, photographs, microfilms, or microfiche. The Berman Amendment was passed as part of a campaign that drew on the First Amendment to promote free trade in ideas. It did have an important impact on limiting the intellectual and cultural nature of the Cuba embargo. The new law was implemented in February 1989.[125]

Finally, in the closing moments of the Reagan administration, Senator Claiborne Pell (D-R.I.) visited Cuba and returned convinced that at least a moderate improvement in relations was possible. Pell said that Washington should lift its embargo on medicine and reconsider plans to launch TV Martí (a television counterpart to Radio Martí).

Overall, however, though a few lone rangers in Congress continued to promote anti-embargo legislation through the Reagan era, their numbers had dwindled precipitously from the wide-ranging support this position had commanded during the Ford and Carter years. The decided lack of congressional initiative during this period reflected the Reagan White House's strong stand against Cuba. As in the past, a parochial legislature proved unwilling to challenge the executive branch about an issue of importance to the administration. A domestic united front, however, still did not yield the foreign-policy results desired.

The Cuba Lobby Grows

The Reagan White House found an ideal partner in the right-wing Cuban-American group called the Cuban American National Foundation, or CANF. Organized in the shadow of the Reagan victory, CANF advocated a hard-line policy toward Cuba that included tightening the embargo. Composed mostly of wealthy, white, conservative Cuban-American businesspeople, CANF and its Washington political action committee (Free Cuba PAC) worked closely with the Reagan administration, shepherding anti-Cuba legislation through Congress. TV Martí, for example, was the idea of CANF's director, Jorge Mas Canosa.[126] CANF ensured that its interests were met through lucrative campaign contributions to important congressional leaders; between 1982 and 1992, the Free Cuba PAC donated more than $1 million to congressional candidates.[127] CANF received ultimate recognition when President Reagan appeared at an organization fundraiser in May 1985.[128]

CANF's growing recognition and power during the 1980s was directly attributable to the partnership it formed with the Reagan White House.[129] It never represented the majority opinion of the Cuban-American community;[130] in a 1988 Gallup poll, for example, the Cuban-American community was almost evenly divided on the sanctions issue.[131] Cuban exiles have formed groups in opposition to CANF; however, none has proved to be as successful as the foundation.[132] They lack the financial resources that CANF commands and have not found as many sympathetic ears in Washington policymaking circles.[133] Nonetheless, repeated surveys have indicated that the Cuban-American community is far from monolithic, and that at least half of the Cuban-American community does not support the anti-embargo position championed by CANF.[134]

Interestingly, the U.S. public during the Reagan years did not favor the embargo either. A majority of U.S. citizens polled in 1988 reported that they would favor talks with Cuba on improving relations, a position CANF strongly opposed.[135] Nevertheless, U.S. public opinion on Cuba has never played an important role in policy formation. Infrequent polls have been taken over the years in occasional efforts to determine how the U.S. public feels about the embargo. There is little or no correlation between public opinion and embargo policy.[136]

Business Interests Decline

Business interests in Cuba dropped sharply during the Reagan years when it became apparent that there was little likelihood of change in the embargo laws. Early in the administration's first term, at least one trade mission visited Cuba, including representatives from a major food company and from a financial enterprise.[137] In 1981 George Pillsbury, a director of his family's food company and a Minnesota state senator, told a conference on U.S.-Cuban trade relations in Washington that the U.S. trade embargo against Cuba represents "economic illiteracy . . . on the part of the people in our country who make foreign policy."[138] Noel Blackman, president of Shore Lobster and Shrimp Company in New York, echoed Pillsbury's sentiments, calling the U.S. trade embargo "odd and self-defeating." But business interest in Cuba dwindled to just about nothing until the last year of Reagan's tenure, reflecting lack of momentum from the White House.

In 1988, sensing a change in Reagan policy toward Cuba, major U.S. companies began arriving on the island at the rate of about two a week, according to a Commerce Department official.[139] In June 1988, Johns Hopkins University sponsored a well-attended conference in New York City on opportunities for U.S.-Cuban trade. In a related development, the Port Authority of New York and New Jersey visited Cuba in December of that year and returned advocating that the embargo be lifted.[140] On the whole, however, during the Reagan years, U.S. business interests reflected the congressional and White House position and avoided challenging U.S. trade policy toward Cuba.

Conclusions about Reagan Efforts

The Reagan administration policy toward Cuba is most noteworthy for its systematic attempt to extend the embargo both domestically and internationally. Though successful at tightening the embargo at home, the Reagan administration encountered one roadblock after another abroad. Despite Reagan White House pressures, Cuba was able to restructure its debt and reestablish relations with Latin American nations.

Though the Cuban economy was far worse in the late 1980s than it was in the 1970s, this shift was less a function of Reagan's policies toward the island than of Cuba's hard-currency problems, emanating primarily from exogenous shifts in the world price of sugar. At the end of the Reagan era, the Soviet-Cuban friendship remained solid, and Cuba had certainly drawn no more closely to the capitalist political-economic orbit. The single goal that the Reagan administration could claim it achieved was that of curtailing Cuba's internationalism in Africa. Under Reagan administration mediation, Cuba signed the historic tripartite agreement ending its military commitment in Angola. Notably, however, Cuba's acquiescence came not as a result of U.S. hostility, but as a result of U.S. efforts at negotiation.

As Chapter 5 demonstrated, Cuba has traditionally responded to U.S. pressure by defensively "circling the wagons," and likewise, when the United States has relaxed tension, so too has Cuba. Cuba responded to Carter's hesitant initiatives toward the island by releasing five thousand political prisoners; in contrast, when the Reagan administration increased pressures on Cuba, Castro suspended the immigration agreement his government had signed with the United States and refused to repatriate 2,746 "undesirable" immigrants who had fled the island during the Mariel exodus. When the Reagan administration did, finally, sit down at a negotiating table with Cuba, Cuba proved far more responsive than it had been during years of hostility.

In sum, by the end of the Reagan era, it had become clear that economic sanctions against Cuba principally served to appease a single interest group in the United States: one element of the Cuban-American community. It was evident that the embargo had long since ceased to be effective at achieving foreign policy goals. Many Cuba-watchers thus speculated that the incoming Bush administration would be more pragmatic and less ideological than its predecessor in its dealings with Cuba.

The Reagan administration bequeathed Bush a nearly airtight sanctions policy that had reversed the liberalizations of the 1970s. There was only one significant aspect of the embargo left to tighten: that of subsidiary trade. Under pressure of a presidential election, President Bush closed off subsidiary trade once again.

Notes

1. Cuban officials estimate that for every cent drop in the world market price of sugar, Cuba loses about $70 million. *Reuters,* June 3, 1982, and January 30, 1983; *The Economist,* March 2, 1985, p. 67; *Fortune,* September 16, 1985, p. 120.

2. Margarita Zimmerman, "Cuba Looks East as Crisis Deepens," *Financial Times,* October 29, 1986, p. 4. In 1987, with the oil prices half of what they were only three years earlier, Cuba lost $150 million on its oil. See Peter Engardio and Elizabeth Weiner, "Cuba Is Living on Borrowed Time," *Business Week,* December 14, 1987, p. 52.

3. Hurricane Kate (November 1985) caused Cuba's sugar crop to drop to 7 million tons from 8 million tons. See R. C. Longworth, "Bad Breaks Raise Cain with Economy," *Chicago Tribune,* p. C1. The drought led to a 12 percent drop in sugar production in 1986 and 1987. See Engardio and Weiner, "Cuba Is Living on Borrowed Time," p. 52; see also *Latin American Newsletters,* July 14, 1988, p. 1.

4. "Notes on Parameters of Cuban Economic Adjustment Process," *Chronicle of Latin American Economic Affairs,* Latin American Institute, University of New Mexico, November 11, 1986.

5. "Cuba: Report on 1987 Economic Performance," *Chronicle of Latin American Economic Affairs,* Latin American Institute, University of New Mexico, July 5, 1988.

6. Karen DeYoung, "Cuba's Trade Troubles Bring Economic Change," *Washington Post,* February 4, 1985, p. A1.

7. Longworth, "Bad Breaks Raise Cain with Economy," p. C1; R. C. Longworth, "Embrace of U.S. Doesn't Reach Washington," May 20, 1986, p. C1.

8. *Reuters,* April 18, 1988.

9. Zimbalist, "Dateline Cuba: Hanging On in Havana," p. 156. Figure also restated at joint conference of McGill University and University of Havana in Havana, May 7, 1996.

10. *United Press International,* June 9, 1985. Cuba more than tripled its nickel capacity between 1959 and 1985. See *Fortune,* September 16, 1985, p. 120. Cuba also began exporting medicines. See *McGraw Hill's Biotechnology Newswatch,* Vol. 6, No. 6., March 17, 1986, p. 3; *Chemical Week,* May 7, 1986, p. 71. For information on Cuba's parallel markets, see R. C. Longworth, "Under Castro, the System Is Broken—But Working," *Chicago Tribune,* May 18, 1986, p. C1. For information on Cuba's tourist industry, see Joseph Treaster, "Cuba Hopes to Cash In on West's Wanderlust," *New York Times,* June 8, 1985, p. 2. The parallel markets were closed in November 1990. The Cuban government explained its action by saying, "these markets—far from continuing to be an option for the working class—have essentially become places where parasitic and anti-social individuals and professional by-standers gather. . . ." See *Foreign Broadcast Information Service,* November 19, 1990, p. LAT-4.

11. See Engardio and Weiner, "Cuba Is Living on Borrowed Time," p. 52.

12. *New York Times,* June 17, 1982, p. D1; *New York Times,* May 11, 1984, p. A2; *Financial Times,* April 21, 1982, p. 5; *The Economist,* April 27, 1982, p.78; *Financial Times,* June 27, 1985, p. 3. For detailed information on the joint venture law, see Kaplowitz and Kaplowitz, "New Opportunities for U.S.-Cuban Trade."

13. *CubaINFO,* December 20, 1990, Vol. 2, No. 20, p. 4.

14. "Cuba Broadens Bid for Western Trade," *Facts on File,* July 10, 1981, p. 477 B2.

15. "Cuba Hopes to Increase Non-Traditional Exports," *Reuters,* November 4, 1988.

16. *Financial Times,* January 6, 1987, p. 4.

17. In 1986, for example, Cuba sold sugar to the Soviets at 45 cents per pound when the world price was 8 cents per pound. Cuba purchased Soviet oil at $14 per barrel, and sold it on the world market at $35 per barrel. See *Chicago Tribune,* May 19, 1986, p. C1. Some argue that the Soviet subsidies did not amount to a significant number, because of differences in calculating exchange rates. For a detailed explanation, see Wayne Smith, testimony, U.S. Congress, *Cuba in a Changing World: The United States–Soviet–Cuban Triangle,* p. 12.

18. *Fortune,* September 16, 1985, p. 120. A *Reuters* report noted that the re-export of Soviet oil earned Cuba $750 million in 1985, or 42 percent of total exports to capitalist markets. *Reuters,* September 4, 1986.

19. *Chicago Tribune,* May 19, 1986, p. C1.

20. Carl Migdail, "Why Castro's Cuba Chases the Yankee Dollar," *U.S. News and World Report,* December 9, 1985, p. 18. There are discrepancies in estimates of

Soviet aid to Cuba, ranging from $1 billion to $7 billion. See Jiri Valenta, testimony, U.S. Congress, *Cuba in a Changing World: The United States–Soviet–Cuban Triangle*, p. 63.

21. John Hoyt Williams, "Havana's Military Machine: On Castro's Island Most of the Population Is Under Arms," *The Atlantic Monthly*, Vol. 262, No. 2, p. 18.

22. Terri Shaw, "Soviets Boosting Aid to Cuba by 50 percent," *Washington Post*, April 12, 1986, p. A20.

23. *Financial Times*, June 27, 1985, p. 3; DeYoung, "Cuba's Trade Troubles Bring Economic Change."

24. In November 1981, Secretary of State Haig met with Cuban Vice-president Carlos Rafael Rodriguez, and in March 1982, President Castro met with General Vernon Walters, President Reagan's Latin American emissary. In both cases, the conversations proved fruitless, probably because the Reagan administration lacked a sincere interest in dialogue. Wayne Smith, chief of the U.S. Interests Section in Cuba at the time, wrote of the Walters visit: "That visit was a charade aimed at giving the impression of a willingness to talk where in fact no such willingness existed." For a full account of the Walters-Castro talk, see Smith, *The Closest of Enemies*, pp. 256–258.

25. James Nelson Goodsell, "Cuba Signals It Would Rather Talk than Fight with the U.S.," *Christian Science Monitor*, July 26, 1984, p. 7.

26. *Reuters*, November 4, 1988.

27. *Associated Press*, February 9, 1988.

28. The author was in Havana at this time and saw the television programs.

29. See George Gedda, "Cuba Shows More Friendship to the U.S., but Clear-Cut Reason Is Evasive," *Associated Press*, February 9, 1988.

30. Lewis Tambs, ed., "A New Inter-American Policy for the Eighties: Report of the Committee of Santa Fe" (Washington, D.C.: Council for Inter-American Security, 1981), p. 46–47. See also Brenner, *From Confrontation to Negotiation*, p. 32.

31. Tambs, "A New Inter-American Policy for the Eighties: Report of the Committee of Santa Fe," pp. 46–47. Among other things, this report advocated (1) increased material and financial assistance to governments and movements resisting the Cubans; (2) direct action against Cuban forces overseas through covert or overt actions; (3) direct action by the U.S. State Department to discourage U.S. citizens from visiting Cuba; (4) active diplomatic efforts to encourage countries with close ties to Cuba to downgrade their relations; (5) efforts to convince the OAS and the UN to seek sanctions against Cuba; (6) direct radio broadcasts to Cuba.

32. *Washington Post*, September 20, 1981, p. A28; Brenner, *From Confrontation to Negotiation*, p. 32.

33. Brenner, *From Confrontation to Negotiation*, p. 32.

34. See, for example, the *Report National Bipartisan Commission on Central America*, Washington, D.C., 1984; U.S. Departments of State and Defense, "The Soviet-Cuban Connection in Central America and the Caribbean," Washington, D.C., March 1985; *Washington Post*, November 15, 1981, p. A1.

35. See Rich, "Cuba's Role as Mediator in International Conflict," pp. 119–139.

36. For in-depth review of Cuba's involvement in Central America, see Erisman, "Central America on the Cuban Foreign Policy Agenda," pp. 165–182.

37. See Kaplowitz, "An Appropriate U.S. Response to Soviet and Cuban Policies in Central America," in Smith, *The Russians Aren't Coming*.

38. *U.S. News and World Report*, April 6, 1981, p. 20.

39. Morley, *Imperial State and Revolution,* p. 363. Secretary of State George Shultz said in 1987, "We want to see Mr. Castro stop being a subversive force in our hemisphere and then we are ready to normalize things with him. . . . We would like to see a change in Cuba, see Cuba rejoin and be a part of the trends of the Americas, be democratic, be open, have a market-based kind of economy and trade with us." *Reuters,* March 19, 1987.

40. Cuban "front" companies were companies set up and controlled by the Cuban government but located in third countries. They are discussed in further detail below.

41. *United Press International,* November 18, 1981. Philip Brenner notes: "No one in the Reagan administration actually believed that enforcing the economic embargo would bring Cuba to its knees, as the Kennedy administration had hoped. But there was some expectation . . . that economic pressure could influence political and social dynamics within Cuba to the U.S. advantage." Brenner, *From Confrontation to Negotiation,* p. 33.

42. *New York Times,* August 27, 1981, p. 7.

43. See, for example, *Washington Post,* September 20, 1981, p. A28.

44. *Washington Post,* April 19, 1987, p. A19.

45. For information on U.S. threats to use force against Cuba see *Washington Post,* November 15, 1981, p. A1; *United Press International,* November 14, 1981; *Associated Press,* December 14, 1981; *Reuters,* December 14, 1981; *Facts on File,* December 18, 1981, p. 937 E2; *U.S. News and World Report,* March 29, 1982, p. 22; *The Economist,* May 1, 1982, p. 58; *Washington Post,* April 19, 1987, p. A19.

46. *The Economist,* May 1, 1982, p. 58.

47. *Washington Post,* April 19, 1987, p. 19.

48. The agreement called for the implementation of UN Resolution 435 (providing for the independence of Namibia through free and fair elections); the departure of all South African forces from Namibia; the staged withdrawal of Cuban troops from Angola with on-site verification by the UN; and the respect by all parties of the principle of noninterference in the internal affairs of the states of southwestern Africa. See Marshall, "Cuba's Relations with Africa: The End of an Era," p. 52.

49. *Business Week,* July 4, 1988, p. 52; *Los Angeles Times,* June 14, 1988, p. 2.

50. *Federal Register,* Vol. 47, No. 76, April 20, 1982. See Krinsky and Golove for more detail on identifying "professional researchers," *Economic Measures Against Cuba,* p. 118.

51. The ban was challenged on First Amendment grounds and was upheld by the Supreme Court on the grounds that a citizen's constitutional freedom to travel abroad, "standing alone [is] insufficient to overcome the foreign policy justifications" for the travel ban. See *Washington Post,* July 1, 1984, p. C6; *Travel Weekly,* July 9, 1984, Vol. 43, p. 2; *Associated Press,* June 28, 1984.

52. Smith, *The Closest of Enemies,* p. 258.

53. *Federal Register,* Vol. 47, No. 227, November 23, 1983.

54. More than half of the front companies were located in Panama. The rest were primarily in Mexico and other Central American countries. The types of products supplied to Cuba in this manner included consumer goods, hardware, computers, and durables such as television sets. See *New York Times,* August 23, 1986, p. 3.

55. *New York Times,* August 23, 1986, p. 3; *Chicago Tribune,* August 23, 1986, p. 6; *Associated Press,* August 23, 1986; *New York Times,* August 31, 1986, Section 4, p. 15.

56. *New York Times,* August 11, 1986, p. A1.

57. *New York Times,* August 23, 1986, p. 3.

58. *Report to Congress on Measures to Enhance Restrictions Against U.S. Imports from Cuba, as Required by Section 1911 of the Omnibus Trade and Competitiveness Act of 1988,* p. 6, in Krinsky and Golove, *Economic Measures Against Cuba,* p. 120.

59. Krinsky and Golove, *Economic Measures Against Cuba,* p. 121.

60. *Federal Register,* November 23, 1988; *States News Service,* November 23, 1988; *Reuters,* November 23, 1988; *Bureau of National Affairs,* International Trade Reporter, November 30, 1988.

61. *Federal Register,* November 23, 1988.

62. *New York Times,* February 12, 1981, p. 9; *Washington Post,* February 12, 1981, p. A2; *Associated Press,* February 12, 1981.

63. *Washington Post,* July 8, 1981, p. A8; *New York Times,* July 6, 1981, p. 2; *New York Times,* July 27, 1981, p. 14; *Christian Science Monitor,* October 1, 1981, p. 9; *United Press International,* November 24, 1981. The Cuban publications included *Granma* and *Bohemia.* By July 1981, about thirty thousand publications had accumulated in Boston since the Treasury Department began enforcing the law.

64. *New York Times,* October 7, 1981, p. B10.

65. *Associated Press,* October 8, 1981.

66. *New York Times,* August 30, 1984, p. A3.

67. *Associated Press,* February 19, 1985; *International Trade Reporter,* February 27, 1985.

68. *Houston Post,* January 8, 1989.

69. *Newsweek,* December 7, 1981, p. 54. When Secretary of State Haig addressed the OAS general assembly in St. Lucia, he accused Cuba of embarking on "a systematic campaign of increasing violence against its neighbors." Mr. Haig gave no specifics on what kind of cooperative effort should be launched to curtail Cuban activities. See *Reuters,* December 4, 1981.

70. *Reuters,* November 22, 1983.

71. Rich, *The U.S. Embargo Against Cuba,* p. 34.

72. *Federal Register,* Vol. 47, No. 20, January 29, 1982.

73. Ibid.

74. *Associated Press,* August 13, 1984; *Associated Press,* November 28, 1985.

75. *Latin American Newsletters,* August 5, 1983, p. 1.

76. *Federal Register,* Vol. 49, No. 189, September 27, 1984. See also Kanako Yamaoka, "Cuban-Japanese Relations in Japanese Perspective: Economic Pragmatism and Political Distance," in Kaplowitz, *Cuba's Ties to a Changing World,* pp. 33–46, esp. p. 39.

77. *Reuters,* November 22, 1983. See also *Metals Week,* Vol. 55, No. 32, August 6, 1984, p. 8.

78. *New York Times,* December 6, 1986, p. 37.

79. Krinsky and Golove, *Economic Measures Against Cuba,* p. 124.

80. Doxey, *International Sanctions,* p. 11. See also Miyagawa, *Do Economic Sanctions Work?* pp. 16–23.

81. Sources differ on the amount of hard currency debt Cuba incurred. See *Financial Times,* September 1, 1982, which called Cuba's hard currency debt $3 billion. *Business Week* said it was $1.2 billion (*Business Week,* September 20, 1982).

82. Cuba requested to delay all payments on the principal that would fall due between September 1982 and 1985, followed by a stretchout on repayments over the next ten years. See *Business Week,* September 20, 1982, p. 56; *Financial Times,* March 23, 1982, p. 4.

83. *Latin America Regional Report,* August 20, 1982, p. 8, in Morley, *Imperial State and Revolution,* p. 340.

84. *Miami Herald,* November 6, 1982, p. 21A; Morley, *Imperial State and Revolution,* p. 341.

85. Morley, *Imperial State and Revolution,* p. 341. See also *Wall Street Journal,* December 27, 1982, p. 12; *Reuters,* January 30, 1983; and Perez-Stable, "Castro Takes the Economy in Hand," p. 298.

86. Cuba wanted 10.5 years repayment and five years grace (accorded most Third World countries) and received 8.5 years and a three-year grace period. Morley, *Imperial State and Revolution,* p. 342; *Financial Times,* March 3, 1983, p. 4.

87. *Latin American Newsletter,* May 10, 1985; Morley, *Imperial State and Revolution,* p. 343.

88. *Latin American Newsletters,* May 10, 1985, p. 2.

89. *New York Times,* June 5, 1985, Section D, p. 2. The National Bank of Cuba issued Cuba's annual economic report for 1985. In it the bank asked Western creditor banks and governments to reschedule $258 million of its medium- and long-term debt in convertible currency due in 1985, "on conditions not less favorable than those granted or in the process of being granted to several Latin American countries." See also *Latin American Newsletters,* May 31, 1985, p. 6; *Washington Post,* June 5, 1985, p. A29.

90. *Reuters,* August 8, 1985. Cuba rescheduled $250 million of Paris Club government-to-government debts in 1984 and $156 million in 1985. See *Reuters,* July 9, 1987.

91. The British Midland Bank established a 30 million pound credit line to boost British exports to the island. *Financial Times,* July 31, 1985, p. 3; *Financial Times,* August 21, 1986, p. 5.

92. *Financial Times,* May 1, 1986, p. 4.

93. Cuba's Banco Nacional proposed a repayment period of twelve years with three years' grace for the $100 million due in 1986. The banks offered to reschedule $75 million of the amount over ten years with six years' grace. *Financial Times,* May 7, 1986, p. 10; Morley, *Imperial State and Revolution,* p. 345.

94. *New York Times,* July 29, 1986, Section D, p. 9; *Chronicle of Latin American Economic Affairs,* Latin American Institute, University of New Mexico, July 16, 1987.

95. *Chronicle of Latin American Economic Affairs,* Latin American Institute, University of New Mexico, July 28, 1987.

96. *New York Times,* March 16, 1988, p. 13; *Associated Press,* March 15, 1988.

97. "Castro Spurns Soviet-Style Reforms," *Facts on File,* September 2, 1988, p. 648 E2.

98. See Morley, *Imperial State and Revolution,* pp. 345, 365.

99. Doxey, *International Sanctions,* p. 144.

100. See *Latin American Newsletters,* September 25, 1981, p. 7; *Latin American Newsletters,* November 6, 1981, p. 2.

101. Don Oberdorfer, "Haig Asks Joint Action on Cuba," *Washington Post,* December 15, 1981, p. A20.

102. The first was to assist Cuba in its offshore oil exploration, and the second was to purchase 100,000 tons of Cuban sugar. See Alan Riding, "Mexico Stresses Ties with Cuba in an Apparent Rebuff to Reagan," *New York Times,* February 21, 1981, pp. 1, 6.

103. Manuel R. Gomez, "Mexico's Latin Policy," *New York Times,* October 15, 1981, p. 27.

104. "Cuba: Notes on Preparations for Trade Expansion with Mexico, Brazil and Uruguay," *Chronicle of Latin American Economic Affairs,* Latin American Institute, University of New Mexico, October 28, 1986.

105. John Arden, "Speculation on Cuba Trade," *Financial Times,* January 15, 1982, p. 4; Warren Hoge, "Brazilians Favor Cuban Trade Ties," *New York Times,* February 7, 1982, p. 9; Jim Brooke, "Brazilian Businessmen Eye Cuban Market," *Washington Post,* February 3, 1982, p. A16.

106. Donna Rich, "Brazil and Cuba Strengthening Relations," *InfoBrazil,* May, 1988, p. 6.

107. Hoge, "Brazilians Favor Cuban Trade Ties," p. 9.

108. Marlise Simons, "Brazilians and Cubans: An Unlikely Courtship," *New York Times,* April 16, 1987, p. 8; Morley, *Imperial State and Revolution,* p. 359.

109. *CubaINFO,* Vol. 3, No. 3, February 28, 1991, pp. 2–3.

110. Joseph Treaster, "Castro Builds Relations with South America," *New York Times,* May 19, 1985, p. 1.

111. Morley, *Imperial State and Revolution,* p. 362.

112. Tad Szulc, "Cuba's Emergence, America's Myopia," *New York Times,* May 5, 1985, Section 4, p. 25; "New Uruguayan Government Lifts Ban on Trade with Cuba," *Christian Science Monitor,* April 11, 1985, p. 5.

113. Elaine Sciolino, "Reagan's Mighty Efforts to Condemn Cuba," *New York Times,* March 24, 1987, p. 28. The nations voting against the United States included Argentina, Nicaragua, Peru, Colombia, Mexico, and Venezuela. Brazil abstained, and Costa Rica voted with the United States.

114. Morley, *Imperial State and Revolution,* p. 366.

115. *Associated Press,* November 12, 1981.

116. Brenner, *From Confrontation to Negotiation,* p. 33.

117. Ibid., pp. 38–39.

118. *States News Service,* April 29, 1987.

119. *States News Service,* May 19, 1987.

120. *Associated Press,* March 28, 1981.

121. *International Trade Reporter,* Bureau of National Affairs, January 23, 1985.

122. Ibid., February 11, 1987.

123. Ibid., June 15, 1988.

124. *United Press International,* July 14, 1987.

125. Golove, "A History of U.S. Regulatory Policy Toward Cuba," p. 18; Krinsky and Golove, *Economic Measures Against Cuba,* p. 120.

126. Gaeton Fonzi, "Who Is Jorge Mas Canosa?" *Esquire,* January 1993, p. 89.

127. Andrew Zimbalist, "Impact of Blockade," p. 5; Jorge Mas Canosa, testimony, U.S. Congress, *Cuba in a Changing World,* p. 155; Alfonso Chardy, "Cuban Foundation Chief Tops Donor List," *Miami Herald,* October 9, 1992, p. 2B.

128. See Brenner, *From Confrontation to Negotiation,* p. 72.

129. Peter Slevin, "Washington Gives Cuban Foundation Clout, Legitimacy," *Miami Herald,* October 11, 1992, p. 20A.

130. Lee Hockstader and William Booth, "Cuban Exiles Split on Life After Castro," *Washington Post,* March 10, 1992, p. A1.

131. According to Gallup, almost 40 percent of those polled indicated that they would like to see the embargo "eased or ended altogether." See Rich, "U.S. and Cuba: Trading Partners?" p. 36.

132. The Cuban American Coalition, the Cuban American Research and Education Fund, the Cuban Democratic Platform, and the Social Democratic Party of Cuba in Exile are some of the Cuban-American groups opposed to the CANF agenda.

133. Marquis, *Miami Herald,* September 28, 1992, p. 1A.

134. See, for example, a survey conducted by Strategic Research Corporation, showing that 39.7 percent of Hispanics in the United States are against the embargo, 20 percent in favor. In Miami, 40 percent of Hispanics are against the embargo, 36 percent in favor. Sixty percent of Hispanics in Miami are Cuban-Americans. See Marcelina Miyares, president of the Cuban Committee for Democracy, testimony, U.S. Congress, *Free Trade with Cuba Act,* p. 229.

A Florida International University public opinion poll of Cuban-Americans in Dade county found that 43 percent of those surveyed supported a dialogue with the Cuban government. See Alicia M. Torres, executive director of the Cuban American Committee Research and Education Fund, testimony, U.S. Congress, *Free Trade with Cuba Act,* March 25, 1994, p. 243.

135. *Associated Press,* June 28, 1988.

136. Ramon Cernuda, testimony, U.S. Congress, House Foreign Affairs Committee, *Promoting Democracy in Cuba,* March 25, 1992, p. 30.

137. *Latin American Weekly Newsletters,* August 7, 1981, p. 3.

138. *Washington Post,* October 18, 1981, p. H10.

139. *The Financial Times,* November 15, 1988, p. 8.

140. Interview with Arlene Alligood, December 5, 1988. Alligood brought a group of port authority representatives to Cuba to assess the island's prospects.

7

The Cuba Embargo After Soviet Collapse: 1989–1993

President Bush's tenure coincided with Cuba's worst economic crisis since the revolution of 1959. Between 1990 and 1993, the country's economy shrank by 34 percent.[1] The immediate cause of this economic decline could be found in the political changes occurring in the Soviet Union. Soviet President Mikhail Gorbachev could ill afford to continue subsidizing the Cuban economy, and Cuba's sharp rejection of the reforms in the Soviet Union was eventually reflected back in dramatically reduced trade and aid packages from its former favorite ally.[2]

The changes in the Soviet Union and the concurrent transformation of the Soviet-Cuban relationship formed the backdrop for U.S. policy toward Cuba during the Bush years. During the late 1980s and early 1990s, the former Soviet Union was undergoing a revolution from within that sent tidal waves halfway around the world. Despite the fact that President Gorbachev visited Cuba in April 1989 and signed grandiose treaties of friendship and economic collaboration with Castro's government, Cuba began to experience major declines in essential imports from the Soviet Union.

In 1988, 85 percent of Cuban trade had been with the former Soviet Union and Eastern Europe. That year, the country's global trade was about $13 billion, of which $7.5 billion was in imports. Cuba's total trade with the West at that time amounted to $1.7 billion, of which $953 million was in imports. Cuban trade with former COMECON nations declined by two-thirds between 1989 and 1992, a heavy blow for a country that had depended on COMECON for over four-fifths of its imports.[3] For example, Soviet deliveries of oil dropped 16 percent in 1991 alone.[4] The primary reasons for this economic sea change were (1) the end of socialism in Eastern Europe, and hence of the COMECON, and (2) the demand, even before the end, that all trade be conducted in hard currency.

In addition to the enormous decrease in trade benefits, other Cuban aid from the Soviet Union dropped commensurately. Soviet military aid to Cuba had been estimated at about $1.2 billion annually; economic and military aid combined accounted for 20 percent of Cuba's GNP.[5] In 1989, for example, nearly one-fourth of all Soviet foreign aid (about $5 billion out of an estimated total of $21.6 billion) had gone to Cuba.[6] This figure dropped to zero in 1992.[7]

Terms of trade between the two countries, as well as amounts, also changed. In July 1990, for example, it was announced that, beginning the following January, all trade between Cuba and the Soviet Union would be conducted in freely convertible currency.[8] Assistant Secretary of State for Inter-American Affairs Bernard Aronson estimated that as a result Cuba would lose $1.5 billion to $2.5 billion in support from the Soviet Union—effectively cutting Soviet aid to Cuba by half.[9]

Beyond the immediate troubles introduced into the Cuban economy by the collapse of Communist regimes in the Eastern bloc, Cuba continued to suffer from the enduring U.S. embargo. The country's Central Planning Board calculated in 1992 that for the period 1960 to 1990, the total estimated cost of the embargo to Cuba was approximately $38 billion.[10]

Cuba dealt with the new economic downturn by turning to non-Communist countries for increased trade and investment.[11] Trade between Cuba and the West increased by 56 percent in 1989 not only in response to the suspension in Cuba's trade with the former Eastern bloc but also as a result of its own amended, more flexible Cuban trade laws.[12] In 1989, in their search for new partners and new trade options,[13] Cuban trade officials began to creatively, pragmatically, and realistically reinterpret the Cuban Joint Venture Law. Established in 1982 and also known as "Law 50," this statute had promoted very few joint ventures. By early 1992, however, Cuban officials confirmed that more than one hundred ventures had been jointly entered into by Cuban enterprises and foreign partners. Spanish investments comprised the major portion of these, accounting for $28 million in 1990.[14] Roughly half of the joint ventures were in tourism and biotechnology. Other examples of increased flexibility in Cuban trade policy included cooperative production arrangements, free trade zones, and associations in third countries.[15] Cuba also responded to the changes in the former Soviet Union by increasing its trade with U.S. subsidiaries during this period.

In addition, the Cuban government turned to the Far East for improved diplomatic and trade relations.[16] Japan responded by reducing Cuba's existing debt to $14 million, down from $700 million in 1989. By 1989, seventeen Japanese firms had branch offices in Cuba.[17] Cuba's relations with China improved steadily as well; at the end of 1988 China was Cuba's third largest supplier of consumer goods, and in 1989 its second largest purchaser of sugar. By 1990, Cuban-Chinese trade had tripled its 1987 level to reach $500 million, and moreover, the trade balance favored Cuba.[18]

Within its own hemisphere, Cuba likewise found ways to mitigate the impact on its economy of the collapse of the Soviet Union and the Eastern bloc. Cuba's trade with Latin America nearly doubled from about $335.7 million in 1988 to $600 million in 1990.[19] For example, in 1990 Latin America imported more than 636,000 tons of Cuban sugar, a fivefold increase from 1988 levels. In addition, Canada nearly tripled its imports of Cuban sugar over the same period.[20]

Bush Takes the Helm: An Overview

The Bush administration arrived at the White House amid much speculation that it would take a more pragmatic stand on Cuba and continue the liberalizing trend initiated by the Reagan administration in its latter days. These expectations were based on the signing of the Angola agreement in 1988, which alleviated a great deal of the tension that had existed between the United States and Cuba for over a decade. Moreover, it was noted, Bush lacked the ideological passion that had shaped Reagan administration foreign policy, particularly in its early years.

The Bush administration did not, however, follow suit on easing the embargo. In a foreshadowing of things to come, early on in Bush's tenure, the Treasury Department issued a pamphlet entitled "Cuba: What You Need to Know About the U.S. Embargo."[21] The pamphlet reiterated the U.S. government's prohibition on all "buying from or selling to Cuban nationals" and noted that the legislation affects "*all* U.S. citizens and permanent residents wherever they are located." At the same time, Secretary of State James Baker III sent a cable to U.S. embassies saying, "Cuban behavior has not changed sufficiently to warrant a change in U.S. attitudes."[22] In fact, the Bush administration echoed Reagan's antagonism toward Cuba at its most extreme and systematically went about finding and closing loopholes in the embargo.[23]

Anti-Cuba efforts of the new Republican White House also included continued condemnation of Cuba in the UN for human rights violations, pressure on the Soviet Union to cut aid to Cuba, and an offensive on allied trade with the island.[24] In a November 1991 speech before the United Nations, Cuba's Ambassador Ricardo Alarcón cited twenty-seven instances of trade contracts that had been interrupted in response to U.S. pressure.[25] The Cuban UN delegation charged that the United States had supplemented the embargo with an "extralegal" campaign to disrupt third-country trade and investment with Cuba. Charges against the United States included coercing a Spanish company, *Tabacalera,* from pursuing a joint venture in tourism with the Cubans; pressuring a Brazilian airline company, VASP, against investing in the Cuban airline, *Cubana;* preventing India from selling rice to Cuba; and discouraging petroleum exploration and development off Cuban coasts.[26]

In March 1990, Assistant Secretary of State Aronson enunciated new conditions for a change in U.S. policy toward the island: "If Cuba holds fully free and fair elections under international supervision, respects human rights and stops subverting its neighbors, we can expect relations between our two countries to improve significantly."[27] This speech was noteworthy in that it altered the focus of the embargo from Cuba's foreign relations to its domestic policies. Changes on the world scene had dictated this shift: because the Soviet Union was imploding, old fears about Soviet expansion through Cuba into Latin America were no longer of concern to U.S. policymakers or to the constituents they represented.[28] Combined with the fall of the Soviet Union, with the removal of Cuban troops from Africa, and peace processes in place in Central America, Cuban foreign policy did not appear as threatening as it once did. Nonetheless, despite an altered international climate, as Carter's reformers had discovered a decade ago, there was simply not enough political capital to be gained from lifting the embargo. Thus, unable any longer to point to a national security threat, U.S. politicians had to find new reasons to justify an old policy. In a sense, then, the Bush White House inherited an antiquated policy that it could not reject but could only mold to fit the new international (and domestic) political arena. Hence, it made domestic reform in Cuba a prerequisite to eliminating sanctions.

Sanctions theorists Hufbauer and Schott have argued that there is a correlation between the success of a sanctions policy and the nature of its foreign policy goals.[29] As we have seen, theorists have found that sanctions are most successful when minor changes in the target nation are sought.[30] Over time the principal aims of the embargo had been to oust the Castro government and to curtail Cuban action abroad (a main objective of the embargo since the 1960s). The Bush administration's new focus on changing Cuba's domestic political and economic system still qualifies, however, as a "major foreign policy goal" according to Hufbauer and Schott's designations. Warning that sanctions applied with such goals in mind are successful only about one quarter of the time, their theory helps to explain the continued failure of the embargo to achieve its aims.

The pinnacle of Bush administration policy toward Cuba came only three months before it left Washington, during the reelection campaign, when President Bush signed into law the Cuban Democracy Act (CDA). This legislation effectively turned back the clocks on the embargo to the pre-1974 period when U.S. subsidiaries located in third countries were precluded from the Cuba trade. The antecedents and consequences of the CDA are examined in detail in the following pages.

Amendments to the Cuba Embargo, 1989–1992

The first change to the Cuba regulations during the Bush administration was in reference to the Berman Amendment of 1988, which had exempted the import or export of informational materials from the embargo.[31] Issuing amendments to bring the regulations into conformity with Berman, OFAC, according to Krinsky and Golove, took a narrow reading of the exemption and limited its scope to the tangible items already in existence at the time of a given import or export contract. A U.S. party, therefore, could not finance the creation of new informational material or pay an advance to a Cuban national. Live telecasts, news wire feeds, and other electronic transmissions were excluded altogether, as was travel to Cuba to negotiate transactions in informational materials. Paintings, drawings, or sculpture were also excluded.[32] In March 1991, OFAC lifted its embargo on Cuban artworks in response to a lawsuit claiming that the importation of these artworks was protected by the Berman Amendment.[33]

The Treasury Department also amended the embargo legislation to unblock the share of an estate of a deceased Cuban national that passes to a U.S. resident, or a resident of a country in an authorized trade territory. In other words, Cuban émigrés could inherit their share of a deceased relative's estate located in the United States, even if the deceased relatives were blocked Cuban nationals at the time of their deaths.[34]

In August 1989, OFAC for the first time imposed a limitation on the amount an authorized U.S. traveler could carry to Cuba to cover expenses: $100 per day.[35] The following month, OFAC updated its list of companies and individuals who were alleged Cuban nationals for the purposes of the embargo. By this time, there were over 270 names on the list;[36] names continued to be added consistently during the next four years.[37]

In another action in October 1989, OFAC announced that charter flights between Miami and Havana would have to arrive or depart from Miami during general business hours of the U.S. Customs Service.[38] Although the ostensible purpose of this new requirement was to ensure the presence of enough customs service agents to obtain compliance with the embargo's restrictions, its effect was to increase the cost of travel between Cuba and the United States. This restriction was made effective October 9, 1990.[39] Nearly a year beforehand, in November 1989, Congress had already acted to substantially expand OFAC's staff and budget, citing the need for more effective enforcement of the Cuba sanctions.

In September 1991, OFAC began restricting the amount of payments U.S. citizens with family in Cuba could send to their relatives. First, according to the new rulings, remittances to the household of a close relative in Cuba could not exceed $300 every three months; the prior figure had been $500. OFAC also limited to $500 the amount of money U.S. citizens could remit to a Cuban national to help finance a temporary visit to the United States. Finally, OFAC limited to a total of $500 annually the amount of money an individual could pay the Cuban government for issuing visas or for renewing Cuban passports issued to Cuban-Americans.[40] In a slight loosening of the restrictions, six months later, in April 1992, OFAC announced that it would license shipments of humanitarian gifts, provided that their value did not exceed $100 per month, and provided that each recipient was sent no more than one such gift per month.

Also in April 1992, OFAC, acting under presidential directive, closed U.S. ports to any third-country vessel carrying goods or passengers to or from Cuba or carrying goods in which a Cuban national had an interest.[41] This restriction was similar to the embargo legislation in effect until 1975 when the U.S. repealed it to conform to the OAS resolution permitting each country to determine its own trade relations with the island.[42]

Most important, in October 1992 President Bush signed into law the Cuban Democracy Act (CDA), which significantly expanded the U.S. embargo against Cuba in a number of ways. First, the CDA prohibited subsidiaries of U.S. companies located in third countries from trading with Cuba. (See Appendixes 10 and 11 on pp. 219–220.) Second, it prohibited third-country vessels from loading or unloading any freight in the United States for 180 days after departing a Cuban port. Third, the CDA provided the Treasury Department for the first time with the authority to impose civil fines up to $50,000 and to order the forfeiture of property for violation of the embargo regulations. Fourth, it authorized the president to declare that countries that provide "assistance" to Cuba are ineligible for aid from the U.S. government. Furthermore, that same month, Congress passed legislation increasing criminal penalties for knowing violations of the TWEA to a maximum of $1 million in fines for corporations and $100,000 for individuals; ten years imprisonment; and the forfeiture of any property concerned in the violation.[43] The CDA's elimination of subsidiary trade was, however, the most far-reaching and hence the most controversial aspect of the Bush administration's legacy in regard to Cuba.

The Cuban Democracy Act

In 1975, the United States had amended the embargo to allow U.S. companies located in third countries to trade with Cuba under very specific conditions. Chapter 5 traced this change in policy to pressure from U.S. allies who complained vigorously about the restrictive extraterritorial regulations. In contrast, the CDA[44] was passed by the U.S. Congress in the shuffle of 1992 election-year politics. The ostensible goal of its author, Congressman Robert Torricelli (D-N.J.), was to speed up the demise of the Castro government by tightening the economic noose around Cuba. Responding to concerns about the welfare of the Cuban people, Torricelli argued:

> I would suggest that having the Cuban people *not* suffer is not an option. They are suffering, and they're suffering terribly. And indeed, an entire generation has been lost. The only question is whether the international community, those people who believe in human rights and the concepts of

> democracy, are at this late date going to develop a strategy to lessen the degree of pain, and shorten the life of the Castro government, so that finally this nightmare can end. That is the founding principle of this legislation.[45]

The moral underpinnings of the Torricelli bill are dubious indeed. In addition to the moral question, however, to argue that creating greater suffering in Cuba will lead more quickly to Castro's demise is ignorant of reality. All indications from the Cuban people (from dissidents to the religious) have been that they desperately want the embargo lifted, not tightened. The Cuban people simply don't believe that more suffering will lead quickly to "democracy," as Torricelli promised; in the six years since the CDA became law, Castro remains as firmly entrenched in Cuban society as ever. History has shown that punitive action against Cuba has rarely helped the United States achieve its goals on the island.

Torricelli's keen commitment to Cuban democracy may have stemmed more from his close association with the Cuban American National Foundation than from a true concern for the Cuban people.[46] The Cuban American National Foundation PAC (Free Cuba PAC) has donated more than $1,000 each to more than half of the Torricelli bill's twenty-two original House sponsors.[47] Torricelli himself became one of the largest recipients of CANF funds once he championed the pro-embargo position. Furthermore, his ambitions to run for senator of New Jersey, a state with a sizable Cuban population, also helped explain his sudden profound interest in the issue.[48]

A highly controversial law, the CDA has a rather involved history in the halls of Congress and the White House. In July 1989 Senator Connie Mack (R-Fla.) first introduced legislation—known as the "Mack Amendment"—that would have precluded all trade between U.S. subsidiaries and Cuba.[49] Foreign governments, U.S. corporations, and even the U.S. State Department strongly criticized the Mack Amendment. In fact, for three years in a row (1989–1992), the State Department under Bush went on record opposing the legislation. Its rationale was explained in a 1989 cable to U.S. embassies abroad: "We permit [subsidiary trade] because we recognize that attempting to apply our embargo to third countries will lead to unproductive and bitter trade disputes with our allies."[50] Notably, Congress passed the Mack Amendment as part of the 1991 trade bill, which Bush then vetoed.

Congressman Torricelli introduced the CDA in 1992, sparking numerous hearings, heated debate, and many revisions. At first the Republican White House opposed the legislation for the same reasons it had opposed the Mack Amendment. In the context of presidential elections, however, Bush's position fell victim to partisan competition for Florida's electoral votes. His endorsement of Torricelli came in May, just two weeks after Bill Clinton told an audience at a campaign fund-raiser in Little Havana

(Miami) that he supported the bill. "I think this administration has missed a big opportunity to put the hammer down on Fidel Castro and Cuba. I have read the Torricelli bill and I like it," Clinton chided.[51]

In a highly politicized and publicized move, President Bush signed the CDA into law while visiting Miami on a campaign stop. Absorbed entirely in parochial campaign issues, he failed to invite Democratic Congressman Torricelli to attend the signing of the foreign policy legislation he had authored. Interestingly, Bush won the Miami vote by a smaller margin than the Republicans had won it by in any previous election; moreover, he had to fight hard for that margin.[52]

Evolution of Subsidiary Trade

In the years between 1975, when it was first permitted, and 1990, trade between Cuba and subsidiaries of U.S. corporations had proceeded moderately. When the COMECON countries began collapsing, however, subsidiary trade jumped almost 300 percent; as we have seen, subsidiaries of U.S. corporations in third countries began replacing the Soviet bloc as Cuba's trade partners. Specifically, in 1988, 215 license applications for trade with Cuba were made to the U.S. Treasury Department. (See Appendix 8 on p. 218.) The result was $246 million of subsidiary trade, and the balance of trade that year favored Cuba. This level of trade was typical for the entire ten-year period from 1980 to 1989.[53] Throughout that decade, the export/import ratio for total trade between Cuba and U.S. subsidiaries remained more or less balanced.[54] Two years later, however, in 1990, the number of license applications increased by 50 percent, and the value of U.S. subsidiary trade with Cuba almost tripled, reaching $718 million in 1991. By 1990, Cuba had become a net *buyer* from U.S. subsidiaries. Cuban imports accounted for 76 percent of its total trade with these firms. Thus, the terms of trade changed in favor of U.S. subsidiaries.[55]

In Fiscal Year (FY) 1992, which ended just prior to the signing of the CDA, total trade between Cuba and U.S. subsidiaries dipped to about $500 million. The 30 percent drop in total trade from the previous year's level was due primarily to a decrease in sugar import by U.S. subsidiaries. The 1991–1992 sugar harvest in Cuba had fallen by more than 15 percent, from an annual average of 8–9 million tons in the 1980s to 7 million tons.[56] Despite the decline in total trade between U.S. subsidiaries and Cuba in 1992, U.S. subsidiaries actually exported 6 percent (roughly $21 million) *more* to Cuba than in the previous year. 1992 saw $407 million worth of goods exported to Cuba from U.S. subsidiaries, $24 million more than the 1991 figure.

It is important to note that even at the height of U.S. subsidiary–Cuban trade in 1991, subsidiaries accounted for only 18 percent of total Cuban trade. The balance of trade in 1992 heavily favored U.S. subsidiaries; 82

percent of all trade conducted between U.S. subsidiaries and Cuba were exports to Cuba, and 18 percent were imports from Cuba.

Types of Goods

Consumable goods comprised the overwhelming majority of trade between U.S. subsidiaries and Cuba. (See Appendix 9 on p. 218.) In 1992, for example, consumables accounted for 91 percent of this trade, a direct reflection of the collapse of the Soviet Union and Eastern bloc and of Cuba's activities in the world's markets. This figure represented a threefold increase in Cuban food imports from U.S. subsidiaries since 1988.

Opposition to the Cuban Democracy Act

Extraterritorial expansion of the embargo in the 1990s attracted widespread opposition. The CDA's unpopularity was expressed through bilateral formal protests, blocking legislation, regional diplomatic protests, and United Nations resolutions. The following section of this chapter explores the scope and nature of the opposition. Foreign nations were angered over the extraterritoriality of the legislation. U.S. corporations, dissidents living in Cuba, Cuban exiles in Miami, and members of the religious community also expressed a range of concerns about the new law.

Canada, Britain, and the European Community. Even before President Bush signed the bill into law, Canada and Britain had issued blocking orders against the proposed legislation. In October 1990, Justice Minister Kim Campbell issued an order barring Canadian subsidiaries of U.S. corporations from complying with U.S. measures precluding subsidiary trade, and requiring such companies to report any directives relating to such measures to the Canadian attorney general. Canadian Foreign Affairs Minister Joe Clark called the proposed legislation "an intrusion into Canadian sovereignty" in a 1990 letter of protest to U.S. Secretary of State James Baker. Trade between Canadian subsidiaries of U.S. companies and Cuba totaled $34.7 million in 1991.[57] That same year, total Cuba-Canada trade reached $280.7 million.

In September 1991, British Trade Secretary Peter Lilley warned the U.S. Congress that he would block the effects of the Mack Amendment by invoking the Protection of Trading Interests Act (PTIA), which protects Britain's sovereignty against extraterritorial trade measures promulgated by other nations. Lilley noted, "It is for the British government, not the U.S. Congress, to determine the U.K.'s policy on trade with Cuba. We will not accept any attempt to superimpose U.S. law on U.K. companies."[58] Following through on Lilley's warning, shortly before the CDA was signed into law, Britain acted to circumvent the U.S. legislation by invoking the

PTIA. British exports to Cuba had amounted to $46.2 million in 1991, and imports from the island were valued at about $20 million.[59] That same year, U.S. subsidiaries based in Britain conducted $21.75 million worth of trade with Cuba.[60]

U.S. subsidiary companies in Britain and Canada were caught in a quandary: either they violate the U.S. law or their home country's law. On the one hand, the U.S. law carries civil penalties up to $50,000 as well as possible confiscation of any property involved. On the other hand, host countries' blocking legislation also carries heavy penalties. Canada's blocking order, for example, fines Canadian-based subsidiaries up to $8,500 or five years imprisonment for *heeding* the CDA.[61]

After the CDA became law, opposition to the new legislation continued to flood Washington. The European Community warned the United States that "the extension of [the embargo] has the potential to cause grave damage to the transatlantic relationship."[62] In mid-September 1993 the European Parliament called on the European Community to ignore the CDA. The European Community stood to lose $500–600 million in trade because of the new law.[63]

Other countries oppose the CDA. Mexico and Japan also formally complained to the U.S. government about the new extraterritorial legislation. Mexican Foreign Minister Fernando Solana called the CDA a violation of "the essential principles of international law, especially non-intervention," explaining that "the decision of one state to establish commercial links with others is an expression of its sovereignty and is not subordinated to the will of a third. Commercial activities and exchanges which take place [involving] Mexico or companies based in our country will be conducted exclusively by Mexican law." On September 30, 1992, the Mexican Congress approved a resolution condemning the CDA.[64]

The following November, the Mexican foreign ministry issued a statement warning U.S. subsidiaries in Mexico not to recognize the new U.S. law. The statement read: "It is unacceptable for companies established in our country to try to place a higher value on foreign legislation in Mexican territory than national legislation."[65]

Mexican President Carlos Salinas de Gortari risked the wrath of the U.S. Congress and the White House when he told his Latin American counterparts in July 1993 that "the blockade [of Cuba] is completely unacceptable in a sovereign nation."[66] Salinas's move was particularly bold since he was committed to gaining U.S. support for the North American Free Trade Agreement (NAFTA) and was therefore generally careful during that period not to ruffle feathers in Washington. Furthermore, the influential CANF had condemned Mexican trade with Cuba and linked CANF's support of NAFTA to the eradication of Mexican-Cuban trade. Nevertheless, Mexican commercial action echoed Salinas's sharp nationalist message. U.S.

subsidiaries located in Mexico quadrupled their level of trade with Cuba between 1991 and 1992.[67]

Nobuo Miyamoto, Japanese ambassador to Cuba, likewise expressed opposition, commenting that "the Japanese government is affected by the law, since it contains articles involving third countries." Ambassador Miyamoto went on to state that the "problem with the law is that [the CDA] constitute[s] the extraterritorial application of U.S. domestic legislation . . . which is not permitted in international law."[68]

Opposition to the CDA also came from Argentina, Bolivia, Chile, Costa Rica, the Dominican Republic, Honduras, North Korea, Uruguay, Venezuela, and Vietnam.[69] At a meeting of mayors, municipal officers, and legislators from over twenty Spanish-speaking nations, a resolution opposing the Torricelli bill was issued and sent to United Nations Secretary-General Boutros-Ghali.[70]

U.S. corporations. U.S. corporations have quietly and consistently registered their opposition to the CDA. In October 1991, Brendan Harrington, a public affairs attorney at Cargill Inc., said his company leads the fight against efforts by Congress to prevent U.S. subsidiaries in third countries from dealing with Cuba. "If Cargill is denied access to the Cuban market," Harrington said, "European and Japanese traders would be very happy to take up the slack."[71] Prior to CDA, Cargill conducted the largest amount of subsidiary trade with Cuba, primarily through its subsidiary based in Switzerland.

Two other U.S. corporate giants have also taken a public stand against CDA. In August 1992, United Technologies (parent company of Otis Elevator) opposed the CDA in testimony before the U.S. Senate. Otis had been selling $10 million of goods a year to Cuba through subsidiaries in Mexico and Spain. Continental Grain also opposed the legislation; Daryl Natz, a spokesman for the company, pointed out that "our competitors who aren't subsidiaries of U.S. companies will get the business." Continental Grain had been selling several million dollars of grain to Cuba annually through its subsidiaries in South America, Canada, and Europe.[72]

Despite these instances of high-profile though temperate protest, the eighty-plus U.S. corporations affected by CDA did not mount an organized opposition. Many said they were wary of alienating members of Congress aligned with CANF. Furthermore, they feared CANF's ability to organize boycotts in Florida or New Jersey, where many Cuban-Americans live.[73]

Dissidents/Exiles. Even Cubans who have been jailed for their opposition to the Castro government opposed the CDA. Cuban dissident Elizardo Sanchez Santa Cruz wrote a letter to the *New York Times* opposing the tightening of the embargo. "Continuing economic pressures against the Cuban government will not bring about change," wrote Sanchez. "On the contrary, they provide Fidel Castro with excuses for his government's economic shortcomings and civil rights violations."[74]

Similarly, Eloy Gutierrez Menoyo, a Cuban exile who spent twenty-two years in prison in Cuba, wrote an op-ed published in the *Miami Herald.* In it he pointed out, "Why not admit that communism has lasted longer wherever an embargo has been imposed? Vietnam, China, North Korea, and Cuba are clear examples. . . . Even under the tightest possible embargo and without significant changes in U.S. policy toward the island, Fidel Castro could shrewdly manage to cling to power."[75]

There are, of course, those in the exile community who support the CDA. CANF had a heavy hand in writing the legislation and in overseeing the bill's passage through Congress and the White House.[76]

Religious community. Members of the Cuban Catholic Church were also among vocal opponents of the CDA. The Catholic Bishops of Cuba issued a statement declaring their "rejection of anything that might increase the great economic difficulties which the Cuban people are currently suffering. . . . Total embargoes affecting trade in essential products, including food and medicines, are ethically unacceptable, violate the principles of international law and are always contrary to the values of the Gospel."[77]

Since the enactment of the CDA, the U.S. group Pastors for Peace has been sending material aid bound for Cuba across the U.S.-Mexican border in a direct challenge to the embargo.[78] In 1993, moreover, Pastors for Peace successfully sponsored a twenty-four-day hunger strike to release a school bus intended for shipment to Cuba that had been impounded by the Treasury Department in Laredo, Texas.[79] Finally, during Pope John Paul II's historic visit to Cuba in January 1998, he condemned the U.S. embargo of Cuba calling it "unethical." He also asked Cuba to open to the world and the world to Cuba.[80]

The United Nations. On November 24, 1992, just one month after the CDA became law in the United States, the UN General Assembly resoundingly passed a resolution introduced by the Cuban government against the U.S. embargo of Cuba. The resolution, entitled "The Need to Terminate the U.S. Economic, Trade and Financial Blockade Against Cuba," expressed concern over the U.S. extraterritorial laws and their impact on the sovereignty of nations, entities, and individuals. The resolution directed UN Secretary-General Boutros-Ghali to prepare a report on the implementation of the resolution calling on all nations to "refrain from promulgating and applying laws and measures . . . directed at . . . strengthening and extending the economic, commercial and financial embargo against Cuba."[81]

When Cuba brought a similar resolution before the UN in 1991, it failed to gain the votes necessary for passage. The CDA was the exact instrument President Castro needed to secure UN support for his anti-embargo position. After the passage of the CDA with its extraterritorial measures, only two countries voted with the United States against the UN resolution: Israel and Romania.[82]

Even the U.S. State Department had predicted that the impact of the CDA would be to make the United States a pariah among its allies. In congressional hearings on Torricelli's proposed legislation in April 1992, Principal Assistant Secretary for Inter-American Affairs Robert S. Gelbard referred to the anti-embargo resolution that failed in the UN in 1991, testifying that "had the embargo applied to U.S. companies in third countries Cuba would have likely won the UN debate."[83] He was correct.

In response to the 1992 UN vote, U.S. State Department spokesman Joe Snyder announced that the nonbinding resolution would not affect U.S. policy toward Cuba or enforcement of the embargo. Between 1993 and 1997, the UN voted to support the Cuban position in numbers increasingly favorable to Cuba; in 1997, the vote was 143 to 3 against the Cuba embargo, with only the United States, Uzbekistan, and Israel opposed.[84] Ironically, despite their vote, both Uzbekistan and Israel trade with Cuba.

Theorists point out that embargoes are sometimes seen as inhumane acts that can result in a loss of prestige to the sender nation.[85] Certainly, its embargo of Cuba has caused the United States to lose moral standing in the international arena. The embargo violates the provisions of GATT, the UN General Assembly Declaration on the Principles of International Law, and the UN General Assembly Charter of Economic Rights.[86] The high-profile UN condemnations of 1992, 1993, 1994, 1995, 1996, and 1997 are a principal example of the moral costs associated with the U.S. sanctions policy. Many nations spoke out early on in the UN General Assembly against the proposed Cuban Democracy Act (CDA), opposing the extraterritorial aspects of the law and in some cases referring specifically to the costs of the embargo to the people of Cuba. For example, the delegate representing the nonaligned nations said of the CDA: "punitive economic action on such a scale will inflict even greater hardship on the people of Cuba and impede their development aspirations."[87]

Domestic opposition. Domestic groups in the United States have also publicly moved to condemn the U.S. embargo of Cuba. The American Public Health Association (APHA), for example, testified before the U.S. Congress, denouncing the Cuban Democracy Act "as destructive to both the Cuban and American people." The APHA called the bill "an attempted attack on the health and well-being of an entire population."[88] As previously mentioned, the U.S. religious group Pastors for Peace has led several caravans of buses filled with medicines, food, and other humanitarian aid destined for Cuba, which have been detained by U.S. customs officials at the U.S.-Mexican border amid much public fanfare.[89] Finally, the Freedom to Travel Campaign led a delegation to Cuba in July 1994. The United States responded to the planned trip by freezing the campaign's travel funds. Notably, upon publicity of the seizure of its funds, the group received spontaneous donations from individuals across the United States to allow the Cuba trip to proceed as scheduled.[90]

There is little doubt that many within the United States, and a majority around the world, see the U.S. embargo as an inhumane act. The United States has suffered embarrassing UN votes against its Cuba policy year after year. Yet widespread domestic and international condemnation has not inhibited U.S. policymakers from proceeding with even more stringent measures, or from unblushingly attempting to convince allies to participate in the Cuba embargo.

A strategy less contemptuous of world opinion might yield more international support and might even aid the United States in achieving some of its goals in Cuba. Ironically, while the United States is losing prestige from its extraterritorial law, the Cuban government has benefited. The CDA fueled President Castro's long-term efforts to blame the island's economic hardships on the United States, and, as we have seen, it enabled the Castro government to gain unprecedented international support in the UN.

The CDA's Impact in the Commercial Arena

U.S. Treasury and State Departments say companies comply. OFAC reports that no new licenses for subsidiary trade were granted after October 24, 1992.[91] Moreover, the Treasury Department states that no enforcement actions were taken because companies are "simply abiding by the law." Serena Moe, senior counsel to OFAC, noted that "a lot of companies have found business reasons to avoid trade. Nobody wants to be the test case, so companies are ducking." Moe added that she expects that if companies are compelled to trade with Cuba because they face a blocking order in their host country they will voluntarily disclose that to OFAC.[92]

Not surprisingly, the State Department reports no difficulties in obtaining compliance with the orders. Bob Fretz, a Cuba desk officer at State, comments, "We are always, always, always looking [for violators of the subsidiary trade laws]" and that "there are no cases [of violations] that we are aware of."[93]

Canada's bark is worse than its bite. It is clear that the CDA has taken a toll on subsidiaries based in Canada. For example, Eli Lilly of Canada Inc. and H.J. Heinz Co. of Canada Ltd. both rebuffed opportunities to sell goods to Cuba in 1993. Sources at both subsidiaries said that their head offices in the United States refused to permit the trade deals.[94]

Despite its bravado before the enactment of the CDA, the Canadian government in effect "wimped out"—as one Canadian scholar put it.[95] According to a 1993 article in the Toronto *Globe and Mail,* the Canadian Justice Department failed to act on about twenty cases of alleged violations of Canada's blocking order against the CDA. Under the Canadian Foreign Extraterritorial Measures Act, the Canadian Department of External Affairs is supposed to refer alleged violations of the Canadian blocking order to the Canadian Justice Department for prosecution. Apparently the Department of External Affairs has done its part in referring the cases to the Justice Department. Nonetheless there has never been a single prosecution in Canada under the Foreign Extraterritorial Measures Act.[96]

It is important to bear in mind Canada's particular vulnerability to U.S. economic pressure: 80 percent of Canadian exports go to the United States. Any blemish on this trade partnership would be particularly troublesome for Canada.[97]

European-based subsidiaries respond. The story from Europe is a bit muddled. According to a report prepared by the European Parliament in late September 1993, the CDA "is putting serious obstacles in the way of EC-Cuba trade and could even lead to a secondary embargo imposed on EC exports in the United States."

According, however, to David Jessup of the quasi-governmental British West India Committee, the CDA in reality has had little direct effect on subsidiary trade based in Europe. He suggested that U.S. subsidiaries are finding alternative legal methods to continue trading with Cuba. The Cubans, for their part, "have found creative new ways of doing business abroad—they have changed their buying patterns," Jessup said, noting that Cuban trading companies are located and operating around the world, "even in as obscure a place as Liechtenstein." He also observed that British companies are doing an "incredible amount of trade" with Panama, the Dominican Republic, and Switzerland, among other places. Trade between Britain and Curaçao, he remarked for example, accelerated in 1992. Jessup attributes Britain's increase in trade with these countries to creative strategies by British-based U.S. subsidiaries in relation to the CDA. "Companies," Jessup said, "find ways of doing business."[98]

U.S. parent corporation comments. As noted earlier, the U.S.-based agribusiness conglomerate Cargill Inc. was among the most active companies involved in U.S. subsidiary–Cuba trade. Questioned about the firm's compliance with CDA, Brendan Harrington, of Cargill's Washington office, was circumspect. Harrington stated that "Cargill is an ethical company. We are not going to break U.S. law." He did criticize the CDA, however, and did not minimize its negative impact on his company. "Unilateral sanctions backfire on U.S. companies. All the CDA is going to do is hurt U.S. competitiveness," he stated.[99]

According to Harrington, Cargill began feeling the impact of the law almost immediately. Direct trade between Cargill's subsidiaries and Cuba is clearly prohibited, but Cargill's indirect trade also took a blow from the new legislation. Much of the international agricultural commodities trade is contract trade, also known as "string trade." Most of it takes place on paper: companies buy and sell contracts. A contract to purchase sugar, for example, may easily be bought and sold twelve to fifteen times. If Cuba shows up anywhere in that string of trade, under the new law the U.S. corporation is forced to default on the contract, thereby incurring a penalty. (In the past, the U.S. company simply needed to apply for a license from the Treasury Department.) Cargill may therefore be forced out of the sugar trade because Cuba is such a major factor in the international sugar market: Harrington points out that Cargill is hesitant to get involved in contract trade for sugar because it is highly likely that Cuba will in fact show up in the string trade.[100] "If Cuba appears anywhere, Cargill must default—that is, pay—to get out of the contract. This obviously does not hurt Fidel Castro," Harrington noted. "Who gets hurt? The U.S. company." He concluded, "It is stupid to sacrifice U.S. market share on the altar of a political gesture."[101]

Taken together, information on whether or not companies comply with CDA regulations is contradictory. The U.S. government, for obvious reasons, says yes. Subsidiary corporations, also for obvious reasons, say yes. Canadian-based subsidiaries do seem to have curtailed their trade, while European-based subsidiaries may be finding their way around the letter of the law. The question of compliance remains somewhat ambiguous; probably all parties are correct to a certain degree.

Impact of CDA on U.S. Subsidiaries

It is clear is that the CDA has taken a toll on U.S. subsidiaries. Many people, including some U.S. government officials, say the act hurts U.S. businesses more than it harms Cuba. Serena Moe at OFAC laughed when questioned on the matter. Her response: "Who do you think the law hurts the most? Of course it hurts U.S. subsidiaries."[102]

Some subsidiaries, particularly those in the agribusiness sector, engaged in substantial amounts of business with Cuba. Though the figures remain classified, it is safe to assume that the trade cutoff was felt by those companies in several ways, including the loss of profits and markets. Although actual profits earned by the large agricultural traders may have been relatively small, future market potential has suffered significantly. As other foreign companies fill the vacuum left by departed U.S. subsidiaries, they reduce the competitive advantage U.S. firms will need when Cuba becomes open to them again.[103] Furthermore, certain increasingly finite resources in Cuba—beach front property and oil and mining rights, for example—are being divided up now among principal trade competitors of the United States.

As we have seen, although the business community can play an important role influencing trade policy and can even hinder an embargo through public opposition, it has been hesitant to take political action in the Cuba case. Even after the profitable subsidiary trade was threatened, U.S. corporations were reluctant to respond. Congressional aides reportedly had a difficult time finding companies willing to testify before Congress in opposition to the proposed legislation. As mentioned earlier in this chapter, of the more than eighty companies doing business under the subsidiary trade component of the embargo, only two or three agreed to publicly testify against the bill.[104] According to congressional staffers, not only did they fear retaliation from the powerful conservative Cuban lobby, but several companies and individuals reported having been harassed by the Federal Bureau of Investigation after taking public stands against the Cuba embargo in the past.[105] Though the Cuba market was interesting to many companies, especially those already engaged in the Cuba trade through their subsidiaries, it was generally not worth it for them to risk current domestic market share as well as government intimidation.

Impact of the CDA on Cuba

Even a U.S. Treasury Department official reports that Cuba has been largely successful in finding new sources to replace those previously occupied by U.S. subsidiaries.[106] Because most of the trade between these companies and Cuban entities was in fungible goods, the task hasn't been as formidable as it could be. Nonetheless, Cuba has had to pay inflated prices to import these goods, and has experienced difficult interruptions in domestic supplies as it located new trade partners. Moreover, theorists note that embargoes entail incalculable opportunity costs to the target nation, especially when other countries are hesitant to trade with the target because of sender nation restrictions.[107] As we have seen above, U.S. pressure to prevent foreigners from investing in Cuba has yielded results.

Sanctions Theory and the CDA

Sanctions theory warns that multilateral embargoes sometimes break down because different actors bear unequal burdens in relation to the sanctions, and the burden on a single country or group of countries may ultimately prove intolerable.[108] As Cuba's most important trade partner before the original embargo was invoked, only the United States was dramatically impacted by the sanctions policy. It was only after the United States pulled out of Cuba, thereby opening a market for other nations, that these other nations were directly affected.[109]

The 1992 tightening of the embargo under the CDA did therefore have an adverse impact on those companies and countries that moved into the Cuba market after 1975. By the time CDA was invoked, total trade between subsidiaries of U.S. companies and Cuba had reached over $718 million, and most of this was in exports to Cuba by a handful of corporations. Hence, the reinvocation of extraterritorial sanctions in 1992 may have had a greater impact on foreign countries than did the original embargo because Cuban hard currency trade levels had increased. The CDA has also frightened potential investors away from the Cuban market and has forced independent companies already involved in the Cuba trade to close up shop as well, for fear of pressure from the United States.[110] On the other hand, as we have seen, certain companies have taken advantage of the tightening of the embargo and moved into the Cuba market as U.S. subsidiaries have left.[111] These advantages notwithstanding, Gareth Jenkins of *Cuba Business* argues that if the embargo is lifted, "European business is likely to end up with a smaller slice of a larger cake, and so on balance, may even benefit commercially."[112]

All in all, then, the sanctions had differing impacts on nations involved in the Cuba trade. Because trade with Cuba accounted for only a small percentage of most countries' trade prior to 1959, little international protest over the embargo was heard in the early years. As time went on, however, other countries began to capitalize on U.S. withdrawal from the island and to invest in and trade with Cuba. The burden of the CDA thus fell on these nations more than on the United States, and opposition to the new sanctions was therefore much greater than protests elicited in the early 1960s after the original embargo was invoked.

Sanctions theory also argues that sanctions are less effective when they attempt to dislocate trade between the target and third nations. This chapter has demonstrated that extraterritoriality has not been effective in producing desired goals. Even though the United States was successful at gaining some international compliance, the CDA sparked widespread and forceful opposition and achieved neither Castro's overthrow nor democratic change in Cuba.

Sanctions theory also warns that sanctions are more likely to be effective when different players in the sender nation have similar agendas and common policy goals. As we have seen illustrated in several instances, the Cuba sanctions have often been shaped by campaign promises made in the heat of presidential elections rather than by real concern over U.S. interests abroad. Presidential candidates have historically used the Cuba issue to appeal to specific domestic constituencies. In addition to interparty conflict, various policymaking bodies within the U.S. government have also failed to achieve a unifying, sustaining vision for U.S.-Cuban relations (as previous chapters have demonstrated). A policy shaped less by parochial electoral concerns and more by common policy goals would no doubt produce more effective results.

Conclusions: After the Soviet Collapse

The embargo policy was based largely on a Cold War paradigm: it was established in order to prevent Soviet encroachment into the Western hemisphere through Cuba. With the collapse of the Soviet Union, the old rationale for the embargo had ceased to exist, and it thus would have made sense for the White House to update a policy that was three decades old. Without Soviet military and economic aid, Cuba could no longer threaten U.S. national security. Nonetheless, the Bush and later the Clinton White Houses chose to maintain the antiquated policy and to continue systematic hostile action against the island neighbor of the United States. Rather than using U.S. national security as rationale for the policy, the politicians now turned to issues of morality. In a nutshell, they argued that economic warfare against Cuba was in the long-term best interest of the Cuban people. The twisted reasoning behind this policy, as explained by CDA sponsor Robert Torricelli, claims that by increasing short-term suffering in Cuba, the CDA will more quickly bring Castro's reign to an end. That was six years ago, and there is no "end" in sight.

The stricter embargo did not help Washington achieve its Cuba goals. While the Cuban economy went into a tailspin during this period, it was due primarily to the collapse of the Soviet Union and not to the embargo. Meanwhile, as a result of the tighter sanctions, the United States has lost the UN vote on the embargo every year since the CDA was passed. Moreover, members of the religious community in Cuba and the United States as well as Cuban dissidents and public interest groups began publicly calling the embargo policy a failure and advocating dialogue with Cuba. On the streets of Havana, popular discontent did rise, though it was never sufficiently strong or organized to lead to the overthrow of the Castro government.

Perhaps then, the symbolic goal of the sanctions—signaling to constituents that the U.S. government still cared about bringing Castro down—was the only achievable goal. Even this goal floundered, however, when large segments of the U.S. public began pushing for a lifting of the embargo. Though Bush left office with sanctions in place that were stricter than any since the 1960s, few observers expected the embargo to yield desired results in the short term. A democratic Cuba with an open economy was still years away.

Notes

1. "Cuba Output Rises Despite U.S. Curbs," *Chicago Tribune,* July 25, 1996, p. 12N; "Cuba's Two Nations," *The Economist,* April 6, 1996, p. S10. Rodriguez, "*La economia de Cuba ante la cambiante coyuntura internacional,*" p. 9; Raul

Taladrid, Vice-president of the Cuban Agency for Economic Cooperation, personal interview, February 26, 1992.

2. Until 1987, Soviet trade with Cuba had been increasing about 10 percent a year. But in 1988, Cuba's imports from the USSR fell by 8 percent, and exports to the Soviet Union fell 14 percent. In 1990, however, Soviet trade with Cuba climbed by 8.7 percent over 1989. See Clyde H. Farnsworth, "Deep Cut Is Reported in Soviet-Cuba Trade," *New York Times,* January 16, 1989, p. D5; Don A. Schanche, "Castro Rubbing Soviets in Cuba Wrong Way—But They'll Be Patient," *Los Angeles Times,* January 15, 1989, p. 14; Robert Graham, "Why Perestroika Is Bad News for Castro," *Financial Times,* April 1, 1989, p. 3; Larry Rohter, "A Caribbean Communist Seeks New Friends," *New York Times,* April 2, 1989, Section 4, p. 1; Julia Preston and David Remnick, "Soviet in Cuba Criticizes Export of Revolution," *Washington Post,* April 4, 1989, p. A1; Julia Preston, "East Block Turmoil Bodes Ill for Trade and Aid in Cuba," *Washington Post,* January 22, 1990, p. A1; Don A. Schanche, "Castro's Power, Cuba's Future Hinge on Continued Economic Bond with Soviets," *Los Angeles Times,* May 6, 1990, p. A12. Cuba also experienced lags in deliveries from the Soviet Union. See "Perestroika Hits Island's Supplies," *Latin American Weekly Report,* February 15, 1990, p. 9.

3. Andrew Zimbalist, "The Cost of the U.S. Embargo and its Extraterritorial Application to the Cuban Economy," in Krinsky and Golove, *Economic Measures Against Cuba,* pp. 127–128.

4. Dominguez, testimony, U.S. Congress, *Cuba in a Changing World,* p. 22; Eusebio Mujal Leon, testimony, U.S. Congress, *Cuba in a Changing World,* p. 40; Jiri Valenta, testimony, U.S. Congress, *Cuba in a Changing World,* pp. 47–60. See also *CubaINFO,* November 19, 1990, Vol. 2, No. 19, p. 2.

5. Purcell, "Cuba's Cloudy Future," p. 114. Jorge Mas Canosa reports that Cuba received $100 billion in Soviet aid in the period 1960–1992. Canosa, testimony, U.S. Congress, House Foreign Affairs Committee, March 18, 1992 (distributed at the hearing), p. 6.

6. Schanche, "Castro Rubbing Soviets in Cuba Wrong Way," p. 1.

7. Hon. Robert S. Gelbard, Ambassador, Principal Deputy Assistant Secretary of State, Bureau of Inter-American Affairs, statement to the U.S. Congress, *Cuba Democracy Act of 1992,* p. 216; *Miami Herald,* November 27, 1990, p. 4A; Thomas Ginsberg, *Washington Times,* November 27, 1990, p. A7.

8. *CubaINFO,* December 14, 1990, Vol. 2, No. 20, pp. 2–3.

9. *CubaINFO,* August 7, 1990, Vol. 2, No. 13, p. 5. Soviet scholar Sergio Mikoyan refutes this figure. In a *New York Times* editorial, Mikoyan wrote that the CIA uses an exchange rate of .62 ruble to the dollar, when in actuality, the rate of exchange is 28 rubles to the dollar. So instead of paying $10 for Cuban commodities worth $3 on the world market, Mikoyan wrote, the Soviets were only paying $2 for $3 worth of commodities. *New York Times,* July 2, 1991, p. A17.

10. Zimbalist, "The Cost of the United States Embargo," p. 130.

11. Dominguez testimony, *Cuba in a Changing World,* p. 22.

12. Gillian Gunn, "Will Castro Fall?" Foreign Policy, No. 79, Summer 1990, pp. 138–139. See also Grabendorff, "The Relationship between the European Community and Cuba," pp. 96–106.

13. *CubaINFO,* Vol. 3, No. 15, October 4, 1991, p. 5.

14. See Kaplowitz and Kaplowitz, "New Opportunities for U.S.-Cuban Trade," pp. 4, 5–8.

15. For more information on this, see Kaplowitz and Kaplowitz, "New Opportunities for U.S.-Cuban Trade," p. 10; *CubaINFO,* Vol. 3, No. 4, March 15, 1991, p. 2.

16. James Kingston, "Cuba Sees Hard Currency Earnings Boost from 1992," *Financial Times,* November 21, 1989, p. 7.

17. Franz Schurmann, "Castro Shows Interest in Wooing Japan and Making Money," *Chronicle of Latin American Economic Affairs,* Latin American Institute, University of New Mexico, April 25, 1989.

18. Gunn, "Will Castro Fall?" p. 137; Fernandez, "Cuba's Relations with China: Economic Pragmatism and Political Fluctuation," p. 25; Charles Lane, "Brezhnev with a Beard," *Newsweek,* August 6, 1990, p. 25.

19. Vasconcelos, "The Limits and Possibilities of Cuban-Brazilian Relations," p. 191. See also James Brooke, "Castro Says He May Trade More in Latin America," *New York Times,* March 17, 1990, p. 3; "Cuba Trade with Latin America Increasing," *Reuters,* November 6, 1989. By 1994, Latin America was Cuba's largest trading partner.

20. Alvarez, "Cuba's Sugar Industry in the 1990's," p. 19.

21. *CubaINFO,* Vol. 1, No. 3, August 11, 1989, p. 4.

22. William Schneider, "U.S., Cuba, Wary of Accepting Change," *National Journal,* Vol. 21, No. 18, May 6, 1989, p. 1150.

23. Smith, testimony, U.S. Congress, *Cuba in a Changing World,* p. 13.

24. *CubaINFO,* September 7, 1990, Vol. 2, No. 14, pp. 1–2; *CubaINFO,* June 19, 1991, Vol. 3, No. 10, pp. 1–2; *CubaINFO,* July 5, 1991, Vol. 3, No. 11, p. 2. Congress initiated a heightened propaganda war against Cuba in the form of T.V. Martí.

25. See Ambassador Ricardo Alaracón's address to the UN General Assembly Plenary Meeting, November 13, 1991, reprinted in Krinsky and Golove, *Economic Measures Against Cuba,* pp. 347–355. In 1994, U.S. journalist Saul Landau reported that the Cuban government said that eight of every ten potential foreign investors were scared off by U.S. government intimidation. National Public Radio, "Talk of the Nation," September 27, 1994.

26. For an excellent review of each of these cases, and more, see Krinsky and Golove, *Economic Measures Against Cuba,* pp. 97–104. The VASP airline deal is discussed in *CubaINFO,* Vol. 3, No. 14, September 14, 1991, p. 5.

27. Bernard Aronson, Assistant Secretary of State for Inter-American Affairs, testimony, U.S. Congress, *Cuba in a Changing World,* p. 93; *CubaINFO,* March 20, 1990, Vol. 2, No. 5, p. 1.

28. Smith, "Comments on Soviet and Cuban Perspectives," in Smith, *The Russians Aren't Coming,* p. 154.

29. Hufbauer and Schott, *Economic Sanctions Reconsidered,* Second Edition, pp. 54–55.

30. Minor goals may be related to specific policies in a target government such as drug trafficking or human rights issues. Such goals may appear minor to outside audiences, but they may be of burning importance to the target nation. See Hufbauer and Schott, *Economic Sanctions Reconsidered,* Second Edition, p. 50.

31. Day, "Economic Sanctions Imposed by the United States Against Specific Countries: 1979–1992" (Congressional Research Service Report).

32. Krinsky and Golove, *Economic Measures Against Cuba,* pp. 122–123.

33. Ibid., p. 125. For information on a lawsuit against the U.S. Treasury Department, see Ken Jenkins, "Poster Importer's Art Clashes with U.S. Policy," *Washington Post,* February 8, 1990, p. V1; *CubaINFO,* Vol. 1, No. 10, December 20, 1989, p. 5; *CubaINFO,* Vol. 3, No. 6, April 11, 1991, p. 1.

34. Golove, "A History of U.S. Regulatory Policy toward Cuba," p. 19.

35. Day, CRS Report, p. 484; *Federal Register,* August 25, 1989.

36. General Manuel Noriega of Panama was designated an agent of Cuba by

the Bush administration. Krinsky and Golove, *Economic Measures Against Cuba,* p. 123. See also "Administration Declares Noriega a Cuban Agent," *Los Angeles Times,* October 28, 1989, p. A15; Lawrence Knutson, "Noriega Was Conduit for Banned Cuban Trade with U.S., Panel Says," *Associated Press,* January 20, 1990.

37. *CubaINFO,* Vol. 1, No. 10, December 20, 1989, p. 4.

38. *CubaINFO,* Vol. 1, No. 8, November 9, 1989, pp. 2–3.

39. Krinsky and Golove, *Economic Sanctions Against Cuba,* p. 124.

40. Ibid., p. 125; *CubaINFO,* Vol. 3, No. 15, October 4, 1991, p. 1.

41. Day, CRS Report, p. 485.

42. Krinsky and Golove, *Economic Measures Against Cuba,* p. 125.

43. Ibid., pp. 125–126.

44. Much of the information on the Cuban Democracy Act comes from the article "U.S. Subsidiary Trade with Cuba: Pre and Post the Cuban Democracy Act," written by this author for a conference entitled "Cuba In the International System: Normalization and Reintegration," September 23-25, 1993, Carleton University, Ottawa, Canada. An updated version of the presentation was published: Donna Rich Kaplowitz, "U.S. Subsidiary Trade with Cuba: Pre and Post the Cuban Democracy Act," in Archibald Ritter and John Kirk, eds., *Cuba in the International System: Integration and Normalization* (MacMillan Press, 1995).

45. Rep. Robert Torricelli, testimony, U.S. Congress, House Foreign Affairs Committee, "Promoting Democracy in Cuba," March 25, 1992, electronic transmission through Federal Information Systems Corporation, Federal News Service, 1992.

46. Christopher Marquis, "Embargo Bill Shows Exiles' Influence," *Miami Herald,* September 28, 1992, p. A1; Christopher Marquis, "Tighten Embargo on Cuba," *Miami Herald,* September 25, 1992, p. 1A; Christopher Marquis, "Bush to Sign Cuba Bill in Miami," *Miami Herald,* October 23, 1992, p. 1A.

47. *National Journal,* February 20, 1993, pp. 449–453.

48. Alligood, "U.S. Subsidiary Trade to End?" p. 1.

49. See "Proposed Legislation Would Ban All Trade Between Cuba and U.S.," *International Trade Reporter,* April 11, 1990; *CubaINFO,* July 27, 1989, Vol. 1, No. 2. p. 1.

50. "Cuba Sanctions Amendment in the State Authorization Bill," from U.S. State Department to U.S. embassies in Brussels, Paris, and Ottawa, September 1989.

51. Peter Slevin, "Bush Signs Law Aimed at Castro: Duking It Out for Voters in Miami," *Miami Herald,* October 24, 1992, p. 1A; *CubaINFO,* Vol. 4, No. 6, May 18, 1992, p. 2. Andrew Zimbalist notes, "As in previous U.S. Cuba policy maneuvers over the past decade, it is clear that the chief aim for American politicians in the Cuban Democracy Act was to appease the rich and influential members of the Cuban American National Foundation (CANF)." See Zimbalist, "Dateline Havana," p. 151. See also Wayne Smith, "The End of the Cold War? U.S.-Cuban Relations Remain Unchanged," *Los Angeles Times,* September 13, 1992, p. M2.

52. See *Miami Herald,* November 11, 1992, p. 2B; *Miami Herald,* November 5, 1992, p. 22A; *New York Times,* October 31, 1992, p. 6.

53. "Special Report, An Analysis of Licensed Trade with Cuba by Foreign Subsidiaries of U.S. Companies," April 1990, Office of Foreign Assets Control, U.S. Department of the Treasury, Washington, D.C. These figures all come from the U.S. Treasury Department "Special Report." They are probably inflated. According to Brendan Harrington, a public affairs attorney for Cargill Inc., only about 15 percent of the licensed trade is actually carried out. Harrington explained that there is no penalty for overestimating the amount of trade that may take place, while there is

a penalty if a company underestimates. Therefore, nearly all companies request licenses for more trade than they actually expect to conduct. Telephone interview with Brendan Harrington, public affairs attorney, Cargill, Inc., Washington, D.C., September 15, 1993.

54. The average export/import ratio for 1980–1989 was 51/49. This number was calculated from the U.S. Treasury Department "Special Report," 1990.

55. In 1992, the balance of trade evened out a bit but continued to favor U.S. subsidiaries by a ratio of 53 percent to 47 percent.

56. See *CubaINFO,* Vol. 5, No. 9, July 16, 1993, p. 9.

57. Helen Simon, "U.S. Allies Angered by New Cuba Bill," *Business Latin America,* October 26, 1992.

58. British Embassy Press Secretary Michael Price stated, "We made clear that there will be provisions within the legal system which will prevent subsidiaries operating out of Britain from complying [with Torricelli]." See *CubaINFO,* Vol. 4, No. 11, October 2, 1992, p. 1; *Wall Street Journal,* November 1, 1991, p. A19; *Globe and Mail,* October 31, 1990, p. A1; *Globe and Mail,* November 1, 1990, p. A1.

59. *Reuters,* "Britain Acts to Circumvent U.S.-Cuba Trade Ban," The Reuter European Community Report, October 21, 1992. See also *CubaINFO,* Vol. 5, No. 8, June 18, 1993, p. 5.

60. U.S. Treasury Department, "Special Report," 1993.

61. See *CubaINFO,* Vol. 4, No. 12, October 27, 1992, p. 2.

62. The Cuban Democracy Act impacts $625 million of the $750 million in annual EC-Cuban trade. See *The Financial Times,* October 9, 1992; *The Gazette,* October 9, 1992; *Agency France Press,* October 8, 1992; *CubaINFO,* Vol. 4, No. 12, October 27, 1992, p. 2.

63. Simon, "U.S. Allies Angered."

64. *Nuevo Herald,* October 1, 1992, p. 1A; *CubaINFO,* Vol. 4, No. 12, October 27, 1992, pp. 2–3.

65. *Washington Times,* November 22, 1992, p. A14; *CubaINFO,* Vol. 4, No. 14, December 4, 1992, p. 3.

66. David Schrieberg, "Anti-U.S. Winds Blow from the South," *Sacramento Bee,* July 17, 1993, p. A12.

67. According to the U.S. Treasury Department, U.S. subsidiaries located in Mexico increased their trade from $5.3 million in 1991 to $21.93 million in 1992. Other locations showing an increase in trade with Cuba included France, Germany, the Netherlands, and Spain. See "U.S. Treasury Department, Special Report, 1993."

68. *Granma International,* November 22, 1992, p. 13. See also *CubaINFO,* Vol. 4, No. 14, December 4, 1992, p. 3.

69. See *CubaINFO,* Vol. 4, No. 13, November 13, 1992, pp. 3–4.

70. Foreign Broadcast Information System, Latin America, October 14, 1992, p. 3.

71. "U.S. Companies Sidestep Embargo on Cuba," *Chicago Tribune,* October 21, 1991, p. 5.

72. Simon, "U.S. Allies Angered."

73. Alligood, "U.S. Subsidiary Trade to End?" p. 1.

74. Elizardo Sanchez, "Let Fidel Castro Lead the Way," *New York Times,* August 26, 1993. Sanchez had spent ten of the previous twelve years in Cuban prisons.

75. Eloy Gutierrez Menoyo, "To the Exile Community, The Whole World Dialogues, So Why Not Cubans?" *The Miami Herald,* August 27, 1993, p. 17A. Other members of Cuban human rights groups also expressed opposition to the

CDA. A letter shown to the author was sent from Hector Aguilera, Alvarez Oscar, Ramon Cernuda, Jose Fernandez, Ariel Hidlago, Hubert Jerez, and Jorge Valls to members of the U.S. Congress, February 13, 1992.

76. Alfonso Chardy, "Torricelli Bill Backer Urged Exile Unit," *The Miami Herald,* September 25, 1992, p. 21A.

77. *CubaINFO,* Vol. 4, No. 12, October 27, 1992, p. 3.

78. See *CubaINFO,* Vol. 4, No. 14, December 4, 1992, p. 4; *CubaINFO,* Vol. 4, No. 15, December 18, 1992, p. 2.

79. The U.S. Treasury Department had permitted all but one of ninety-five vehicles loaded with goods bound for Cuba to cross the border. They forbade the export of the bus, however, because it was not considered "humanitarian goods." The pastors stated that the bus would be used to bring children to Sunday school and church services. See *CubaINFO,* Vol. 5, No. 11, Sept. 3, 1993, pp. 2–3, and Vol. 5, No. 10, August 6, 1993, p.1.

80. *New York Times,* January 22, 1998, p. A1; *CubaINFO,* Vol. 10, No. 2, January 29, 1998, p. 1.

81. See Krinsky and Golove, *Economic Measures Against Cuba,* pp. 13–84.

82. Fifty-nine countries voted in favor of the resolution, 71 abstained, and 42 did not appear for the vote. Among those voting in favor of the resolution were Canada, France, Mexico, Venezuela, Brazil, Chile, Colombia, Ecuador, China, India, New Zealand, Indonesia, Spain, and Uruguay. Among those abstaining were Britain, Germany, Belgium, Denmark, Greece, Ireland, Italy, Luxembourg, Netherlands, Portugal, and Russia. See *CubaINFO,* Vol. 4, No. 14, December 4, 1992, p. 2.

83. Statement by Robert S. Gelbard before the Committee on Foreign Affairs, House of Representatives, April 8, 1992.

84. *CubaINFO,* Vol. 6, No. 15, November 22, 1994, p. 3. *New York Times,* November 13, 1996; *CubaINFO,* Vol. 9, No. 15, November 13, 1997, p. 1.

85. Doxey notes: "Wreaking economic havoc on an impoverished developing country which is already unable to meet the basic needs of its people hardly commends itself as appropriate action, even if the foreign or domestic policy of the country concerned merits an international response." Doxey, *International Sanctions in Contemporary Perspective,* p. 145.

86. Andrew Zimbalist, testimony, U.S. Congress, *Free Trade with Cuba Act,* p. 210.

87. Krinsky and Golove, *Economic Measures Against Cuba,* p. 68.

88. Victor Sidel, APHA, testimony, U.S. Congress, House Committee on Foreign Affairs (distributed at the hearing), no page numbers marked. See also Krinsky and Golove, *Economic Measures Against Cuba,* p. 61.

89. *CubaINFO,* Vol. 6, No. 3, February 18, 1994, p. 4. See also *CubaINFO,* Vol. 5, No. 11, September 3, 1993, pp. 2–3.

90. *CubaINFO,* Vol. 6, No. 9, July 1, 1994, p. 1.

91. Telephone interview with Clara David, Office of Foreign Assets Control, U.S. Treasury Department, August 31, 1993.

92. Telephone interview with Serena Moe, senior counsel at the Office of Foreign Assets Control, U.S. Treasury Department, September 13, 1993.

93. Telephone interview with Bob Fretz, U.S. Department of State, September 7, 1993.

94. Jeff Sallot, "Don't Let Washington Call the Shots," *Globe and Mail,* July 16, 1993, p. A17.

95. Telephone interview with Dr. John Kirk, September 9, 1993.

96. Sallot, "Don't Let Washington Call the Shots," p. A17.

97. Telephone interview with Jeff Sallot, Foreign Affairs Correspondent for the *Globe and Mail,* September 14, 1993.

98. Telephone interview with David Jessup, British West India Committee, September 14, 1993.

99. Telephone interview with Brendan Harrington, public affairs attorney at Cargill's Washington office, September 15, 1993.

100. For an excellent explanation of "string trade" and the CDA, see William R. Pearce, Vice Chairman of the Board, Cargill Inc., letter submitted for inclusion, U.S. Congress, *Cuban Democracy Act of 1992,* pp. 265–271.

101. Interview with Brendan Harrington, September 15, 1993.

102. Telephone interview, Serena Moe, September 13, 1993.

103. Simon, "U.S. Allies Angered."

104. United Technologies and Cargill agreed to testify in Senate hearings in August 1992.

105. Series of telephone interviews with several congressional offices, including those of Senator Dodd and Congressman Rangel, August 1992, October 1993.

106. Telephone interview, Serena Moe, U.S. Treasury Department, September 13, 1993.

107. Hufbauer and Schott, *Economic Sanctions Reconsidered,* pp. 60–61, 64.

108. Leyton-Brown, "Extraterritoriality in the United States Trade Sanctions," p. 255.

109. Some nations believe that *if* the embargo were lifted, they would lose their market presence in Cuba. The Canadian trade attaché in Havana made this comment to the author in Havana, January 1988.

110. Telephone interview with David Jessup, British West India Committee, September 14, 1993. See also Saul Landau, note 25 of this chapter.

111. Faxed letter from Wolf Grabendorff, Director of IRELA, Spain, to Donna Rich Kaplowitz, September 10, 1993.

112. Gareth Jenkins, "Fractured Blockade," *Cuba Business,* Vol. 8, No. 6, July-August, 1994, p. 8.

8

The Phoenix Rises Again: Cuba, 1993–1997

If the first years of the decade were characterized by Cuba's economic free fall, the middle years of the 1990s were years of modest growth for the island. Cuba's economy hit bottom in 1993; in four years its GDP had plunged by 34.8 percent.[1] Exports fell by 70 percent and imports plummeted 75 percent between 1989 and 1993.[2] In 1994, however, the economy grew a slight 0.7 percent, followed by a 2.5 percent jump in 1995. In 1996, the Cuban economy expanded an impressive 7.8 percent, outstripping a 5 percent official forecast for the year, as well as the 3.5 percent average rate of growth among other Latin American nations. In 1997 the growth rate was 4 percent.[3]

Exports increased 33 percent in 1996, with tourism representing the major "motor" of the economy—increasing by 41 percent over the previous year. Over one million people visited Cuba in 1997, making tourism the most important foreign currency earner on the island: The tobacco sector grew by 40% between 1996 and 1997. Tourism brought more than $1.7 billion to Cuba in 1997 gross earnings.[4] Meanwhile, in 1996 the nickel sector showed a 31 percent growth rate, citrus grew by 38 percent, and fish production by 74 percent. Sugar production increased slightly over 1995 levels, which were the lowest they had been in thirty years.[5]

Certain basic indicators also pointed to the fact that the crisis was easing. Electrical blackouts, which in 1993 had sometimes lasted twenty hours a day, were nearly eliminated. Increased gasoline supplies led to more traffic in the streets, and road repair and construction were renewed. Finally and most important, food shortages were eased by late 1996.[6] Cuba thus weathered the storm and survived. In fact, a number of basic indicators held steady even during the crisis years. Cuba's infant mortality rate actually dropped from ten per thousand live births in 1989 to 7.9 per thousand in 1996. Life expectancy improved from 74.5 in 1986 to 77 years in 1996, and between 1989 and 1996 the literacy rate improved from 96 percent to 98 percent.[7]

Though Cuba's growth rate appears impressive, the figures are relative to figures for the preceding five-year economic crisis (1989–1993). Hence, despite vigorous growth, Cuba's general standard of living remained well below 1989 levels. For example, although exports grew 33 percent in 1996 over the previous year, this growth was completely counterbalanced by increased imports, primarily in the food and oil sectors.[8] The trade deficit was financed with short-term credits obtained at high interest rates, sending Cuba's hard currency debt up to an estimated $11 billion in 1996.[9] Economist Andrew Zimbalist suggests that at the current rate of growth, it will take until the year 2015 for Cuba to regain its 1989 GDP levels.[10]

The Cuban government feared that the positive data generated by the island's economic recovery would fuel rising popular expectations that couldn't be met. One Cuban economist said that although things are better now, people's expectations have also risen. "Until people get two pieces of bread every morning instead of one, they will not think things are better. People are actually more angry and anxious now than they were when the crisis was more severe," he said.[11] Hence the Cuban government began issuing warnings to curb expectations.[12] Vice-president Carlos Lage announced in a news conference in July 1996 that the Cuban economy was expected to more than double in 1996, but immediately urged citizens to bear in mind that Cuba had started recovery "from a very low point."[13] In an unprecedented move, the Cuban government also acknowledged that public patience was wearing thin and that the economic crisis had brought inequalities that cost the government popular support.[14] A longtime master at manipulating public opinion, the Cuban government probably bargained that it would be better to openly address rising but doomed expectations than to sweep disappointment under the rug where it could grow out of control.

Market-Oriented Reform

Cuba's economic recovery was based on a two track strategy: sectoral and market-oriented. As we have seen, despite the impressive figures for the mid-1990s, the Cuban government still remained more cautious than optimistic in 1997. With deep reservations, it allowed further carefully calibrated market-oriented reform to pave the way for continued economic growth.

As Chapter 7 showed, during the first few years of the economic free fall, Cuba responded to the macroeconomic crisis with a sectoral strategy. Between 1989 and 1993, Cuba sought to raise import capacity and growth by promoting nontraditional exports: primarily tourism and biotechnology. (Until 1989, 77 percent of Cuban exports had been concentrated in a single commodity: sugar.) The sectoral strategy, however, proved to be somewhat problematic. Although biotechnology and pharmaceutical exports accounted for roughly $200 million in income by 1993—and were projected to reach a billion dollars by the year 2000—these revenues were not sufficient to stem the mounting economic crisis. Biotechnology was also limited by its large consumption of foreign exchange and by the market power of competitive multinational pharmaceutical companies.

Tourism did grow steadily, with gross revenues increasing by 500 percent between 1989 and 1995 (from $165 million to $1 billion). In fact, by 1995, tourism had replaced sugar as the island's main foreign currency earner, and its earnings are projected to double by the turn of the century. Nonetheless, the tourism industry demands high levels of imports, cutting real profits to less than a third of income earned. Moreover, the appearance of rich foreigners and the growing wealthy class of Cubans who work in the tourism industry have aggravated political tensions in the country.

With the persistence of the economic crisis, the government sought a more systemic strategy for recovery and in 1993 began to introduce market mechanisms into the Cuban economy. The first major move in this direction was the 1993 law that depenalized use of the U.S. dollar. This change was a direct consequence of the earlier reforms to attract tourism and foreign investment. Since the dollar economy had begun to expand and black market activities to skyrocket, the government decided to capitalize on the illegal activity and legalize dollar holdings. On July 26, 1993, Castro proclaimed, "Today, life, reality . . . forces us to do what we would have never done otherwise . . . we must make concessions." He then announced the following liberalizations: (1) Cubans would be permitted to have foreign currency and to buy directly in special stores; (2) the government would introduce a national currency that would be convertible (made effective in December 1994); (3) bank accounts in dollar denominations would be permitted; and (4) Cubans could pay for the services of other Cubans in dollars.[15] In conjunction with the 1993 law, shops were opened where local Cubans could buy imported consumer goods.

Two major goals of this new legislation were successfully met: the thriving black market in dollars was significantly weakened, and remittances sent to Cubans from family members abroad increased, until they were limited by U.S. law in 1994.[16] The price of the dollar on the black market dropped from 125 pesos in 1993 to 18 pesos in 1996.[17] By 1996, it was estimated that between 25 and 40 percent of the Cuban population had access to U.S. dollars.[18]

In 1994, the Cuban government introduced two reforms intended to stimulate private initiative. First, restrictions on self-employment were eased in specific sectors, a measure that effectively eliminated the Cuban state as the sole employer or instigator of economic activity. Currently, there are 200,000 Cubans working for themselves in a hundred different occupations, ranging from hair stylists and plumbers to taxi drivers, carpenters, electricians, tailors, shoemakers, and home restaurant owners (known in Cuba as "paladares").[19] Since private wage labor is prohibited, self-employed persons have not been allowed to legally hire workers other than family members. Taxes instituted in 1996 on private enterprise caused this sector to shrink somewhat—from a high of 208,000 participants in early 1996 to 200,000 at the end of the year.[20]

Second, in 1993 the Cuban government transformed state farms into worker-run cooperatives. These cooperatives have the right to use the land (but not own it outright), have ownership of the crop, own bank accounts, and elect their own management. By the end of 1994, between 70 and 75 percent of Cuba's farming land was in the hands of private cooperatives.

In September 1994, the Cuban government reestablished farmers' markets, allowing agricultural producers to sell surplus goods at market prices. In order to offer these goods for sale, farmers must first satisfy their preestablished quota (around 80 percent of their output) and must pay taxes. The farmers' markets have been successful on several fronts—increasing agricultural production, sopping up excess currency in people's pockets, and improving the value of the Cuban peso.

The agricultural sector—the most liberalized sector of the Cuban economy—has, however, introduced old vices and imbalances into that economy. For example, although the state sets artificially low prices for agricultural products (often 1/35 of those set by the free market), farmers have quickly become among the most affluent groups in Cuban society because the farmers' markets have brought them tremendous economic gain; their savings represent 75 percent of total private savings.[21] Moreover, because demand is so high, some prices at farmers' markets have become prohibitive, raising consumers' wrath.

The government response in the spring of 1996 was to increase taxation on agricultural producers, a policy with certain drawbacks. First, some producers were forced out of the market altogether.[22] Second, most Cubans view taxation as anathema—a detested element of capitalism and the most blatant symbol that capitalism is creeping into Cuban socialism. The Cuban government has attempted to explain the need for taxes on the basis of social justice. The tax system, they say, will iron out the inequalities now prevalent in Cuban society, although no doubt it will take some years for the system to reach a comfortable equilibrium. Meanwhile, though taxing farmers and cooperatives has been controversial, for most Cubans, access to farmers' markets has meant an improvement in their lives. At least, the presence of the farmers' markets has symbolized to many of them that the sense of shortage is over.[23]

In December 1994, the Cuban government also introduced artisan or crafts markets where Cubans can sell light manufactures, everything from shoes to sandwiches. These markets have also been tremendously popular, and many public places in Cuba that were previously empty are now filled with small vendors selling anything and everything to the public. The geography of Cuban public space has been transformed.

The Cuban government has also begun to correct its own finances so as to prevent future inflation. Taxes, reduced subsidies to unprofitable state firms, and an increase in certain key state prices reduced the fiscal deficit from 40 percent of the GDP in 1993 to 7 percent in 1994. Jose Luis Rodriguez, minister of economy and planning, in 1997 set a goal of reducing this figure further to 2 percent.[24] While official government strategy for alleviating the deficit emphasized efforts to reduce expenditures in the national economy, Cuba's recovery efforts clearly also focused on attracting foreign trade partners.

Foreign Investment

Foreign direct investment is the cornerstone of Cuba's efforts to redirect its trading patterns. (See Appendix 12 on p. 221.) Toward this end, in 1995 Cuba passed a liberal foreign investment law replacing its 1983 joint venture law. Under the new legislation, foreigners are no longer limited to 49 percent ownership of joint ventures but are now allowed to own Cuban enterprises outright in nearly every sector of the economy. Foreign investors are also allowed to repatriate profits, and the new law permits independent arbitration processes in disputes over property rights and in cases of compensation for expropriation.[25] Additional reforms aimed at attracting new trade partners include cooperative production agreements, free trade zones, autonomous enterprises, and third party marketing and management agreements.

Though the total volume of Cuban trade as of the time of this writing has not reached 1989 levels, participation of Latin American, Western European, and Canadian trade partners has grown substantially. Non-Cuban entities now hold ownership in companies ranging from tourism and communications to mineral extraction and agriculture. According to 1997 figures, 260 joint ventures were operating in Cuba, involving fifty-seven countries in forty areas of the economy. The foreign investment projects totaled up to $5 billion.[26]

Closer relations with other Latin American and Caribbean nations have also been a key component of Cuba's reintegration in the world economy. The Cuban foreign trade minister called the region "more than ever, a priority objective of Cuban foreign policy." This is partly a pragmatic response on Cuba's part to the economic demands it faces in the 1990s, but it also reflects Cuba's long-term commitment to Latin American integration. By 1996, Cuba had established full diplomatic relations with every South American country.[27]

Sanctions theory cautions that an embargo's chances of success are diminished if the nations circumventing the embargo are neighbors.[28] Clearly, in the wake of Cuba's successful campaign to increase trade with

Latin American nations, the embargo's chance of succeeding steadily corroded. Latin America's share of Cuba's total trade increased to 30 percent in 1993 from less than 5 percent before 1988. By 1994, the Latin American region was Cuba's largest trade partner. More than 41 percent of Cuba's imports now originate in the region.

Mexico is Latin America's (indeed, the world's) largest investor in Cuba, with substantial investments in telecommunications and oil refining. For example in 1994, in Cuba's largest-ever foreign investment deal, the Mexican Grupo Domos signed a $1.5 billion deal to overhaul Cuban telecommunications. In addition, as we have seen, Mexico-Cuba trade has been active, particularly in the cement, textiles, and glass industries. Mexican imports from Cuba rose from $8 million in 1988 to over $80 million in 1993.

Canada has also taken a major piece of the Cuban pie. Notably, Sherritt International of Canada committed half a billion dollars to nickel extraction and oil exploration, and other Canadian firms have invested in transportation, agriculture, tourism, communications, and finance.

No doubt many potential foreign investors have been dissuaded from entering the Cuba market because of the extraterritorial reach of the Cuban Democracy Act. In 1994, Saul Landau reported that eight out of ten would-be investors in Cuba were directly persuaded against such investments by the U.S. government.[29] Nevertheless, Cuba has signed joint ventures and embarked on foreign investment projects with firms from Argentina, Australia, Brazil, Canada, France, Germany, Great Britain, Israel, Italy, Jamaica, Mexico, Russia, and Spain, as well as others. Hence, despite U.S. pressure, the Cuba market has shown impressive growth.

In conclusion, the Cuban government has been able to reverse a downward economic spiral by embracing methods it once scorned. Legalization of the dollar, taxation, and foreign ownership of Cuban property were, only a few short years ago, abhorred by Cuban socialists. Today, they are the very nuts and bolts of Cuba's economic recovery. In short, despite President Fidel Castro's characteristic socialist hyperbole, the foundation of the Cuban economy has shifted from predominantly socialist in orientation to moderately capitalist, or at least mixed. The socialist economy endures principally in rhetoric but less so in fact.

Although the road ahead may be unclear, it is certain that, once having embarked upon this path of economic reform, there is no turning back for Cuba. The most fundamental reason for this is quite simple: if the present government of Cuba wants to remain in power—which it clearly does—it must at least ensure that the population has access to the bare necessities. In the new post–Cold War configuration of the world, lacking a strong ally to subsidize the economy, the Cuban government concluded that economic liberalization was the only way to ensure basic necessities to the population—the very core of its own political survival. Hence, the Cuban government swallowed the bitter fruit of economic liberalization and came out ahead.

Enter The Clinton Administration/Track II

If the Cuban economy has quietly but irreversibly taken on a shape the United States always demanded, this salutary turn of events seems to have gone unnoticed in Washington. As Chapter 7 recounted, the Clinton administration rode into Washington on the coattails of the Torricelli legislation and, as this chapter will show, it has overseen the most rigorous tightening of the embargo in its thirty-five year history.

Under the tutelage of Richard Nuccio, a former Torricelli aide who was given the role of "Special Advisor to the President and Secretary of State for Cuba," one of the administration's first moves on Cuba policy was to expand what has become known as the "Track II" provision of the Cuban Democracy Act. Most of the CDA's provisions tightened the embargo against Cuba, but two of the bill's provisions called for liberalized telecommunications links with the island, and for strengthening elements of civil society in Cuba through increased communication and humanitarian aid programs. Nuccio capitalized on these two openings by encouraging humanitarian organizations and human rights groups to set up activities in Cuba, and by overseeing liberalization of the U.S. telecommunication policy with Cuba. In July 1993, the State Department issued guidelines for establishing more "efficient and adequate" telephone communications services between the United States and Cuba. Fifteen months later, five U.S. companies received approval from the Federal Communications Commission to provide direct telecommunications services to the island. The telecommunications companies were allowed to improve both satellite and undersea cable links between the two countries for the first time since the embargo took effect in 1962.[30]

Among the initiatives sponsored by the Track II provision was federal funding for a flagship project under the directorship of Freedom House, a conservative New York–based human rights group aimed at Cuba under the tutelage of Cuban-American activist Frank Calzon. The half-million-dollar federal grant was to be used for disseminating information in Cuba, providing humanitarian assistance to victims of political repression, providing supplies and equipment to "democratic groups inside the country," and sponsoring visits to Cuba by U.S. experts and activists from countries that have undergone recent political and economic transitions.[31]

It was misguided to think that Havana would accept such measures, even under the guise of "aid," and especially from an organization backed by U.S. government funding and headed by a man with no political credibility on the island. No doubt Havana scorned this type of intervention more keenly than it did the tightening of the embargo. The Cuban government's reaction to Track II predictably demonstrated not only its ineffectiveness but its counterproductivity: Track II quelled the very voices it was trying to accentuate. In response to the initiative, Raul Castro said: "This is the 'other war' . . . with the objective of undermining us ideologically from within. We are ready to prepare a response capable of confronting the entire dimension of that political ideological terrain."[32] Havana then moved to intensify a crackdown against dissidents and, more important, against formerly loyal party members who advocated political and economic liberalization. New restrictions were placed on all forms of contacts with Americans, and hard-line party officials were transferred into key positions at the University of Havana. Reformers within the Castro government who had been pushing for a gradual political and economic opening in Cuba found themselves under attack. Between 45 and 150 Cuban scholars grouped in two think tanks dedicated to the study of the United States and Europe—many with close intellectual links to U.S. scholars—were arrested or detained. Many lost their jobs.[33]

It is no surprise that the U.S. Track II policy backfired. Sanctions theory has long cautioned that sanctions may be counterproductive and fail because they strengthen belligerent elements in the target country and increase the defensiveness of the target government.[34] We have seen, furthermore, that Cuba has traditionally responded to U.S. pressure by circling the wagons. This time, those who paid the price for U.S. pressure were legitimate Cuban advocates of market reform and democratic transition.

In August 1996 Nuccio was replaced by Stuart Eizenstat as Special Representative for Promotion of Democracy in Cuba. Eizenstat, formerly of the Commerce Department, backed off from the failed Track II approach and focused on attempting to recruit international support for the Helms-Burton law (discussed below), or at least to soothe U.S. allies incensed by the extraterritorial reach of the law.[35]

Amendments to the Embargo

Both minor and major changes were made to the embargo during Clinton's early years in office. In July 1993, the administration ordered the Treasury Department to prevent companies providing telephone service to Cuba via Canada from continuing such service. The Office of Foreign Assets Control sent letters to seven domestic U.S. companies that operate through Bell Canada, ordering them to terminate such service or face prison sentences and hundreds of thousands of dollars in fines. Treasury and White House officials contended that the Cuban government earned revenues from calls originating in the United States.[36]

U.S. policy toward Cuba reached a crisis point in mid-1994 when Castro, in response to riots in Havana in early August, announced that his government would no longer prevent Cubans from leaving the country. Within the month, more than thirty thousand Cubans set sail for the United States on makeshift rafts and flimsy boats. After eight days of negotiations between the United States and Cuba, the two countries signed a new immigration accord reversing decades of policy. Cuba agreed to "take effective measures in every way it possibly can" to prevent the illegal departure of Cubans to the United States, and the United States agreed to grant twenty thousand immigrant visas per year to Cubans. The Clinton administration also reversed its longstanding welcome of Cuban refugees. Until that point, Cubans who reached U.S. shores illegally were granted permanent resident status in the United States. This policy had the effect of encouraging illegal emigration from the island and frustrating the many thousands of Cubans who sought legal methods of coming to the United States but were repeatedly denied visas.[37]

In an addendum to the immigration agreement of September 1994, the two countries agreed in May 1995 to parole into the United States the vast majority of Cubans then being held at the Guantánamo naval base. Twenty-one thousand Cubans who left the island in the summer of 1994 had been held at the base for nearly a year until agreement on their fate was reached. The United States also agreed to return to Cuba all Cuban emigrants intercepted at sea. Cuba agreed to ensure that no action would be taken against the returned migrants.[38]

As fallout from the crisis, the Clinton administration instituted several changes to the embargo in an effort to further tighten the noose around Castro's neck. Most important, in October 1995 the administration rescinded the general license under which professional researchers, journalists, and Cuban-Americans could travel freely to Cuba. Under the new measures, all travelers who had previously fallen into the general license category now had to apply for a specific license each time they wanted to travel to the island. This significantly tightened the embargo and led to numerous "travel challenges" by various academic groups.[39] It also reduced the number of charter flights between the two countries.[40]

In addition, the Clinton administration moved at this time to ease the sanctions slightly in a few areas. Full-time undergraduate students were now allowed to study in Cuba, Western Union was permitted to open offices in Cuba to facilitate communication between Cubans in the United States and on the island, and U.S. nongovernmental organizations (NGOs) were permitted to send material and financial assistance to Cuban NGOs.[41] In February 1997, the U.S. government also permitted ten U.S.-based news organizations to open offices in Havana.

Helms-Burton

The apex of Clinton policy toward Cuba came in March of 1996 when President Clinton signed the Helms-Burton legislation (also known as the Cuban Liberty and Democratic Solidarity Act) into law. Among other things, the law punishes foreign companies that do business with Cuba and reverses the historic prerogative of the president to control the Cuba sanctions. The White House had opposed the measure (first introduced in February 1995), on the same grounds that the Bush administration had originally opposed the Cuban Democracy Act: the White House argued that the extraterritorial nature of the Helms-Burton legislation would provoke strong reaction from our allies and trading partners.[42] However, after the Cuban air force shot down two civilian aircraft piloted by the anti-Castro group "Brothers to the Rescue" in February 1996 (an election year), the Clinton administration bowed under palpable pressure and signed the bill into law.[43]

The Helms-Burton legislation contains numerous new provisions that significantly change the embargo. First, it codifies into law all executive orders in effect March 1, 1996, relevant to the U.S. embargo against Cuba, thereby eliminating the power of the president to respond with "calibrated measures" to Cuban actions. The bill legislates that the embargo will remain in effect until a "transition government" is in place in Cuba that fulfills eight requirements and that has made demonstrable progress in four "additional factors." The list of requirements the transition government must fulfill includes the legalization of all political activity; the release of all political prisoners; the dissolution of Cuba's Department of State Security and all its local branches; a public commitment to free and fair elections within eighteen months, with the participation of multiple parties and under international observation; an end to interference with U.S. broadcasts to Cuba; and the absence of Fidel and Raul Castro from the transition process.[44]

Most controversial among the bill's provisions was Title III of the law, which deals with property claims in Cuba. Title III makes liable in U.S. courts anyone who "traffics" in—that is, "sells, transfers, distributes, manages, or otherwise disposes of, purchases, leases, receives, possesses, obtains control of, uses or otherwise acquires or holds an interest in"—property confiscated by the Cuban government on or after January 1, 1959. In other words, if a Cuban plantation owner left Cuba in 1959, and in the late 1990s a Spanish company built a hotel on the old plantation, the former Cuban citizen, if he or she is now a U.S. citizen, can sue the Spanish company in a U.S. court for "trafficking in confiscated property." The U.S. court is therefore exercising jurisdiction over actions of a foreign company that took place in a foreign land, for the benefit of someone who was, at the time of his loss, a foreign citizen.[45] Helms-Burton also denies entry visas to the United States to officers or stockholders in the "trafficking" companies.

On the other hand, the legislation contains a clause allowing the president to suspend the effective date for Title III for renewable periods of up to six months if he certifies that the suspension is necessary to the U.S. national interest and that it will expedite a transition to democracy in Cuba. This loophole was added at the last minute to make the entire legislation more palatable for Clinton, who was giving up significant executive power under Helms-Burton. Recognizing that the controversial Title III would be the most problematic for U.S. allies, Clinton has in fact used the loophole to postpone indefinitely allied wrath. In a face-saving measure in January 1997, he declared his intent to suspend the measure indefinitely "as long as U.S. allies keep pressing Cuba for reforms."[46] This action, which left the law standing while partially suspending its application, placated neither the law's critics nor its supporters. Senator Jesse Helms expressed anger at the president's waiver and called it a "terrible mistake that emasculates the legislation."[47]

Despite the fact that the White House seems to have placed Title III on permanent freeze, the U.S. State Department has created a new unit dedicated to organizing claims for property confiscated by the Cuban government—precisely what Title III intends for the State Department to do. The new unit is charged with collecting and analyzing information from all available sources on whether property in Cuba claimed by a U.S. national has been confiscated by the Cuban government.[48] The State Department believes that there may be grounds for 75,000 to 200,000 additional claims, over and above the 5,911 certified claims already registered with the Foreign Claims Settlement Commission.[49] (See Appendixes 3 and 4 on p. 212.)

In another clause, Helms-Burton subjects individuals traveling unlicensed to Cuba to a civil penalty of $50,000 (previously the crime carried only criminal penalties). The law also bans imports of sugar products from countries that import Cuban sugar; it instructs U.S. representatives at international lending bodies to vote against admitting Cuba and reduces U.S. contributions to those organizations by the amount of any aid they grant to the island; and it withholds quantities of aid to Russia and other former Soviet states equal to the amount those countries provide Cuba in military and intelligence aid. Finally, the legislation authorizes the president to establish an exchange of news bureaus between the United States and Cuba, provided they are fully reciprocal, and instructs the director of the United States Information Agency to convert television broadcasting to Cuba to ultra-high frequency (UHF). Proponents of this change claim that ultra-high frequency is more difficult for Havana to block.[50] However, independent communications experts argue that UHF signals have even less range than VHF, making it more difficult to transmit the signal to Cuba and easier for the Cubans to jam it.[51]

At the same time that Clinton announced he would sign Helms-Burton, he instituted two additional measures that further tightened the embargo. First, he ordered further restrictions on travel within the United States by Cuban officials who reside here, and he limited visits by Cuban officials to the United States. Second, he suspended all charter air travel from the United States to Cuba indefinitely.[52] Restricting charter flights amounted to putting money in Castro's pocket because U.S. travelers were often forced to use Cuban carriers through third countries rather than booking direct flights from Miami.

Goals Assessment: Helms-Burton Sponsors

There are multiple, overlapping layers of goals for this new legislation. Undoubtedly Senators Jesse Helms and Dan Burton, the bill's authors, have long been ideological enemies of the Castro government and share a genuine interest in removing Castro from power. The provisions within Helms-Burton that punish companies that trade in property formerly owned by Cuban-Americans are ostensibly designed to deny foreign investment to Cuba and thus bring the economy down. As in decades past, however, U.S. policymakers in this case as well erroneously calculated that the Castro government would tumble as a result of its economic deprivation. As has been noted, embargo theorists compute that sanctions imposed to achieve major policy changes are generally unsuccessful;[53] furthermore, in the specific case of Cuba, economic deprivation has actually created greater political unity and strength in the target nation. Given the historical and theoretical evidence, then, Helms and Burton probably introduced the legislation with only faint hope that the new law would be the straw to break the camel's back. Short of effecting change in Cuba, the two legislators probably believed the measure would have symbolic impact: it would demonstrate to interested parties that they still cared about ridding Cuba of Castroism.

No doubt Helms and Burton were also interested in indulging Cuban-Americans who have long clamored for restitution of property rights on the island—and who have generously contributed to political campaign coffers. According to data provided by the Center for Responsive Politics, from January 1987 to June 1994 the Cuban American National Foundation, its members, and various CANF supporters have contributed over $250,000 to the campaign funds of four influential congresspeople: Rep. Dan Burton (R-Ind.) received $12,150, Ileana Ros-Lehtinen (R-Fla.) received $127,565, Robert Torricelli (D-N.J.) received $53,150, and Robert Menendez (D-N.J.) received $69,873.[54] The provisions in Helms-Burton that allow Cuban-Americans to sue foreigners in U.S. courts appeal directly to this domestic constituency.

Attempting to overthrow Castro and pandering to Cuban-Americans have long been embargo goals. Helms-Burton, however, offers two new twists on all previous incarnations of the Cuba embargo. First, the bill significantly limits presidential power by codifying into law executive orders related to the Cuba sanctions. Helms and Burton have taken from the president the power to lift the embargo and have given that power to the parochial Congress, where there is little incentive to soften an anticommunist law.

Second, the bill spells out exactly what domestic changes have to take place within Cuba before the embargo is lifted. For decades, the embargo was ostensibly imposed to prevent Cuba from engaging in "revolutionary" foreign policy. Slowly, as Cuba tamed its foreign ambitions, and as geopolitics shifted away from an East-West prism, this rationale for the embargo lost its meaning. By the early 1990s, U.S. policymakers shifted stated embargo goals to focus on domestic changes within Cuba. The Helms-Burton legislation codifies into embargo law goals for the transformation of Cuba's domestic situation. From now on, no president can carefully calibrate responses to Cuban actions and take small steps to lift parts of the embargo. The embargo's raison d'être is now embedded in the legislation itself: a transition government fulfilling twelve criteria laid out by Helms-Burton now dictates when the embargo can be lifted.

Clinton's Goals for Helms-Burton

No doubt President Clinton shared some of the sponsors' goals for the legislation. It is likely that he too is interested in presiding over the end of the Castro government, as all U.S. administrations before him have been. He has also shown his own interest in pandering to the Cuban-American community; Cuban-Americans have proved generous contributors to Democratic Party fundraising in Florida,[55] and, more significantly, they represent a key vote in that important swing state. In fact, South Florida's Cuban-American population voted to reelect Clinton in higher numbers than a Democrat has received previously from that community. Thirty-six percent of Cuban-Americans reportedly voted for Clinton in 1996, compared with 22 percent in 1992.[56]

Clinton's main concerns with the legislation came from its extraterritorial impact, as well as the limits it places on his own powers. Before the Cubans shot down the Brothers to the Rescue plane, the Clinton administration had testified against the bill in Congress. Secretary of State Warren Christopher had cited the administration's objections to "the extent to which passage would limit the president's autonomy in conducting foreign affairs, constrain the United States' ability to assist a transition government in Cuba, burden the U.S. court system with lawsuits filed against foreign companies that have invested in properties nationalized since 1959, and invite widespread repudiation from and trade barriers by major U.S. allies."[57]

Nonetheless, when the Cubans shot down the Cuban-American civilian aircraft during an election year, Clinton felt cornered into signing the bill. Senator Bob Dole, GOP candidate for president, had long since registered his support for the measure and had criticized the Clinton administration for "not doing enough" about Castro.[58] In all probability, Clinton did not want to be perceived as being "soft on communism" during an election year and thus yielded to demands pressed on him once again by a Republican Congress, a Republican presidential candidate, and the wealthiest elements in the Cuban-American constituency.

Hence, domestic motives were undoubtedly the most important influence on Clinton's decision to sign the legislation. As previous chapters have demonstrated, the embargo of Cuba has evolved most during presidential election campaigns when candidates commit themselves to actions in order to attract votes. In early 1996, a U.S. presidential election year, the embargo became the tightest in its thirty-five year history.

Foreign Response to Helms-Burton

Sanctions theory warns that when sanctions are applied extraterritorially, allies may not support them, and may even openly oppose them.[59] Embargoes are less successful when the sender state attempts to dislocate trade between the target and third nations. Even before it became law, Helms-Burton was subject to "unadulterated, undiluted anger," in the words of U.S. Commerce Department's Stuart Eizenstat.[60] The European Union (EU), for example, issued this statement: "The EU cannot accept that the United States should seek through unilateral legislation to determine and restrict the EU's economic and commercial relations. . . . This extraterritorial extension of U.S. jurisdiction has no basis in international law."[61] Canada and Mexico also issued strong official protest against the proposed legislation, and later instituted blocking orders to prevent their companies from obeying U.S. extraterritorial laws.[62]

The Rio Group of fourteen Latin American nations issued a statement categorically rejecting the law, "which violates the principles and norms established by international laws and the United Nations and the Organization of American States charters. . . . " Numerous individual countries as well issued statements condemning the law, including Mexico, Canada, Colombia, India, Britain, and Chile.[63]

In the weeks before the U.S. presidential election in November 1996, the European Union, in an unprecedented move, brought an action against the Helms-Burton legislation before the World Trade Organization (WTO).[64] The EU seeks a ruling on the legislation's illegality under international trade rules via the WTO's dispute resolution process.[65] Throughout 1997, EU and U.S. representatives attempted to reach an agreement over the most controversial aspects of the law. Negotiations centered on EU opposition to Title IV, which bars executives of foreign companies benefiting from expropriated U.S. properties in Cuba from entering the United States, and Title III, which would open U.S. courts to lawsuits against foreign corporations that benefit from expropriated U.S. properties in Cuba. The Clinton administration maintained that the WTO is "not competent" to rule on Helms-Burton, which the United States views as a matter of national security and not a trade dispute. Washington hoped to persuade the Europeans to adopt "binding principles" to inhibit "future acquisition" of expropriated property in Cuba in return for waiving Title IV. By early 1998, the two sides had still failed to reach an agreement.[66]

Meanwhile, retaliatory legislation was passed in all fifteen EU states, prohibiting European countries from obeying the Helms-Burton provisions and permitting them to countersue U.S. companies in European courts.[67] On this side of the Atlantic, Mexico followed suit, and Canada too, on January 1, 1997, passed legislation allowing Canadians to seek recovery in their courts for any losses they suffer as a result of Helms-Burton.[68] Mexico and Canada both, furthermore, initiated a complaint against the United States under the North American Free Trade Agreement. On another front, the Juridical Committee of the Organization of American States unanimously found that Helms-Burton "does not conform to international law."[69] Finally, twin votes in the UN Security Council and General Assembly overwhelmingly condemned the U.S. embargo of Cuba and specifically the Helms-Burton legislation.[70] Notably, the single most public condemnation of the U.S. embargo came in January 1998 with the historic visit of Pope John Paul II to Cuba. In his parting address, in front of cameras from all over the world, the Pope called the U.S. economic sanctions against Cuba "oppressive economic measures, unjust and ethically unacceptable, imposed from outside the country."[71]

Cuba has responded to Helms-Burton with legislation of its own. In January 1997, Cuba passed a law penalizing U.S. citizens who seek restitution of their expropriated properties under the Helms-Burton provisions. Significantly, the law recognizes the right of individuals to seek compensation for their losses prior to the 1959 revolution, once the United States and Cuba negotiate an agreement. However, it excludes U.S. citizens from any indemnification settlement if they take action against Cuba under Helms-Burton. The Cuban law also allows Cuban citizens to sue for claims of "theft, torture, corruption and murder" from Batista era officials who now reside in the United States. Finally, it allows Cubans to pursue damage claims against the United States stemming from U.S. military and economic action against the island.[72]

Hence, we see that U.S. efforts under Helms-Burton to make the Cuba embargo multilateral have prompted allies to condemn the policy and refuse to abide by it, just as sanctions theory warned. Moreover, U.S. international prestige was tarnished when Helms-Burton became law. The United States was subjected to World Trade Organization review, retaliatory legislation from nearly all our close trade partners, and continued UN votes against U.S. Cuba policy, by ever widening margins. The 1997 vote was 143 to 3, in favor of Cuba.

Despite this outpouring of condemnation and countermeasures, Washington continued to play the Helms-Burton card. When presidential candidate Bob Dole criticized the White House for doing little to implement the law, the Clinton administration put four foreign companies on notice that their joint venture agreements with Cuba rendered them subject to Helms-Burton provisions. Sherritt International of Canada, Mexico's Grupo Domos, Italy's Societa Financiara Telefonica (STET), and Israel's Grupo BM then received letters from the Treasury Department indicating that certain individuals in the companies were excluded from entry into the United States.[73]

Continued U.S. disrespect for the norms of international trade, as well as Helms-Burton's relative failure to stifle the interest of Cuba's main foreign trade partners, indicates that both passage and implementation of the law have had more to do with domestic U.S. politics than a sincere intention to bring democracy to Cuba. As we have seen, Clinton approved the legislation after a Cuban provocation *during an election year.* He had to respond swiftly and strongly against Cuba lest he subject himself to an onslaught of criticism from the Republican party. Moreover, his actions to enforce Helms-Burton came after candidate Bob Dole raised the subject on the campaign stump. Clinton simply did not want to risk losing the South Florida vote, no matter how high the price.

Domestic Response to Helms-Burton

Business community. By the time Helms-Burton was signed into law, it was no secret in the U.S. business community that U.S. firms were the biggest losers in the continued embargo against Cuba. Estimates of lost potential business opportunities with Cuba range from $1 billion to $15 billion annually, and renewed trade between the two countries would represent up to 100,000 jobs in the U.S. economy.[74] Even with the restrictive Helms-Burton law on the books, U.S. businesses flocked to learn about the Cuban market. In 1996 alone, 1,500 U.S. firms (up from 400 in 1990) visited the island, including General Motors, Sears Roebuck, Avis, Hyatt, Sheraton, and the Bank of Boston. Furthermore, in dozens of cases, U.S. companies signed letters of intent to do business once the embargo is lifted.[75]

Trade associations. Not surprisingly, the increasing business interest in Cuba bred a new type of actor during Clinton's first term of office: Cuba-related trade associations. While the different groups varied on whether to enter the Cuba market before or after Castro leaves, their premise was widely the same: to develop partnerships with U.S. businesses now in order to facilitate their eventual entry into the Cuba market. Despite the fact that the embargo had never been stricter, in the mid-1990s U.S.-based organizations were thus already making profits off potential Cuba trade and positioning themselves to capitalize on eventual trade with the island.[76]

Sanctions theory counsels that the business community's public opposition to an embargo may hinder the policy.[77] As preceding chapters have shown, the U.S. business community has generally followed the White House lead on Cuba: when an administration eased sanctions, businesses visited Cuba, but when sanctions were tightened again, businesses quietly bided their time. With Helms-Burton, for the first time in the embargo's history, U.S. business interest in Cuba appeared deliberately to challenge Washington's policies. Although businesses did not actively trade with Cuba, they openly explored future possibilities in constantly increasing numbers. Some companies began to pressure Washington to lift the embargo, sending notice to both Washington and Havana that unified domestic consent for the policy (if indeed it had ever existed) was crumbling.[78] In 1998 a new coalition called Americans for Humanitarian Trade with Cuba, composed of former U.S. government officials and current business leaders was formed. The coalition advocates lifting the ban on the sale of foods and medicine to Cuba.[79]

Legal community. One sector of the U.S. economy that stood to gain from the Helms-Burton legislation was the legal community. Law firms in Miami and Washington began aggressively searching for clients to defend and prosecute the potential cornucopia of lawsuits that the Helms-Burton law encourages. Numerous conferences on Cuba materialized both before and after Helms-Burton became law. At one conference, businesses paid $800 a person to listen to presentations by attorneys from seven Washington law firms, in addition to foreign-based lawyers, on potential lawsuits that could be brought against foreign companies, as well as international ventures "beyond Cuba."[80]

U.S. Public Consensus Crumbles

Though Helms-Burton undoubtedly appealed to a certain segment of the Cuban-American population, in the mid-1990s the general public became increasingly vocal against U.S. economic coercion of Cuba. This was most obvious in the conservative community, which until this point had advocated for the embargo. Conservative talk show host John McLaughlin returned from a Cuba trip in 1993 and declared that Castro still had the support of the majority of the people, and that the embargo should be lifted. "Now thirty years old, the U.S. embargo has practically no impact. . . . In my conclusion, in my view, the time has come for the U.S. embargo, first on tourism, then on trade, to be lifted."[81] By 1995, an array of conservative political pundits, including William F. Buckley Jr., Gary Jarmin, William Ratliff, and Roger Fontaine; Senator Richard Lugar; as well as major newspapers and magazines, including the *Washington Post, New York Times, Wall Street Journal, Miami Herald, Los Angles Times, Seattle Times, Boston Globe,* and *U.S. News and World Report,* had called for the lifting or easing of the Cuba sanctions, or at least the initiation of serious discussions with the Castro government.[82]

During the mid-1990s, the Clinton administration was also dogged by activist groups championing humanitarian aid and travel to Cuba. For example, in addition to its well-publicized and successful hunger strike at the Mexican border to protest Treasury Department denial of the shipment of a bus to Cuba,[83] Pastors for Peace also sent volunteer construction brigades and more humanitarian supplies to the island throughout the mid-1990s.[84] In 1996, the group began a second hunger strike demanding that the Clinton administration release four hundred computers they were donating to Cuban hospitals. National pressure in response to the hunger strike led the Treasury Department to set up a phone line dedicated to those concerned over the plight of the group.[85] The fast lasted ninety-four days and was ended when the Treasury Department released the computers to the United Methodist Church, which promised to provide Treasury with a list of Cuban clinics and hospitals that would receive the computers.[86] The computers reached Cuba in September 1996 after the Treasury Department issued a license for their release, though the United Methodist Church said it never solicited the license.[87]

The administration also faced pressure from a California-based group called Global Exchange, which organized the Freedom to Travel Campaign, a challenge to the Cuba travel ban. Medea Benjamin, the group's founder, argued that the United States is the only Western democracy that treats travel as a crime. Some 175 people traveled to Cuba "to challenge" the embargo in November 1993. Upon their return, sixty-five of their passports were seized by customs officials for possible prosecution. Several months later, the passports were returned without comment.[88] In June 1994, in an effort to prevent further travel challenges, the Treasury Department froze $48,000 in the bank accounts of the Freedom to Travel Campaign in San Francisco. Treasury actions backfired, however, when donations flooded into the group following publicity of Treasury efforts. Freedom to Travel received an additional $40,000, and many newspapers published editorials supporting the constitutional right to travel.[89] Again, the Treasury Department backed down and released the money belonging to the group.[90] With public opinion swinging against the Cuba sanctions, Treasury most probably did not want to provoke further public debate on the issue.

Impact of Helms-Burton in Cuba

Because Helms-Burton in principle would force foreign investors to abandon their investments in Cuba or face U.S. court battles, the State Department predicted that the legislation would have a "chilling effect" on Cuban commerce. Not surprisingly, little has happened. A Mexican cement company, two Spanish hotel chains, and a Dutch bank did leave Cuba under threat of lawsuits in U.S. courts.[91] Undoubtedly, moreover, new investors who had been exploring the Cuba market before Helms-Burton was passed have backed away. In this regard Cuban Vice-president Carlos Lage admitted that the effects of the legislation "are negative. Not so much in terms of practical application, but because of its intimidating effect."[92] Nonetheless, most foreign companies have remained in Cuba, and in fact, foreign investment grew after Helms-Burton was passed. The number of joint ventures signed with Cuba jumped from 212 prior to Helms-Burton to 260 six months after the bill became law.[93]

As we have seen in previous chapters, sanctions theory warns that economic coercion can lead to political cohesion in the target country.[94] If there was any doubt before Helms-Burton that Castro knew how to manipulate foreign aggression to his advantage, there is no doubt now. Not only have international firms continued to invest in Cuba, but Helms-Burton has served to unify the Cuban people further against the United States, even as the Cuban government enjoys reduced popular support. The language of the Helms-Burton law is widely available in Cuba and is discussed in schools, universities, work centers, and civic organizations. Because the bulk of the legislation focuses more on property claims and less on the stated goal of "assisting the Cuban people in regaining their freedom and prosperity," Castro did not have to be a genius to recognize the powerful affront ordinary Cubans would feel upon understanding the spirit of the law. Cuba scholar Ana Julia Jatar of the Inter-American Dialogue, noted in a *Washington Post* editorial:

> By bringing back the issue of property rights and the division between the "haves" who left and the "have-nots" who stayed, Helms-Burton has reunited the Cuban society behind the Castro government, and deepened feelings of distrust against the United States. Read from Havana, U.S. policy seems more concerned with old properties than with new democracy.[95]

Moreover, in further demonstration of his nationalistic wizardry, Castro sent hundreds of university students—heretofore the most disaffected segment of the population—to the Cuban National Archives to calculate the losses caused by acts of sabotage committed by those who left, so those who stayed can establish the amount of *their* claims. A new sense of nationalism has developed amongst the generation for whom the issues and events of the revolution had only been chapters in history books. Hence, we see once again that sanctions can actually be counterproductive when they cause the population in the target country to unify against a common enemy.

Conclusions

1993–1997 were years of economic growth for the Cuban economy, despite the most severe tightening of the embargo to date. If, after thirty years of failed policy, there remained a smidgen of doubt about the efficacy of Cuba sanctions, these years should lay any doubt to rest. Clinton, following the lead of all eight of his predecessors who have faced Castro, shaped a Cuba policy based more on pandering to a small county in South Florida than on concern for U.S. national security or for the plight of the Cuban people currently residing on the island.

Sanctions theory has long issued stiff warnings that have continued to be unheeded or unheard in Washington. First, sanctions theory has counseled that sanctions tend to be a unifying force in the target country. For almost four decades, Castro has proven himself a master at manipulating economic aggression to his own ends. This was all the more true during Clinton's term when Castro succeeded in rallying support from younger generations who had formerly been the most critical of his government.

Second, sanctions theory admonishes that when sanctions are forced on third parties, they tend to be less successful. Cuba is a case in point. With the enactment of the extraterritorial Helms-Burton legislation, the embargo evoked unprecedented condemnation abroad. Not only did UN votes condemn U.S. policy by increasing margins every year, but U.S. policy was decried in new fora as well, including the World Trade Organization and the Organization of American States. Furthermore, U.S. efforts at expanding the embargo abroad backfired when, after passage of the Helms-Burton law, foreign investors entered the Cuba market at an even faster pace than they had during the preceding period.[96]

Third, sanctions theory cautions that when sanctions aren't supported by influential domestic constituencies, chances of success are diminished. The Clinton administration faced a public increasingly opposed to the Cuba sanctions. U.S. businesses flocked to Havana to study the potential market despite the fact that U.S. laws made it more difficult for them to consider investing than ever in history. U.S. religious and activist groups constantly challenged the embargo in public ways, forcing the Cuba sanctions into public debate. U.S. newspapers and magazines registered their opposition to the embargo in unprecedented numbers. Former Bush and Reagan administration officials who had once championed the embargo now opined against it in every conceivable format. It became embarrassingly apparent that U.S. policy toward Cuba was held hostage by a small group of Cuban-Americans who supported it.

Sanctions theory also warns that economic coercion against a target can lead to the unintended consequence of strengthening hard-liners within the target government. The Clinton administration's blind pursuit of Track II, to support civil society in Cuba through increased contact as well as its embrace of Helms-Burton, backfired. The most legitimate voices for economic and political reform on the island were squelched by the Cuban government in their attempt to ward off U.S. interference.

In short, during Clinton's first term in office, it became utterly, unavoidably apparent that the U.S. embargo of Cuba achieved one goal, and one goal only: appeasement of one segment of the Cuban-American community. No other explanation could explain the irrational behavior of the actors involved.

Notes

1. Caribbean Update, Newsletter, November 1, 1996.
2. *The Economist,* April 6, 1996.
3. Pascal Fletcher, "Recovery in Cuba Outstrips Forecasts," *The Financial Times,* December 27, 1996, p. 4; Janet Matthews Information Services, Quest Economics Database, JMIS Press Summaries, January 6, 1997; *CubaINFO,* Vol. 9, No. 9, July 10, 1997, p. 6.
4. *CubaINFO,* Vol. 9, No. 1, January 15, 1997, p. 7; *CubaINFO,* Vol. 10, No. 1, January 8, 1998, p. 6.
5. "Cuba Output Rises Despite U.S. Curbs: Tourism, Sugar Cited as Economy Rebounds," *Chicago Tribune,* July 25, 1996, p. 12N; Rolando Napoles, "Cuba Economy: Warnings Over Optimism in 1997," *Inter Press Service,* January 8, 1997; Jane's Defense Weekly, April 3, 1996; *CubaINFO,* Vol. 9, No. 16, December 11, 1997, p. 8.
6. Douglas Farah, "Rising Expectations Blur Cuban Economic Revival," *Washington Post,* August 27, 1996, p. A12; Joy Gordon, "Cuba's Entrepreneurial Socialism," *Atlantic Monthly,* Vol. 279, No. 1, January 1997, pp. 18–35; Wayne Smith, "Cuba's Long Reform," *Foreign Affairs,* March/April 1996, p. 103; David Rieff, "Cuba Refrozen," *Foreign Affairs,* July/August, 1996, p. 62.
7. Gordon, "Cuba's Entrepreneurial Socialism"; *CubaINFO,* Vol. 9, No. 1, January 15, 1997, p. 10. Cuba has the lowest infant mortality rate in Latin America, and one of the lowest worldwide.
8. Napoles, "Cuban Economy: Warnings Over Optimism in 1997."
9. Fletcher, "Recovery in Cuba Outstrips Forecasts," p. 4
10. Anita Snow, "Castro Cheers Cuba's Economy on Anniversary," *Austin American-Statesman,* July 28, 1996, p. A25.
11. Farah, "Rising Expectations Blur Cuban Economic Revival," p. A12.
12. Ibid.
13. Minister of Economy and Planning Jose Luis Rodriguez said that serious financial strains would persist in 1997. See Napoles, "Cuba Economy: Warnings Over Optimism in 1997."
14. Farah, "Rising Expectations," p. A12.

15. Ana Julia Jatar, Senior Fellow, Inter-American Dialogue, congressional testimony, June 30, 1995; statement provided to the author.

16. According to one report, remittances from exiles amounted to $800 million a year, the largest foreign currency earner for Cuba. See Rieff, "Cuba Refrozen."

17. "Cuba's Two Nations," *The Economist,* April 6, 1996, p. S10; *CubaINFO,* Vol. 8, No. 12, September 19, 1996, p. 7.

18. Jatar, testimony, U.S. Congress.

19. Smith, "Cuba's Long Reform," p. 101.

20. "Cuba Output Rises Despite U.S. Curbs," *Chicago Tribune,* July 25, 1996, p. 12N; *CubaINFO,* Vol. 8, No. 10, August 1, 1996, pp. 8–10.

21. Jatar, testimony, U.S. Congress.

22. "Cuba's Two Nations," p. S10. Hard currency earnings are taxed on a sliding scale starting at 10 percent and rising to a marginal rate of 50 percent on earnings of $60,000 or more. Cuban officials indicate that peso incomes will someday be taxed as well.

23. Author's interviews in farmers' markets in May 1996. See also Gordon, "Cuba's Entrepreneurial Socialism."

24. Napoles, "Cuba Economy: Warnings over Optimism in 1997." See also Jatar, testimony, U.S. Congress.

25. Scott Studebaker, "Forsaking a $5 Billion Market and an Export Platform," *Latin American Law and Business Report,* Vol. 3, No. 11, November 30, 1995.

26. Douglas Farah, "Cuban Action's Timing Puzzling to Observers; Economy Has Turned Up After Long Fall," *Washington Post,* February 27, 1996, p. A6; Linda Robinson, "Cuba Takes a Stiff Belt," *U.S. News and World Report,* July 29, 1996, p. 36; Charles Thurston, "Cuban Logistics Improve as Capitalism Evolves," Chilton Report, Vol. 95, No. 10, p. 28; Gordon, "Cuba's Entrepreneurial Socialism," pp. 18–30; and Nancy Dunne, "Clinton Suspends Helms-Burton Again," *Financial Times,* January 4, 1997, p. 3.

27. *CubaINFO,* Vol. 8, No. 11, August 29, 1996, p. 6.

28. Doxey, *International Sanctions in Contemporary Perspective,* p. 144.

29. Saul Landau, "Talk of the Nation," National Public Radio, September 27, 1994.

30. *CubaINFO,* Vol. 6, No. 13, October 13, 1994, pp. 2–3; *Communications Daily,* December 6, 1994, p. 5.

31. CubaINFO, Vol. 8, No. 4, March 21, 1996, p. 11.

32. Peter Kornbluh, "Killing Castro Softly," *The Nation,* March 18, 1996.

33. David Rieff, "Defiance and Dollarization," *Foreign Affairs,* July/August 1996. The author was in Havana shortly after the Cuban scholars were detained and discussed the situation with some of them firsthand. See also Kornbluh, "Killing Castro Softly."

34. Bienen and Gilpin, "Evaluation of the Use of Economic Sanctions," p. 14.

35. Nuccio was released from his position in part because of the failure of Track II to accomplish its mission, but also because he faced charges of misconduct unrelated to Cuba, stemming from his earlier position on the foreign affairs subcommittee. In that role, he had leaked secret information about U.S. military links to Guatemalan military officials who murdered a U.S. citizen. See *CubaINFO,* Vol. 8, No. 11, August 29, 1996, pp. 2–3. Eizenstat's efforts were fruitless. On a trip through Canada, Mexico, Belgium, Ireland, Spain, Germany, France, Italy, The Hague, Holland, Denmark, and Great Britain, Eizenstat met only with dissent. See

CubaINFO, Vol. 8, No. 12, September 19, 1996, pp. 1–3; *CubaINFO,* Vol. 8, No. 14, November 5, 1996, p. 1.

36. *CubaINFO,* Vol. 5, No. 9, July 16, 1993, p. 1.

37. *CubaINFO,* Vol. 6, No. 12, September 22, 1994, pp. 1–6; *CubaINFO,* Vol. 6, No. 11, September 1, 1994, entire issue; *CubaINFO,* Vol. 6, no. 16, December 15, 1994, pp. 5–6.

38. Joint Statement of the United States and Cuba, May 1, 1995, White House Press Office. The director of international affairs for the U.S. Immigration and Naturalization Service, Phyllis Coven, said that the immigration agreements of 1994 and 1995 were remarkably successful in reducing the number of illegal Cubans attempting to immigrate to the United States. See *CubaINFO,* Vol. 8, No. 13, October 10, 1996, p. 6.

39. Cynthia McClintock, Philip Brenner, and Wayne Smith, op-ed, *Washington Post,* November 1, 1994.

40. *CubaINFO* Vol. 7, No. 7, May 18, 1995, p. 10. Marazul halted flights to Cuba in April 1995 because of restrictions imposed during the Cuban refugee crisis in the fall of 1994. Marazul had been flying between Miami and Havana for sixteen years.

41. *Federal Register,* October 13, 1995, 31 CFR Part 515.

42. *CubaINFO,* Vol. 7, No. 8, June 8, 1995, pp. 11–12. This issue contains a letter from Wendy R. Sherman, assistant secretary for legislative affairs, that examines point by point the White House position on Helms-Burton. *CubaINFO,* Vol. 8, No. 4, March 21, 1996, p. 2.

43. Brothers to the Rescue had consistently filed false flight plans and had flown over Cuban territory numerous times, dropping anti-Castro leaflets. They had organized a flotilla that tried to penetrate Cuban waters but was turned back. The Cuban government had warned them on several occasions against attempting to violate Cuban air space, saying that aircraft entering Cuba's territory would be shot down. See Farah, "Cuban Action's Timing Puzzling to Observers," p. A6; Carl Nagin, "Backfire," *The New Yorker,* January 26, 1998, pp. 30–35.

44. *CubaINFO,* Vol. 8, No. 4, March 21, 1996, p. 2.

45. Gordon, "Cuba's Entrepreneurial Socialism."

46. "Holding Bad Law at Bay: Clinton Move Boosts Drive to Bring Democracy to Cuba," *Pittsburgh Post-Gazette,* January 9, 1997, p. A10. In December 1996, European foreign ministers voted to link expanded ties to Cuba with human rights improvements and progress toward democracy. See Dunne, "Clinton Suspends Helms-Burton Again," p. 3; *CubaINFO,* Vol. 8, No. 10, August 1, 1996, pp. 1–5.

47. *New York Times,* January 4, 1997, p. A1; *CubaINFO,* Vol. 9, No.1, January 15, 1997, pp. 4–5.

48. *CubaINFO,* Vol. 8, No. 13, October 10, 1996, p. 7.

49. *CubaINFO,* Vol. 8, No. 15, November 21, 1996, p. 2. The original 5,911 claims filed with the commission were valued at $1.8 billion when originally confiscated and are now estimated to be worth approximately $6 billion.

50. *Federal Register,* October 13, 1995, 31 CFR part 515. As of 1997, no U.S. news bureau has opened in Havana. Despite Cuba's authorization to permit CNN to operate out of Cuba, U.S. bureaucratic conflict prevented this from occurring.

51. *Washington Post,* April 1, 1994, p. A19; *Miami Herald,* April 1, 1994, p. 8A; *CubaINFO,* Vol. 6, No. 5, April 8, 1994; BBC, September 6, 1996.

52. *CubaINFO,* Vol. 8, February 29, 1996 (Supplement), p. 5; White House Press Conference, Federal News Service, October 6, 1995; *CubaINFO,* Vol. 7, No. 13, October 12, 1995, pp. 1–6.

53. Hubauer and Schott, *Economic Sanctions Reconsidered,* Second Edition, p. 59.

54. Kurt Shaw, Institute for Policy Studies, April 1, 1995, reprinted in *CubaINFO,* Vol. 7, No. 5, pp. 13–14.

55. *CubaINFO,* Vol. 6, No. 5, April 8, 1994, p. 12.

56. *CubaINFO,* Vol. 8, No. 15, November 21, 1996, p. 10.

57. *CubaINFO,* Vol. 7, No. 5, April 6, 1995, pp. 3–4. See also *Miami Herald,* October 7, 1995, p. 1A.

58. *CubaINFO,* Vol. 8, No. 13, October 10, 1996, pp. 1–2.

59. Doxey, *International Sanctions in Contemporary Perspective,* p. 143; Wallensteen, "Economic Sanctions," p. 121. Hufbauer and Schott, *Economic Sanctions Reconsidered,* Second Edition, p. 95.

60. Gordon, "Cuba's Entrepreneurial Socialism."

61. *CubaINFO,* Vol. 7, No. 5, April 6, 1995, p. 2; *CubaINFO,* Vol. 8, No. 4, March 21, 1996, p. 7.

62. *CubaINFO,* Vol. 8, No. 2, February 8, 1996, p. 4; *CubaINFO,* Vol. 8, No. 14, November 5, 1996, pp. 1–3.

63. *CubaINFO,* Vol. 8, No. 4, March 21, 1996, p. 8.

64. *CubaINFO,* Vol. 8, No. 14, November 5, 1996, pp. 2–3.

65. *Washington Post,* December 4, 1996, p. A28; *New York Times,* December 3, 1996, p. A6; *CubaINFO,* Vol. 8, No. 16, December 12, 1996, pp. 1–2; *CubaINFO,* Vol. 9, No. 15, November 13, 1997, pp. 10–11.

66. *CubaINFO,* Vol. 9, No. 5, April 10, 1997, pp. 1–2; *CubaINFO,* Vol. 9, No. 8, June 12, 1997, p. 2; *CubaINFO,* Vol. 9, No. 14, October 23, 1997, pp. 1–2.

67. Gordon, "Cuba's Entrepreneurial Socialism." See also *New York Times,* October 3, 1996, p. A11.

68. "Law Penalizes Restitution-Seekers," *Chicago Tribune,* January 11, 1997, p. 7N.

69. *CubaINFO,* Vol. 8, No. 8, June 13, 1996, pp. 3–4; *CubaINFO,* Vol. 8, No. 1, August 29, 1996, p. 5.

70. Stefan Halper, "Mixed Effects of Helms-Burton on Cuba," *Washington Times,* December 2, 1996, p. A15.

71. *CubaINFO,* Vol. 10, No. 2, January 29, 1998, pp. 1–12; *New York Times,* January 22, 1998, p. A1.

72. Larry Rohter, "Cuba Measure Strikes Back at the United States," *New York Times,* January 11, 1997, p. 5. It should be noted that the Cubans have always been willing to engage in negotiations with the United States over compensation issues. In 1995, Cuban economist Pedro Monreal presented several formulas on compensation to a Washington conference. See *CubaINFO,* Vol. 7, No. 2, pp. 15–16.

73. Dick Kirschten, "The Big Chill," *The National Journal,* Vol. 28, No. 26, June 29, 1996; *CubaINFO,* Vol. 8, No. 9, July 11, 1996, p. 2; *Agence France Press,* January 3, 1997; *CubaINFO,* Vol. 9, No. 16, December 11, 1997, p. 1.

74. Michael Lyster, "Who's Our Man in Havana?" *World Trade,* August 1996; Gordon, "Cuba's Entrepreneurial Socialism." Gordon quotes conservative estimates of $1 billion. See also Studebaker, "Forsaking a $5 Billion Market and an Export Platform."

75. Lyster, "Who's Our Man in Havana?" p. 16; Gordon, "Cuba's Entrepreneurial Socialism"; *CubaINFO,* Vol. 9, No. 12, September 11, 1997, p. 7.

76. Kirschten, "The Big Chill." Among the trade associations are U.S.-Cuba Business Council, a conservative organization that wants the embargo to be maintained; Shaw, Pittman, Potts and Trowbridge, a Washington law firm that conducts seminars on investments in Cuba; the U.S.-Cuba Foundation, a conservative reli-

gious organization that advocates normalized relations with Havana; and the U.S.-Cuba Trade and Economic Council, headed by John Kavulich, which advocates lifting the embargo. See *CubaINFO,* Vol. 7, No. 2, February 7, 1995, pp. 4–5.

77. Renwick, "Economic Sanctions," pp. 79, 82.

78. Studebaker, "Forsaking a $5 Billion Market and an Export Platform."

79. Dick Kirschten, "The Big Chill," p. 1422; *CubaINFO,* Vol. 6, No. 5, April 8, 1994, p. 4.

80. *CubaINFO,* Vol. 10, No. 2, January 29, 1998, pp. 7–8. Former government officials include: former U.S. Treasury secretary Lloyd Benson, retired Gen. John Sheehan, former deputy secretary of Defense Frank Carlucci, and former trade representative Carla Hills.

81. Broadcast on *The McLaughlin Group,* January 23, 1993, reprinted in *CubaINFO,* Vol. 5, No. 2, February 8, 1993, p. 9. See also *CubaINFO,* Vol. 5, No. 10, August 6, 1993, p. 12; *U.S. News and World Report,* September 26, 1994.

82. Robert Kagan, "Is Castro Convertible?" *The Weekly Standard,* Vol. 1, No. 5, October 16, 1995, p. 36. Former Reagan aide Roger Fontaine testified before Congress that he had long "been an unapologetic supporter of the embargo," and now he believes "it is time to deprive Castro of these convenient scapegoats. . . . He alone should be stuck with the responsibility for economic failure and political repression." William Ratliff, a senior research fellow at the Hoover Institute, also shifted from a pro-embargo to anti-embargo position. See *CubaINFO,* Vol. 6, No. 5, April 8, 1994, p. 5; William F. Buckley, editorial, *The National Review,* August 30, 1994; *CubaINFO,* Vol. 7, No. 3, February 23, 1995, pp. 1–2, 9.

83. *CubaINFO,* Vol. 5, No. 10, August 6, 1993, p. 1.

84. *CubaINFO,* Vol. 6, No. 4, March 17, 1994, p. 2; *CubaINFO,* Vol. 8, No. 2, February 8, 1996, pp. 1–2.

85. *CubaINFO,* Vol. 8, No. 5, April 15, 1996, p. 1.

86. *CubaINFO,* Vol. 8, No. 8, June 13, 1996, p. 5.

87. *CubaINFO,* Vol. 8, No. 12, September 19, 1996, p. 4.

88. *CubaINFO,* Vol. 5, No. 13, October 15, 1993, p. 1; *CubaINFO,* Vol. 6, No. 6, April 29, 1994, p. 2.

89. *National Public Radio,* "Morning Edition," June 24, 1994; *San Francisco Chronicle,* June 22, 1994, p. A14; *CubaINFO,* Vol. 6, No. 9, July 1, 1994, p. 2.

90. *CubaINFO,* Vol. 6, No. 14, November 3, 1994, p. 7.

91. Robinson, "Cuba Takes a Stiff Belt," p. 36.

92. Farah, "Rising Expectations Blur Cuban Economic Revival," p. A12.

93. Dunne, "Clinton Suspends Helms-Burton Again," p. 3. Janet Matthews Information Services notes that the number of joint ventures operating in Cuba increased to 260 in 1996 from 240 at the end of 1995. JMIS, January 6, 1997, p. 1.

94. Doxey, *Economic Sanctions in Contemporary Perspective,* p. 131; Galtung, "On the Effects of International Economic Sanctions," p. 35.

95. Ana Julia Jatar, "Helms-Burton Backfires," *Washington Post,* July 22, 1996, p. A19.

96. *CubaINFO,* Vol. 9, No. 1, January 15, 1997, p. 7. Cuba's *Prensa Latina* suggested that one reason for positive economic performance in 1996 was that the Helms-Burton legislation had the unintended effect of stimulating foreign investment rather than stifling it.

9

The Lessons of the Cuba Sanctions

One of the first foreign policy moves of Clinton's second term in office was to enter into negotiations with North Korea—the only country against which the United States has maintained a sanctions policy of longer duration than Cuba. The U.S. government provided $8.2 million in aid to our former Asian enemy, with an additional $6 million pending. In addition, the Clinton administration licensed the U.S. grain conglomerate Cargill to sell 500,000 tons of grain to North Korea and authorized government payment of half the cost of $50 million a year in heavy fuel oil to be sent to North Korea. United States–North Korean talks also centered on the establishment of liaison offices in each other's capitals.[1] It appeared that the Clinton administration was beginning to punch holes in the forty-seven-year-old sanctions against North Korea. Although the White House publicly maintained that its purpose was to avert famine in North Korea, in fact accelerated U.S. overtures toward that country were rooted mainly in old Cold War competition with China over influence on the Korean peninsula.

Regardless of motivation, the United States appeared for all the world to be making great strides in moving beyond Cold War paradigms in Asia and remaining true to Clinton's famous campaign commitment to build a bridge to a new world order in the twenty-first century. Not so with respect to Cuba. The U.S. approach to its island neighbor at the end of the twentieth century remained hostage to a midcentury foreign policy. As one of her first moves as U.S. secretary of state, Madeleine Albright categorically defended the embargo, arguing that the United States was not isolated in its Cuba policy. During the week when Albright issued her statement, the highest ranking Canadian to visit Cuba in twenty years traveled to Havana to meet with Castro, promising healthy aid and trade packages.[2] No doubt the Canadian move was intended to tweak the U.S. nose over a policy it had long and loudly opposed. Soon after, at Albright's first meeting as secretary of state with the European Union, the transatlantic row over U.S. Cuba policy dominated the agenda.[3]

Within a week of Clinton's second inauguration, the United States Agency for International Development published a report entitled "Support for a Democratic Transition in Cuba." The report was designed to serve as reassurance to Cubans that a postsocialist Cuban economy would not flounder, as has been the case in many Eastern European countries. The report promised between $4 billion and $8 billion (most of it financed by the U.S. government) to a post-Castro transition government that met Helms-Burton requirements.[4] Even adjusted for inflation, this program would cost U.S. taxpayers more than the Marshall Plan that helped Europe recover from World War II. Not surprisingly, Castro angrily responded to the report, reminding the United States that Cuba is "not for sale."[5] Rallying public support on the island, he said, "What most outrages us is that they are trying to buy us. . . . It is shameful that someone should imagine freedom and dignity can be bought, that someone should imagine that for all the gold in the world we would be capable of agreeing to be slaves again. Never will the dragon be allowed to devour the lamb."

Unlike North Korea, Vietnam, and China, where stated U.S. policy has been to ease each country toward democracy through a lessening of tensions known as "constructive engagement," in the Cuba case there was no remission of sanctions, but instead a dangling carrot to seduce Cubans toward democracy. In other words, bribery was not beyond the pale for a president crossing the bridge to the twenty-first century. Clearly, the Clinton administration has learned nothing from the mistakes of its predecessors; from the vantage point of the late 1990s, it appears that the United States, under Clinton's stewardship, is going to haul the excess baggage of a failed Cuba sanctions policy into the new millennium.

This book explains why the Cuba sanctions have not only failed but have at times actually been counterproductive to U.S. interests. It also explores why the United States has been so faithful to a decisively unsuccessful and unpopular policy.

Cuba was targeted from the outset for economic sanctions because of its high degree of vulnerability to U.S. economic coercion. A U.S.-sponsored embargo was certain to exact grave consequences on the dependent island economy, especially because the prior relationship between the two partners had been cordial. At the time the embargo was first considered, the United States accounted for more than two-thirds of Cuba's trade, supplied three-quarters of Cuba's imports, and purchased two-thirds of Cuba's exports. Cuba's economy was inelastic and highly concentrated in sugar production and export. In fact, the United States had been purchasing more than half of Cuba's annual sugar harvest. Sanctions theory uses the benchmark GNP ratio of 50 to 1 as predictive of sanction success. The ratio of the GNPs of the United States and Cuba was 173 to 1 at the time the embargo was initiated. By all estimates, the Cuba embargo has been a thousand times more costly to the Cuban economy than to the U.S. economy.[6]

Moreover, every conceivable form of sanction has been employed in the Cuba case. Export, import, and financial sanctions have been invoked against Cuba during the course of the embargo, rendering Cuba vulnerable to massive attack on its economic welfare. Finally, U.S. efforts to extend the embargo multilaterally met with moderate success in the early years. All in all, in a case of high vulnerability in the target combined with exhaustive use of sanctions instruments by the sender, economic sanctions would stand a good chance of pressuring a hypothetical target government. Cuba, however, was not a hypothetical government. There were real actors involved, and nearly from the beginning, the players ensured that sanctions would not achieve the goals for which they seemed so well suited.

There are three main reasons for the failure of the Cuba embargo to achieve the objectives set out for it. If there is one single reason the sanctions failed, it was because Cuba was able to circumvent the embargo by turning to the Soviet Union. Sanctions theory cautions policymakers that if target nations are able to find alternative sources of supply, the sanctions face difficult odds.

Alternative Sources of Supply

The Cuba sanctions were invoked at the height of the Cold War in the framework of an East-West (i.e., free world vs. communist) polarity. Forcibly cut off from the United States, Cuba was able to turn to the United States' ideological opponent and chief antagonist, the Soviet Union, for assistance. Within three years of the imposition of sanctions, the Soviet Union and Eastern bloc had completely replaced former U.S.-Cuban trade. An astute political thinker in 1960 might have predicted that a Cuba embargo would have been perceived as opportunity in the socialist bloc. The Soviet Union had already demonstrated its willingness to bankroll and back other targets of U.S. embargoes—North Korea, Vietnam, and Egypt. The Cuba embargo presented an almost irresistible opportunity for the Communist bloc to expand into the United States' backyard—an opportunity similar to the one the United States had recognized when it looked for an "ally" in Yugoslavia.

Though the socialist bloc proved to be Cuba's most important trade partner and benefactor, alternative sources of trade with Cuba came from virtually all spheres. Certain Western European countries, as well as Canada, Japan, Mexico, and others, never fully complied with the sanctions. Trade between Cuba and nonsocialist countries reached as high as 41 percent of total Cuban trade. Despite U.S. efforts, credits and financial assistance from nonsocialist countries flowed into Cuba. Even subsidiaries of U.S. corporations in third countries capitalized on the attractive Cuban market between 1975 and 1992 when such trade was permitted. The United States simply did not command enough economic power on a global scale to prevent Cuba from finding alternative trade partners. Hence, the most important reason that the Cuba sanctions failed is that Cuba was always able to obtain essential goods and services from countries willing to break the embargo.

Today, pro-embargo lobbyists argue that the embargo has a greater chance of success now than ever before because the Soviet Union no longer exists and Cuba no longer has a sugar daddy to help pay its tab. While it is true that Cuba no longer can rely on lucrative trade agreements with the former Eastern bloc, Cuba has nonetheless been able to find trading partners among the former socialist nations and, more important, among market economy countries. Hence, while the Cuban economy is undeniably suffering from the loss of its former closest trade allies, it is surviving nonetheless.

Effective Countermeasures

Another important reason that the Cuba sanctions have failed to achieve their intended goals is that U.S. policymakers underestimated Fidel Castro time and again. U.S. policymakers believed that the embargo would succeed in putting enough pressure on the system in Cuba to squeeze Castro out.[7] Sanctions theory by the mid-1960s, however, warned explicitly against such calculations. In his seminal work on economic sanctions, Johan Galtung argued that "value deprivation may initially lead to political *integration* and only later—perhaps much later, or even never—to political disintegration."[8] This is exactly what happened in Cuba. What U.S. policymakers misunderstood—and what proved to be a fatal flaw of the sanctions policy—was that Fidel Castro was popular in Cuba, politically astute, and capable of using U.S. aggression to his advantage. The Cuba sanctions led not to the political disintegration of Cuba, as intended by U.S. policymakers, but to national unity. U.S. economic aggression against Cuba continues to provide Castro with the fuel he needs to bring the Cuban people together to ward off what is perceived from Havana as Yankee imperialism. Castro, for example, can adroitly unite Cuban youth, the most disaffected element of the Cuban population, on an anti–Helms-Burton rally. Moreover, what Cuban (or citizen of any country, for that matter) would welcome U.S. laws that legislate the return of property to owners who left voluntarily almost forty years ago? Hence, a principal reason for the failure of the Cuba embargo is that the sanctions helped the Cuban government rally public opinion behind its anti-embargo position and enabled it to blame many economic shortcomings on U.S. economic aggression.

Goals Hard to Attain

A third major reason that the Cuba embargo did not succeed in its primary goal of ousting Fidel Castro was that the goal was flawed to begin with. Theory suggests that clear, short-term, easily attainable goals are most likely to be achieved through a sanctions policy, and that major changes in the behavior of the target nation are the most difficult to secure by this means.

The overriding goal of the Cuba sanctions has been the overthrow of the Castro government. Other objectives of the embargo, such as disrupting Cuban military adventurism abroad and bringing democracy to Cuba, have been important but subsidiary to the primary goal. The objectives for the Cuba embargo, as enunciated by U.S. policymakers, have fluctuated and have nonetheless almost always been of the "major policy change" variety. Frequent changes in the pronounced objectives as well as the difficulty of achieving the various goals of the embargo led one leading congressman to conclude that in the case of the Cuba embargo, "the goal-post has not just been moved forward. They have taken the goal-post away."[9] Hence, the third reason for the embargo's failure is that its goals were nearly impossible to achieve through any type of economic coercion.

A number of additional factors shed light on why the embargo failed. Each of these reasons, in and of themselves, probably would not have been sufficient to lead to the inefficacy of the Cuba sanctions. Working in concert with one another and with the aforementioned reasons, however, they provide further, powerful explanation of the sanctions' failure to achieve their goals.

Impact on Allies

As we have seen, the Cuba sanctions met with varying degrees of resistance from U.S. allies and neighbors. From the earliest days of the Cuba embargo, some of the United States' most important allies refused to participate in the trade ban. A decade after the invocation of the embargo, any multilateral consensus to abide by the sanctions had crumbled. In recent years, the embargo has subjected the U.S. government to international condemnation, a response even U.S. government officials responsible for invoking sanctions anticipated. Sanctions theory has long warned that when allies are adversely impacted by economic embargoes, chances of success are diminished. In the Cuba case, U.S. allies and trade partners shifted from privately disregarding the embargo in its early years to vociferously opposing it in nearly every appropriate international forum and to enacting blocking orders against it.

Level of Internal Support in the Sender Nation

The embargo of Cuba has been undermined by internal conflict in the United States. Election politics, interagency squabbles, and interest group demands have fundamentally shaped Cuba policy around the internecine feuds of domestic political agendas, rather than long-term and consistent U.S. foreign and national security interests. The single most influential architect of U.S. policy toward Cuba has been the Cuban-American community in South Florida. The wealthiest, most conservative members of this community have held U.S. policy toward its island neighbor hostage to their own parochial interests. In fact, the embargo has evolved to a point at which this community's main concerns dictate the very wording of U.S. foreign policy. As Ana Julia Jatar noted, the Helms-Burton legislation is more concerned with "old properties than with new democracy."[10] Not surprisingly, a policy dictated so exactly by one South Florida county has not been fruitful.

Length of Sanctions

Sanctions that last less than three years are usually more successful than sanctions of longer duration.[11] The longer sanctions last, the more opportunity target nations have to develop methods to circumvent them. The early years of the embargo were the most difficult for Cuba; the island nation was forced to redirect an economy reliant on one patron/benefactor (the United States) to another very different patron/benefactor (the Soviet Union). By the early 1970s, however, Cuba's economy was robust and vital, and at that time, U.S. allies resumed vigorous trade with the island. Furthermore, the enduring embargo has been costly to the United States, both in terms of lost opportunities and international prestige. Today, as Castro opens Cuba's doors to foreign investment, the embargo prevents U.S. companies from competing in a natural market. All in all, over time Cuba has proven capable of weathering the worst of storms: it survived conversion from a market-oriented economy to a socialist one, and it is now demonstrating that it is capable of (at least) surviving the swing back toward a more market-driven model. U.S. allies shake their heads at the anachronistic U.S. foreign policy and then legislate blocking orders to prevent U.S. myopia from reaching their shores.

Embargo Is Successful: A Modest Proposal

This book documents the historical and political evolution of the Cuba embargo. It seeks to explain why an embargo of such impressive magnitude and exhaustive duration has failed to achieve its primary goals. There is, however, another way of thinking about the embargo; perhaps it has not really failed. If one accepts the proposition that the main goal of the embargo had little to do with foreign policy, and everything to do with domestic politics, it could be argued that the embargo has, at least in part, achieved its goal.

Only in the earliest years of the embargo was the U.S. population at large truly concerned about U.S. Cuba policy; even then, to a great extent, it was primarily an issue for businesspeople whose interests on the island were being challenged. The Eisenhower administration did come under domestic attack for not taking action to defend U.S. reputation. For example, conservative columnist George Sokolsky wrote, "The United States needs to take a stand against every speck of a country spitting in our face."[12]

Not since the early 1960s, however, has there been an uproarious cry from the U.S. public to do something about Castro.[13] Nonetheless, successive U.S. administrations have been wedded to the Cuba embargo. Ironically, with the passage of time, and with the entrenchment of the Cuba sanctions as an enduring aspect of U.S. foreign policy, *lifting* the sanctions came to represent a perceived threat to the United States' reputation and domestic image. As Brzezinski argued in the late 1970s, "There is little to be gained from eliminating the embargo, but there is a lot of risk associated with such action."[14] In effect, the burden of proof has fallen on those in the U.S. government who have advocated a return to *normal diplomatic relations* with Cuba rather than on those who want to maintain the sanctions.

It appears that U.S. legislators believe that their domestic political clout is at risk if they oppose the embargo. Even now, in the waning moments of the twentieth century, it is perilous to advocate lifting the sanctions. Legislators who take this position run the danger of being perceived as soft on communism, a risky business even after the end of the Cold War, or they are perceived as admitting that the United States has made a very bad choice for a very long time. There is little political capital to be gained from admitting that a long struggle has failed.[15] There is, however, something to be gained from staying the course: money and votes.

Cuban-American Interests Dominate U.S. Cuba Policy

In the shadow of the Reagan White House a new beast was born: the conservative Cuban-American lobby—the Cuban American National Foundation, founded by the late Jorge Mas Canosa. The Reagan administration nurtured this fledgling group into national prominence, and by the time Reagan left the White House, CANF had unprecedented power over U.S. policy toward Cuba.[16]

A 1997 report released by a nonprofit Washington-based think tank, the

Center for Public Integrity (CPI), concluded: "The Miami-based Cuban American National Foundation (CANF) is dollar for dollar the most effective lobbying group in Washington and has a virtual choke hold on U.S. policy toward Cuba." The study pointed out that because the U.S. public doesn't consider Cuba to be a major priority, CANF has been able to fill this "policy vacuum" with its own agenda.[17]

CANF was successful at its lobbying primarily because its coffers run deep. CANF's political action committee contributed $27 million to federal candidates since 1982.[18] Among one of the top recipients of CANF money is, as we have seen, Robert Torricelli (former congressman from New Jersey, currently senator from the state), who received more than $120,000 in campaign contributions since 1989 from Cuban-American leaders advocating the overthrow of Fidel Castro. According to the CPI study, Torricelli began receiving CANF support at about the same time that he underwent a transformation from an opponent of U.S. sanctions against Cuba into one of the nation's most forceful advocates for intensifying them.[19] After meetings with Jorge Mas Canosa and after accepting CANF campaign contributions, his metamorphosis was complete. According to CPI Chairman Charles Lewis, "In my years here, I've never seen a flip-flop and passage of money in such a dramatic way."[20]

Aside from donating substantial campaign contributions to key members of congress, CANF has had unprecedented direct influence at the policymaking level. For example, under Mas Canosa's stewardship, CANF used its influence to pressure Congress to create Radio and TV Martí, anticommunist broadcast stations that have received more than $280 million in federal money. The foundation also promoted the Cuban Democracy Act (also known as the Torricelli Bill) and the Helms-Burton Act.[21]

CANF's enormous power emerged despite the fact that it never represented the majority opinion of the Cuban-American community nor that of the U.S. public in general.[22] In a 1988 Gallup poll, the Cuban-American community was almost evenly divided on the sanctions issue. A clear majority of U.S. citizens polled in 1988 and 1994 reported that they would favor talks with Cuba on improving relations, a position CANF strongly opposed.[23] A plurality of citizens polled in 1995 believed that the United States should establish normal diplomatic ties with Cuba and lift the embargo.[24]

Representing neither the majority of the Cuban-American population nor the views of the general public, CANF derives its power from three sources. First, it disseminates its substantial financial resources to sway influential politicians and policymakers. Second, it fills the public opinion vacuum left by the majority of U.S. citizens who simply don't perceive Cuba to be a major foreign policy issue.[25] Third, CANF takes a moral high ground, making the argument that the United States has an obligation to depose a terrible dictator ninety miles off its coastline. Those who question the methods supported by the foundation to achieve Castro's demise are labeled as communist sympathizers. For example, the Washington think tank that published information about CANF's financial contributions was attacked in this way by CANF-supported Rep. Lincoln Diaz-Balart (R-Fla.): "Even after 38 years of oppression and infamy, the 'study' . . . shows that there are still those who actively serve Castro's interests in the U.S."[26] Cuban-American leaders called the report "left-wing" propaganda. In other words, CANF did not challenge the conclusions of the study but attacked it on a platform of anticommunism.

CANF has also used techniques based on fear and repression to ensure compliance with its point of view. Conservative columnist Georgie Anne Geyer, a former Mas ally, wrote: "State Department officials admit that Mr. Mas's foundation . . . has been responsible for the fact that the United States has basically formulated no policy of its own toward Cuba because of fear of the foundation's tactics."[27] In Miami, CANF power goes unrivaled. America's Watch, a human rights organization that normally concerns itself with abuses in foreign lands, issued a twenty-nine page report claiming that "a repressive climate for free expression" had been created by anti-Castro Cuban-American leaders who condone violence and intimidation to quiet exiles favoring a softening of policies toward Cuba. Calling Miami the number one terrorist city in the United States, the report noted a score of unsolved incidents from bombings to mob attacks and accused Jorge Mas Canosa (who has since died) and the CANF of fostering that climate of violence.[28]

Given CANF's financial and political power, its intimidation tactics, and the absence of any clearly defined and affluent opposition group, it is likely that many Capitol Hill legislators—perhaps the majority—cast their ballots on pivotal questions related to Cuba with more concern over how their party's votes will play in Miami than the relationship of those votes to reasonable foreign policy goals. Hence, U.S. national interests vis-à-vis Cuba have been taken prisoner by a small group of South Florida caudillos.

Conclusion: From Foreign Policy to Domestic Goals

It is probable that at the start of the embargo, U.S. foreign policy concerns were paramount, and that U.S. legislators truly believed that sanctions would succeed in ousting Fidel Castro from Cuba. Even in the early 1960s, however, both history and theory had already supplied basic lessons in the elements of a successful sanctions policy. Had legislators thought objectively about the political and economic circumstances surrounding Cuba, the United States, and the world at that time, they might have perceived serious flaws in their conception of the Cuba embargo and serious obstacles to the successful achievement of its goals.[29] Nonetheless, U.S. policymakers, unschooled in sanctions theory, probably invoked the embargo in the sincere belief that it would result in deposing Castro.

Over the years, however, as it became painfully obvious that the embargo would not succeed in overthrowing a neighboring government, it likewise became clear that there were compelling domestic reasons to maintain the policy. Because there was little to be gained from championing its removal, and because there were money, votes, and a twisted moral standing to be had from maintaining—even strengthening—the sanctions, the White House and a majority in Congress consistently opted to support the embargo. Hence, it appears that for almost twenty years, the U.S. embargo of Cuba has primarily been a domestic policy instrument. U.S. sanctions against Cuba serve more to placate what has been called a "potent and sometimes fearsome lobby" than achieve political change in Cuba.[30] In this respect, and this respect alone, the embargo can be considered a success.

Notes

1. Barbara Slavin, "North Korea Postpones New York Negotiations," *USA Today,* January 28, 1997, p. 6A; "Seoul Journal Foresees Kim Chong-il Succession in April," *British Broadcasting Corporation Summary of World Broadcasts,* January 27, 1997.

2. Anthony DePalma, "A Top Canadian Visits Cuba, Nettling Washington," *New York Times,* January 23, 1997, p. A3.

3. "Cuba Row to Dominate EU First Meeting with Albright," *Agence France Press,* January 26, 1997.

4. Nick Madigan, "U.S. Pledges Support for Post-Castro Cuba," *Washington Post,* January 28, 1997. The report estimated that between $320 and $720 for each of the eleven million people on the island would be needed in the first six years. See Stanley Moister, "Clinton Pledges Aid for Post-Castro Cuba," *Los Angeles Times,* January 29, 1997, p. A6.

5. National Public Radio, Morning Edition, January 29, 1997.

6. Estimates are that the embargo costs the United States 0.003 percent of U.S. GNP annually and costs Cuba 3 percent of its GNP annually.

7. Saul Landau compared U.S. efforts to squeeze Castro with a toothpaste tube. He said that the United States has always believed that if it simply squeezed hard enough, Castro would come popping out. Instead, the United States has managed to squeeze a lot of other Cubans out of Cuba, but, as in a toothpaste tube, there is always just a bit more at the bottom, and that is where Castro is. National Public Radio, "Talk of the Nation," September 28, 1994.

8. Galtung, "International Economic Sanctions," pp. 26–27.

9. Congressman Charles Rangel, testimony, U.S. Congress, *Free Trade with Cuba Act,* p. 380.

10. Ana Julia Jatar, "Helms-Burton Backfires," *Washington Post,* July 22, 1996, p. A19.

11. Renwick, "Economic Sanctions," p. 80; Hufbauer and Schott, *Economic Sanctions Reconsidered,* Second Edition, pp. 100–101.

12. Carla Anne Robins, *The Cuba Threat,* p. 86.

13. Even in the early 1960s, the U.S. public was far from united on the Cuba issue. A 1963 Gallup poll found that 36 percent of respondents "didn't know" what the United States should do in regard to Cuba. In a 1994 NBC/*Wall Street Journal* poll, only 5 percent of respondents thought that Cuba was the most serious foreign policy issue facing the United States. Bosnia, Russia, Haiti, North Korea, the Middle East, and "not sure" all took priority over Cuba.

14. Smith, *The Closest of Enemies,* p. 100.

15. U.S. Congress, *Toward Improved United States–Cuba Relations,* p. 21.

16. For more information on how the Reagan administration helped organize the Cuban American National Foundation, and hand-picked Jorge Mas Canosa as its leader, see Gaeton Fonzi, "Who Is Jorge Mas Canosa?" *Esquire,* January 1993, p. 121.

17. Phil Whillon, "Report Attacks Cuba Lobby," *The Tampa Tribune,* January 24, 1997, p. 1.

18. *CubaINFO,* Vol. 9, No. 16, December 11, 1997, p. 10.

19. Adam Piore, "Torricelli Hit for Cuban Flip-Flop: Report Says Money Changed Him," *The Bergen Record,* January 24, 1997, p. A3. The report says Mas Canosa began to cultivate a relationship with Torricelli in the late 1980s. At the time, Torricelli was publicly advocating a dialogue with Castro conditioned on human rights concessions and a pullout from Angola. Torricelli even cosponsored legislation to partially lift the embargo on medicine and medical supplies to Cuba.

20. Piore, "Torricelli Hit for Cuban Flip-Flop," p. A3. For a list of recipients of CANF moneys, see Whillon, "Report Attacks Cuba Lobby," p. 1.

21. Whillon, "Report Attacks Cuba Lobby," p. 1.

22. Lee Hockstader and William Booth, "Cuban Exiles Split on Life after Castro," *Washington Post,* March 10, 1992, p. A1.

23. Rich, "U.S. and Cuba: Trading Partners?" p. 36. See also *Associated Press,* June 28, 1988. Time and Cable News Network sponsored the 1994 poll conducted by Yankelovich Partners, September 1994.

24. The Chicago Council on Foreign Affairs, "American Public Opinion and Foreign Policy," February 15, 1995. A majority of U.S. citizens in 1994 advocated ending the embargo in return for Cuba's halting the flow of refugees trying to reach the United States. ABC News poll, March 25, 1995.

25. A CBS/*New York Times* poll conducted in 1994 found that 63 percent of respondents believed that what happens in Cuba is either "not very important" or "somewhat important" to U.S. interests; 35 percent believed what happens in Cuba is "very important." Roper Center Public Opinion Online, September 18, 1994. In a Time/Cable News Network poll conducted in September 1994, 59 percent of respondents said that Cuba represents either "no threat" or a "slight threat" to the United States. Time/CNN poll, September 1, 1994.

26. Whillon, "Report Attacks Cuba Lobby," p. 1.

27. Fonzi, "Who Is Jorge Mas Canosa?" p. 88.

28. Ibid., p. 119. Mas himself took credit for a raid on art dealer Ramon Cernuda's home. He also carried out a boycott of *The Miami Herald,* calling it a "tool of the Castro regime," in response to anti-embargo editorials. *Herald* vending boxes were defaced, and publisher David Lawrence received death threats. See also Peter Slevin, "Jorge Mas Canosa: The Road to Havana," *Miami Herald,* October 11, 1992, p. 1A. Elliott Abrams, former assistant secretary of state for inter-American affairs, said, "An attack from the foundation would hurt you more than an attack by any other Cuban group, and so you avoid it. . . . You say to yourself, if I block this, or attempt to, will the foundation be angry with me?" See also "Jorge Mas Canosa: A Matter of Basic Rights," *The Miami Herald,* February 2, 1992, p. 3C; "Press

Terrorism in Miami," *New York Times,* February 2, 1992, p. A24; David Lawrence, "A Defining Moment for our Community," *The Miami Herald,* February 2, 1992, p. 3C; Jose de Cordoba, "*Miami Herald* Officials Are Threatened as Cuban Exile Controversy Continues," *Wall Street Journal,* February 3, 1992, p. A1; Dagmaris Cabezas, testimony, U.S. Congress, *Cuba and the United States: Thirty Years of Hostility and Beyond,* pp. 283–287; and Sandra Dibble, "Little Havana Museum Is Bombed," *Miami Herald,* June 15, 1990, p. A1.

29. Many of the Cuba-specific variables were available for consideration by the decisionmakers. For example, decisionmakers should have been able to conclude from available evidence and past behavior that the Soviet Union would come to Cuba's aid. It was also possible for decisionmakers to conclude from available evidence that Castro was a popular ruler and that he was skilled at using U.S. aggression to his advantage.

30. William Gibson, "Cuban-American Lobby Rips Report: Study Calls Group 'Potent, Fearsome,'" *Sun-Sentinel,* Fort Lauderdale, January 24, 1997, p. 3A.

Appendixes

Appendix 1. Basic Statistics on Cuba

Area: 110,860 sq. km.

Population: 10,936,635 (July 1995 est.)
1–14 years: 22 percent
15–64 years: 68 percent
65 years and over: 10 percent

Life expectancy at birth: 77.05 years
Male: 74.86 years
Female: 79.37 years

Literacy: 98 percent

Labor force by occupation
Services and government: 30 percent
Industry: 22 percent
Agriculture: 20 percent
Commerce: 11 percent
Construction: 10 percent
Transportation and communications: 7 percent

Communications
Telephone system: 229,000 telephones
20.7 telephones per 1,000 persons
Radios: 2.14 million
Televisions: 1.53 million

Trade partners (by percentage of total Cuban trade) (1995 estimate)

Exports

Russia	15 percent
Canada	9 percent
China	8 percent
Egypt	6 percent
Spain	5 percent
Japan	4 percent
Morocco	4 percent

Imports

Spain	17 percent
Mexico	10 percent
France	8 percent
China	8 percent
Venezuela	7 percent
Italy	4 percent
Canada	3 percent

Foreign Trade (in Millions U.S.$)

	1989	1990	1991	1992	1993	1994	1995
Exports	5400	5415	2980	1779	1137	1314	1526
Imports	8140	7417	4234	2315	2037	1956	2088

Sources: U.S. Central Intelligence Agency, *The World Factbook, 1995,* Central Intelligence Agency, *Cuba: Handbook of Trade Statistics, 1995, Cuba.*

Appendix 2. Cuban Trade for Selected Years, 1958, 1964–1968[1]

	1958[2]		1964[3]		1965[3]		1966[3]		1967[3]		1968[3]	
Year	Amount	Percent	Amount	Percent	Amount	Percent	Amount	Percent	Amount	Percent	Amount	Percent
Exports												
Principal Market												
United States	490	67	0	0	0	0	0	0	0	0	0	0
Other non-Communist countries	225	30	293	41	140	20	148	23	145	20	144	24
Soviet Union	14	2	275	39	375	55	285	45	375	53	280	46
Other Communist countries	5	1	141	20	171	25	207	32	195	27	186	30
Imports												
Principal Market												
United States	543	70	0	0	0	0	0	0	0	0	n.a.	n.a.
Other non-Communist countries	234	30	327	32	220	25	218	24	232	23	n.a.	n.a.
Soviet Union	(–)[4]	(–)[4]	411	41	420	49	479	54	550	56	n.a.	n.a.
Other Communist countries	(–)[4]	(–)[4]	277	27	225	26	203	22	208	21	n.a.	n.a.

Source: Adapted form U.S. Department of Agriculture, Economic Research Service, Foreign Regional Analysis Division, *A Survey of Agriculture in Cuba*, Washington, 1969.

n.a.—not available.

1. All data after 1960 are highly unreliable. They were estimated by using data of reporting countries, and estimating sources were not always comparable.
2. In million Cuban pesos. In 1958, 1 Cuban peso equaled U.S.$1.
3. 1964–1968 data are in million U.S. dollars.
4. Minus means insignificant, if any.

Appendix 3. Claims Awarded Under the Cuban Claims Program of the Foreign Claims Settlement Commission

	To Corporations	To Individuals	Total
Total value, July 1972	$1,578.5 million	$221.0 million	$1,799.6 million
Number of awards			
by value (dollars)			
5,000 or less	258	2,953	3,211
5,000–25,000	234	1,233	1,467
25,001–100,000	140	536	676
100,001–500,000	133	219	352
500,001–1,000,000	41	33	74
Over 1,000,000	92	39	131
Total	898	5,013	5,911
Total value, July 1994	$4,986.1 million	$698.1 million	$5,685.0 million

Source: Foreign Claims Settlement Commission of the United States, *Final Report of the Cuban Claims Program* (Washington, D.C., July 1972); reprinted from the 1972 Annual Report to the Congress.

Note: The mid-1994 values were calculated by compounding annually the 1972 values with the customary FCSC interest rate of 6 percent.

Appendix 4. Claims over U.S.$ 10 Million (1994) Awarded to Corporations Under the Cuban Claims Program of the Foreign Claims Settlement Commission

Corporation	Amount U.S.$ (1994)	Corporation	Amount U.S.$ (1993)
Cuban Electric	845	Pan American Life Insurance	31
ITT	413	United States Rubber	30
North American Sugar	344	F.W. Woolworth	29
Moa Bay Mining	279	Havana Docks	28
United Fruit Sugar	269	Continental Can	28
West Indies Sugar	268	Firestone Tire and Rubber	26
American Sugar	256	International Harvester	26
Standard Oil	226	Owens-Illinois	25
Bangor Punta	169	General Motors	24
Francisco Sugar	166	Chase Manhattan	23
Texaco	158	IBM World Trade	20
Manati Sugar	153	First National City Bank	20
Nicaro Nickel	104	Swift	19
Coca-Cola	87	First National Bank, Boston	19
Lone-Star Cement	80	General Electric	19
New Tuinueu Sugar	74	Libby	18
Colgate Palmolive	45	Goodyear Tire and Rubber	16
Braga Brothers	40	Sears Roebuck	12
Broise Cascade	37	Reynolds Metals	11
American Brands	33	Lykes Brothers	11
Atlantic Richfield	32	Sherwin Williams	11
Burns Mills	31		

Source: Business International Corporation, *Developing Business Strategies for Cuba,* New York, March 1992, p. 76.

Note: The mid-1994 values were calculated by compounding annually the 1960 values using the customary FCSC simple (not compounded) interest rate of 6 percent.

Appendix 5. Composition of Trade, 1989–1994 (Million U.S.$)

	1989	1990[a]	1991[a]	1992[a]	1993[a]	1994[a]
Total Exports	**5,392**	**4,910**	**3,550**	**2,030**	**1,275**	**1,375**
Sugar, molasses, honey	3,959	3,690	2,670	1,300	820	800
Fish	127	125	115	120	90	110
Fruit	139	150	100	50	50	80
Tobacco	85	95	100	95	75	85
Nickel	485	400	245	200	120	130
Medical products	58	130	50	30	20	60
Other	539	320	270	235	100	110
Total Imports	**8,124**	**6,745**	**3,690**	**2,235**	**1,990**	**2,025**
Food	1,011	840	720	450	490	430
Raw material	307	240	140	40	35	30
Fuels	2,598	1,950	1,240	835	750	720
Chemical products	530	390	270	170	150	175
Semifinished goods	838	700	425	195	180	215
Machinery	1,922	1,790	615	350	235	240
Transport equipment	609	590	170	125	80	115
Consumer goods	277	225	90	50	50	80
Other	32	20	20	20	20	20
Trade Deficit	**2,732**	**1,835**	**140**	**205**	**715**	**650**

Sources: Anuario Estadistico de Cuba 1989 and official data from Cuba's trade partners.
a. Estimated from partner trade data.

Appendix 6. Exports by Country of Destination, 1989–1994 (Million U.S.$)

	1989	1990	1991	1992	1993	1994
Total	**5,392.0**	**4,910.0**	**3,550.0**	**2,030.0**	**1,275.0**	**1,375.0**
Europe						
Austria	4.7	2.8	1.1	1.8	2.1	
Belarus				4.1	7.4	
Belgium-Luxembourg	2.4	2.3	4.0	5.2	4.7	6.9
Cyprus	0.4	0.2	0.3	0.6	0.5	
Czechoslovakia	109.4	40.3	5.0	8.8		
Denmark	0.1	0.7	0.4	0.6	0.7	0.6
Finland	18.3	18.5	19.1	18.0	18.3	20.7
France	61.3	52.0	61.1	44.1	39.1	44.1
Germany	20.8	23.3	19.4	20.8	14.3	24.7
Greece	0.1	0.6	4.6	0.1		
Hungary	10.7	2.7	1.2	0.2	0.1	0.1
Ireland	0.4	0.2	0.3	1.9	1.7	
Italy	44.7	52.1	47.7	50.8	33.4	50.3
Netherlands	26.2	22.4	40.1	25.9	27.1	24.0
Norway	0.4	0.1	0.0	0.1	0.1	1.4
Poland	15.4	2.3	0.2	1.3	0.5	0.6
Portugal	22.6	19.1	18.4	26.7	34.8	
Romania	117.2	55.0	2.8	5.2	7.7	17.0
Russia				632.2	436.0	300.5
Slovenia					4.6	
Spain	91.4	80.1	90.8	84.7	64.7	77.9
Sweden	3.3	24.8	6.3	4.6	4.6	0.7
Switzerland	8.1	10.9	7.9	8.1	7.1	8.0
Turkey	0.0	5.7	1.3	0.9	0.0	
United Kingdom	56.3	54.0	31.6	22.9	12.9	16.1
Near East/Asia						
China	229.0	306.2	201.7	182.8	73.6	120.7
Hong Kong	0.2	0.2	0.2	1.0	1.4	0.8
India	10.1	10.4	4.4	4.1	4.0	
Indonesia	6.3	0.1	0.1	0.0	0.1	
Japan	133.4	94.9	141.8	114.7	51.1	63.5
Jordan	0.3	5.2	5.4	0.6	0.1	
Kazakhstan				29.3	3.5	
Malaysia	18.9					
Sri Lanka	0.0	3.7	0.0	0.0		
Syria	15.3					
Taiwan	0.2	1.1	1.2	0.1	2.5	
Thailand	0.0	0.0	0.1	0.3	0.0	
Americas						
Argentina	1.3	0.8	0.7	1.8	1.9	
Barbados	0.1	0.2	0.0	0.2		
Bolivia	0.1	0.3	0.1	0.4	0.2	
Brazil	32.2	102.4	27.6	16.3	9.8	
Canada	52.5	111.5	133.1	212.2	132.6	142.3
Chile	0.0	0.0	3.6	0.1	0.2	0.2
Colombia	0.3	0.4	0.2	3.3	2.9	
Costa Rica	0.5	0.4	0.0	0.7		
Ecuador	0.4	0.2	0.4	0.2	0.4	
Guadaloupe	0.8	0.8	0.6	0.5	0.1	
Honduras	0.0	0.0	0.1	0.0		

Appendix 6 (continues)

Appendix 6 (continued)

	1989	1990	1991	1992	1993	1994
Americas continued						
Martinique	1.2	1.1	0.8	0.6		
Mexico	21.4	53.5	44.4	7.4	4.4	11.8
Nicaragua	6.7	5.1	5.1	2.2	2.9	
Panama	0.2	0.2	0.0	0.3		
Peru	15.3	5.7	0.6	0.3	0.5	
Uruguay	0.1	0.1	0.1	2.1	0.4	5.5
Venezuela	26.2	8.6	17.9	20.7		
Africa						
Algeria	80.7	70.0	52.7	54.3	48.7	
Egypt	11.8	56.2	7.1	8.1	1.1	
Ethiopia	0.5					
Libya	2.6	56.5	28.5			
Morocco	0.4	0.3	0.3	9.2	1.0	0.5
Tunisia	18.5	16.4	11.3	14.3	9.8	7.6
Oceania						
Australia	0.8	0.8	0.4	0.3	0.4	
New Zealand	0.0	0.0	8.8	13.6	0.0	0.1
Others	**4,090.2**	**3,527.1**	**2,487.0**	**357.5**	**200.9**	**425.9**

Sources: Anuario Estadistico de Cuba 1989 and official data from Cuba's trade partners.

Appendix 7. Imports by Country of Origin, 1989–1994 (Million U.S.$)

	1989	1990	1991	1992	1993	1994
Total	**8,124.0**	**6,745.0**	**3,690.0**	**2,235.0**	**1,990.0**	**2,025.0**
Europe						
Austria	6.4	5.5	2.8	1.5	0.9	
Belgium/Luxembourg	34.6	45.1	39.8	21.7	52.4	33.3
Croatia				0.1	1.6	
Cyprus	0.0	0.0	0.0	0.0	2.0	
Czechoslovakia	112.8	75.0	11.6	5.9		
Denmark	15.3	16.4	23.2	9.6	4.7	4.8
Finland	6.9	2.5	3.1	1.8	2.3	0.9
France	49.2	68.6	62.5	90.4	127.3	133.4
Germany	124.3	99.9	123.4	59.4	39.5	40.5
Greece	0.0	0.0	0.1	0.1		
Hungary	47.2	29.0	24.0	8.2	2.5	1.7
Ireland	0.0	9.7	2.2	0.4	6.0	
Italy	81.1	108.3	158.3	101.7	64.5	62.8
Lithuania				0.4		
Netherlands	38.3	37.8	36.0	41.9	58.4	49.8
Norway	1.1	0.9	0.6	0.3	0.2	0.5
Poland	20.1	6.3	3.9	5.9	3.1	2.0
Portugal	1.3	0.9	1.6	0.8	1.8	
Romania	164.4	76.7	0.9	4.9	4.9	8.9
Russia						248.6
Spain	216.3	303.2	284.6	199.0	190.9	288.9
Sweden	28.7	14.9	35.3	9.8	7.6	8.0
Switzerland	32.6	31.5	27.3	24.5	12.0	8.2
Turkey	0.0	0.4	0.0	0.1	0.5	
United Kingdom	87.1	67.2	50.2	49.8	21.0	40.1
Near East/Asia						
Bangladesh	0.0	0.0	1.0	0.0		
China	212.3	271.9	224.4	200.2	177.0	147.2
Hong Kong	0.1	0.3	0.3	0.4	0.6	3.1
India	9.2	5.9	1.1	1.8	0.2	0.0
Indonesia	0.0	0.0	0.3	0.0	13.5	13.9
Japan	54.5	72.7	35.7	17.8	18.2	24.0
Malaysia	0.1	0.0	1.4	0.0	0.5	
Taiwan		0.2	0.3	0.7	0.8	1.1
Thailand	32.6	28.9	15.6	0.0	0.0	
Americas						
Argentina	187.0	163.4	98.9	62.8	71.6	
Brazil	62.3	84.6	65.6	17.2	18.8	25.1
Canada	131.7	132.5	114.4	100.4	107.3	83.6
Chile	0.0	0.0	7.4	4.1	4.5	14.9
Colombia	26.6	19.9	20.1	14.4	20.3	
Costa Rica	0.7	0.6	0.0			
Ecuador	0.0	0.0	0.0	0.7		
Mexico	108.5	102.9	104.4	116.7	188.1	174.0
Netherlands Antilles	18.9	57.0	25.9	12.2		
Nicaragua	14.4	7.6	3.0	4.0	0.4	
Panama	2.6	2.2	1.8	2.0	2.1	
Peru	15.6	9.2	1.1	0.7	1.5	
Trinidad and Tobago	22.3	37.8	4.5	12.0	8.9	
United States	2.9	1.3	1.3	1.1	2.6	4.4

Appendix 7 (continues)

Appendix 7 (continued)

	1989	1990	1991	1992	1993	1994
Americas continued						
Uruguay	15.3	14.1	10.7	0.6	0.6	0.1
Venezuela	28.0	464.4	48.5	79.4	119.8	
Africa						
Algeria	0.0	0.0	10.3	0.1	1.0	
Morocco	0.0	0.0	0.0	1.4	0.0	0.0
Tunisia	7.2	6.0	4.2	3.9	8.9	5.8
Oceania						
Australia	1.8	0.4	0.3	0.0	0.1	
New Zealand	0.0	18.6	46.2	24.2	5.2	8.0
Others	**6,102.4**	**4,248.1**	**1,949.4**	**918.0**	**613.4**	**587.8**

Sources: Anuario Estadistico de Cuba 1989 and official data from Cuba's trade partners.

Appendix 8. Licensed U.S. Foreign Subsidiary Trade with Cuba, 1985–1992

	1985	1988	1990	1991	1992
License applications	256	215	321	285	225
Total exports to Cuba (million U.S.$)	162	97	533	383	407
Total imports from Cuba (million U.S.$)	126	149	172	335	92
Total exports and imports (million U.S.$)	288	246	705	718	499
Export/import ratio	56/44	40/60	76/24	53/47	82/18

Source: Office of Foreign Assets Control, *An Analysis of Licensed Trade with Cuba by Foreign Subsidiaries of U.S. Companies* (Washington, D.C.: U.S. Department of Treasury), July 1991.

Appendix 9. Goods Exported from U.S. Subsidiaries to Cuba, 1985–1992 (Million U.S.$)

	1985	1988	1990	1991	1992
Grain, wheat and other consumables	109	56	500	348	363
Industrial and nonconsumables	53	41	33	36	44
Percentage of consumables in subsidiary exports	67.28	57.73	93.81	90.86	89.19
Percentage of consumables in subsidiary trade	37.85	22.76	70.92	48.46	72.75

Source: Donna Rich Kaplowitz and Michael Kaplowitz, *New Opportunities for U.S.-Cuban Trade* (Baltimore: Johns Hopkins University Press, 1992); *U.S. Treasury Department,* Special Report, 1993.

Appendix 10. U.S. Parent Companies of Foreign Subsidiaries Licensed to Trade with Cuba, 1985–1991

ALCOA
AM International
Aeroquip International
Analytical Technology
Armco
BF Goodrich
Baker Hughes
Barry-Wehmiller
Beatrice Companies
Bonne Bell
Borg-Warner
Bridgestone/Firestone
Buckman Laboratories
Burndy
Butler Manufacturing
Campbell Investment
Carrier
Carter Day Industries
Caterpillar
Central Soya
Champion Spark Plug
Coleman
Combustion Engineering
Continental Grain
Cooper Industries
Corning
Crane
Cummins Engine
Del Monte
Dow Chemical
Dorr-Oliver
Dresser Industries
Drew Chemical
Drexel Burnham Lambert
E.D.&F. Man International Futures
E.I. Dupont
Eli Lilly
Emhart Industries
Envirotech
Exxon
Fischer & Porter
Ford Motor
GK Technologies
GTE International
General Electric
Genlyte Group
Gilbarco
Gillette
Goodyear Tire and Rubber
H.B. Fuller
H.H. Robertson
Hercules
Hoechst Celanese
Honeywell
Hussmann
IBM World Trade
ITT
Ingersoll-Rand
International Multifoods
International Securities Investment
Johnson and Johnson
Johnson Controls
John Fluke Manufacturing
Joyce International
Lubrizol
Litton Industries
McGraw Edison
Manville
Mennen
Minnesota Mining & Manufacturing
Monsanto
Morton International
N.L. Industries
Nynex
Otis Elevator
Owens Corning Fiber
Pfizer
Philipp Brothers
Picker International
Potters Industries
RCA Global
R.J. Reynolds
Raychem
Reichhold Chemicals
Reliance Electric
Richardson Electronics
Rohm & Haas
S.C. Johnson & Son
Joseph E. Seagram & Sons
Sigma-Aldrich
Sybron Acquisition
Stanley Works
TFX Holdings
TRW Teleflex
Tenneco
Toledo Scale
USM
Uarco
Union Camp
Union Carbide
Vulcan Hart
Westinghouse Electric
Worthington International
Worthington Pump

Source: Documents obtained by the author through Freedom of Information Act requests to the Office of Foreign Assets Control of the U.S. Department of Treasury, March 31, 1992.

Appendix 11. Partial List of Goods Sold to Cuba by U.S. Subsidiaries, 1985–1991

agricultural pesticides
air cleaners
aluminum sheets
asphalt manufacturing equipment
automatic transmissions
bottle inspectors
brake fluid
carbon black
cardboard box mfg. equipment
cardpunch machine and sorter
carpentry tools
cement
ceramic glazes
chemical coatings and finishes for leather
compressors
copper concentrates
corn
detergent alkylate feedstock
diesel engines
dry roofing felt
electrical connectors
electrical fuses
electrical plugs
electrical switches
elevators
enamel glazes
enameling furnace components
engineering services for plastics, synthetic leather, ammonia
eyeglass lenses
fertilizer
flour products
flowmeters
fluorescent lamps
food
funeral cars
fuse links
gas pumps and nozzles
gear drive mechanisms
gelatin capsules
glass manufacturing machinery and parts
glass products
hacksaw blades
hydraulic pumps
ice machines
kerosene lanterns
light bulbs
lubricating oils
maize
metal warehouses
micro switches
motors
oats
office furniture
office supplies
oil additives
orthopedic supplies
passenger cars and spare parts
pharmaceutical products
photocopy paper
photographic supplies
plastic products, cutlery, toys
plumbing equipment
plywood
polyethylene bags
polypropylene ropes
polystyrene room dividers
power boilers
power plant equipment, pumps, motors steam-generating
pressing machines
pressurized cables
processing equipment
PVC pipes and fittings
rice
riveting tools
rivets
rock-drilling bits and rods
roller chain and parts
rubber base adhesive
sausage casings
sewer system equipment
sewing machines: industrial parts
soybean meal
spark plugs
sterilizers
sunflower seed oil
synthetic adhesive
telephone exchange equipment
telephone pay stations
telephone subsets
teleprinters: parts
temperature recording equipment
thermostats
tires
traffic light relays
transformers
truck chassis
typewriters
underwater equipment: masks, snorkels, fins
valves: gate, air, three-way, globe
water system equipment
weight scales
wheat flour
x-ray equipment
x-ray film

Source: Documents obtained by the author through a Freedom of Information Act request to the Office of Foreign Assets Control of the U.S. Department of Treasury, March 31, 1992. See also Donna Rich Kaplowitz and Michael Kaplowitz, *New Opportunities for U.S.-Cuban Trade* (Baltimore: Johns Hopkins University Press, 1992).

Appendix 12. Foreign Investment in the Republic of Cuba, 1990–1997

Country	Announced	Committed/Delivered
Australia	500,000,000	10,000,000
Austria	500,000	100,000
Brazil	150,000,000	20,000,000
Canada	941,000,000	100,000,000
Chile	69,000,000	30,000,000
China	10,000,000	5,000,000
Dominican Republic	5,000,000	1,000,000
France	15,000,000	10,000,000
Germany	10,000,000	2,000,000
Greece	2,000,000	500,000
Honduras	7,000,000	1,000,000
Israel	22,000,000	7,000,000
Italy	97,000,000	87,000,000
Jamaica	2,000,000	1,000,000
Japan	2,000,000	500,000
Mexico	2,256,000,000	250,000,000
The Netherlands	300,000,000	40,000,000
Panama	2,000,000	500,000
Russia	25,000,000	2,000,000
South Africa	400,000,000	5,000,000
Spain	350,000,000	80,000,000
Sweden	10,000,000	1,000,000
United Kingdom	75,000,000	50,000,000
Uruguay	500,000	300,000
Venezuela	50,000,000	3,000,000
Total	5,301,000,000	706,900,000

Source: U.S.-Cuba Trade and Economic Council.
http://www.cubatrade.org. July 11, 1997

Note: The figures represent amounts of announced, committed, and delivered investment since 1990 by private sector companies and government-controlled companies from various countries to enterprises within the Republic of Cuba as of January 27, 1997. Information compiled through the media, other public sources, individual discussions with company representatives, non-Republic of Cuba government officials, and Republic of Cuba-based enterprise managers and government officials.

Acronyms

APHA	American Public Health Association
CACR	Cuban Assets Control Regulations
CANF	Cuban American National Foundation
CARICOM	Caribbean Community and Common Market
CDA	Cuban Democracy Act
CIA	Central Intelligence Agency
CMEA	Council for Mutual Economic Assistance
COMECON	Council for Mutual Economic Assistance Countries
EC	European Community
ECGD	British Export Credit Guarantee Department
GATT	General Agreement on Tariffs and Trade
GDP	Gross Domestic Product
LAFTA	Latin American Free Trade Association
LASO	Latin American Solidarity Organization
NAFTA	North American Free Trade Agreement
NATO	North Atlantic Treaty Organization
NGO	Nongovernmental Organizations
NSAM	National Security Action Memorandum
OAS	Organization of American States
OFAC	Office of Foreign Assets Control of the U.S. Treasury Department
PTIA	(British) Protection of Trading Interests Act
SALT	Strategic Arms Limitation Talks
SGA	Special Group Augmented
TWEA	Trading With the Enemy Act
UN	United Nations
WTO	World Trade Organization

Bibliography

Books and Articles

The books in this bibliography fall into two categories, those that deal with the history of Cuba and those that deal with sanctions theory. There are several books devoted primarily to the U.S. embargo that deserve particular attention. *Imperial State and Revolution, the United States and Cuba, 1959–1986*, by Morris Morley, provides the most comprehensive and detailed account of the history of the U.S. embargo of Cuba through 1986. Morley traces the legislative history of the embargo and focuses on U.S. efforts to internationalize the embargo. He bases his work on hundreds of personal interviews and thousands of declassified documents. Michael Krinsky and David Golove in *United States Economic Measures Against Cuba* address the U.S. embargo of Cuba as it relates to the United Nations and international law. In their collection, Krinsky and Golove present valuable UN documents as well as difficult-to-obtain Cuban accounts of the embargo. The National Security Archive Document Set, *Chronology of the Cuban Missile Crisis*, by Peter Kornbluh and Laurence Chang, provides probably the best primary-source collection on the early years of the embargo. Other important sources of information on the embargo are the records of hearings in the U.S. Congress.

Alligood, Arlene. "U.S. Subsidiary Trade to End?" *Cuba Business*, Vol. 6, No. 4, September 1992.

Allison, Graham. *Essence of Decision*. Boston: Little, Brown, 1971.

Alvarez, Jose. "Cuba's Sugar Industry in the 1990's: Potential Exports to the U.S. and World Markets." International Working Paper Series. Gainesville: Food and Resource Economics Department, University of Florida, 1992.

Armstrong, Scott, and Philip Brenner. "Putting Cuba and Crisis Back in the Cuban Missile Crisis." *Los Angeles Times*, November 1, 1987, Part V, p. 3.

Baldwin, David. *Economic Statecraft*. Princeton: Princeton University Press, 1985.

Baloyra, Enrique, and James A. Morris. *Conflict and Change in Cuba*. Santa Fe: University of New Mexico Press, 1993.

Bender, Lynne. *The Politics of Hostility: Castro's Revolution and United States Policy*. Hato Rey, Puerto Rico: Inter-American Press, 1975.

Benjamin, Medea, Joseph Collins, and Michael Scott. *No Free Lunch: Food and Revolution in Cuba Today*. New York: Grove Press, 1986.

Bienen, Henry, and Robert Gilpin. "Evaluation of the Use of Economic Sanctions to Promote Foreign Policy Objectives, with Special Reference to the Problem of Terrorism and the Promotion of Human Rights." Princeton: Unpublished report, April 2, 1979.

Blackburn, Robin. "Prologue to the Revolution." In *The Cuba Reader: The Making of a Revolutionary Society*, edited by Philip Brenner, William LeoGrande, Donna Rich, and Daniel Siegel. New York: Grove Press, 1989.

Blasier, Cole. *The Giant's Rival*. Pittsburgh: University of Pittsburgh Press, 1983.

Blasier, Cole, and Carmelo Mesa-Lago, eds. *Cuba in the World*. Pittsburgh: University of Pittsburgh Press, 1979.

Blight, James, and David Welch. *On the Brink: Americans and Soviets Reexamine the Cuban Missile Crisis*. New York: Hill and Wang, 1989.

Bonachea, Rolando E., and Nelson P. Valdés. *Cuba in Revolution*. New York: Doubleday, 1972.

Bonsal, Philip W. *Cuba, Castro and the United States*. Pittsburgh: The University of Pittsburgh Press, 1971.

Boorstein, Edward. *The Economic Transformation of Cuba*. New York: Monthly Review Press, 1968.

Brady, Lawrence J. "The Utility of Economic Sanctions as a Policy Instrument." In *The Utility of International Economic Sanctions*, edited by David Leyton-Brown. Australia: Croom Helm Publishers, 1987.

Brenner, Philip. *From Confrontation to Negotiation: U.S. Relations with Cuba*. Boulder: Westview Press, 1988.

Brenner, Philip, William LeoGrande, Donna Rich, and Daniel Siegel, eds. *The Cuba Reader: The Making of a Revolutionary Society*. New York: Grove Press, 1989.

Brzezinski, Zbigniew. *Power and Principle: Memoirs of a National Security Adviser, 1977–1981*. New York: Farrar, Straus, Giroux, 1983.

Business International Corporation. *The Cuban Revolution*. Prepared by Siegfried Marks, Foreign Economist. New York: January 1960.

Buzzanell, Peter. "Cuba's Sugar Industry—At the Crossroads." Paper presented at the American Sugarbeet Growers Association Annual Meeting, Clearwater, Florida, January 27, 1992.

Cardoso, Fernando Henrique, and Enzo Faletto. *Dependency and Development in Latin America*. Berkeley: University of California Press, 1979.

Carter, Barry E. *International Economic Sanctions: Improving the Haphazard U.S. Legal Regime*. Cambridge: Cambridge University Press, 1988.

Caves, Richard A., Jeffrey A. Frankel, and Ronald W. Jones. *World Trade and Payments: An Introduction*. Fifth Edition. Glenview, Ill. and London, England: Scott, Foresman/Little, Brown Higher Education, 1990.

Chang, Laurence, and Peter Kornbluh. *The Cuban Missile Crisis, 1962*. New York: The New Press, 1992.

Chang, Laurence, Donna Rich, and Chris Wallace. *Chronology of the Cuban Missile Crisis*. Washington, D.C.: National Security Archive, February 1989.

Chonchol, Jacques. "El primer bienio de reforma agraria (1959–1961)." In *Reformas Agrarias en América Latina*, edited by Oscar Delgado. Mexico City: Fondo de Cultura Económico, 1965.

Cuban American National Foundation. *Blue Ribbon Commission on the Economic Reconstruction of Cuba*. Washington, D.C., and Miami: Cuban American National Foundation, 1991.

Daoudi, M.S., and M.S. Dajani. *Economic Sanctions: Ideals and Experience*. London: Outledge and Kegan Paul, 1983.

de Lima-Dantas, Elizabeth. "Historical Setting." In *Cuba: A Country Study*, edited by James D. Rudolph. Washington, D.C.: Department of the Army, 1987.

Dinerstein, Herbert. "Moscow and the Third World: Power Politics or Revolution." *Problems in Communism* (January-February 1968).

Domínguez, Jorge I. *Cuba*. Cambridge: The Belknap Press of Harvard University, 1978.

———. *Cuba: Order and Revolution*. Cambridge: Belknap Press of Harvard University, 1978.

———. "The Obstacles and Prospects for Improved U.S.-Cuban Relations: A U.S. Perspective." In *U.S.-Cuban Relations in the 1990s*, edited by Domínguez and Rafael Hernández. Boulder: Westview Press, 1989.

———. *To Make a World Safe for Revolution*. Cambridge: Harvard University Press, 1989.

Domínguez, Jorge I., and Rafael Hernández, eds. *U.S.-Cuban Relations in the 1990s*. Boulder: Westview Press, 1989.

Doxey, Margaret. *Economic Sanctions and International Enforcement*. First Edition. London: Oxford University Press, 1971.

———. "Sanctions Revisited." *International Journal* XXXI (Winter 1975–1976).

———. *Economic Sanctions and International Enforcement*. Second Edition. London: York: Oxford University Press, 1980.

———. *International Sanctions in Contemporary Perspective*. London: The Macmillan Press, 1987.

Duffy, Gloria. "Crisis Mangling and the Cuban Brigade." *International Security* 8 (Summer 1983).

Duncan, W. Raymond. *The Soviet Union in Latin America*. New Brunswick: Rutgers University Press, 1960.

———. "Cuba-U.S. Relations and Political Contradictions in Cuba." In *Conflict and Change in Cuba*, edited by Enrique Baloyra and James A. Morris. Santa Fe: University of New Mexico Press, 1993.

Economist Intelligence Unit. *Cuba—Country Profile: 1991–1992*. London: 1992.

Ellings, Richard. *Embargoes and World Power: Lessons from American Foreign Policy*. Boulder: Westview Press, 1985.

Erisman, H. Michael. "Central America on the Cuban Foreign Policy Agenda: Where Does It Stand?" In *Cuba's Ties to a Changing World*, edited by Donna Rich Kaplowitz. Boulder: Lynne Rienner Publishers, 1993.

Erisman, H. Michael, and John Kirk. *Cuban Foreign Policy Confronts a New International Order*. Boulder: Lynne Rienner Publishers, 1991.

Feinsilver, Julie M. *Healing the Masses: Cuban Health Politics at Home and Abroad*. Berkeley: University of California Press, 1993.

Fernandez, Damian. "Cuba's Relations with China: Economic Pragmatism and Political Fluctuation." In *Cuba's Ties to a Changing World*, edited by Donna Rich Kaplowitz. Boulder: Lynne Rienner Publishers, 1993.

Ferro-Clerico, Lilia, and Wayne Smith. "The U.S. Trade Embargo." In *Subject to Solution: Problems in Cuban-U.S. Relations*, edited by Wayne Smith. Boulder: Lynne Rienner Publishers, 1988.

Galtung, Johan. "On the Effects of International Economic Sanctions." In *Dilemmas of Economic Coercion: Sanctions in World Politics*, edited by Miroslav Nincic and Peter Wallensteen. New York: Praeger, 1983.

Garthoff, Raymond. *Intelligence Assessment and Policymaking: A Decision Point in the Kennedy Administration*. Washington, D.C.: The Brookings Institute, 1984.

———. *Reflections on the Cuban Missile Crisis*. Washington, D.C.: The Brookings Institute, 1987.

George, Alexander, David Hall, and William Simons. *The Limits of Coercive Diplomacy*. Boston: Little, Brown, 1971.

Goldston, Robert. *The Cuban Revolution*. New York: Bobbs-Merrill, 1970.

Golove, David. "A History of U.S. Regulatory Policy Toward Cuba." *Cuba Update*, April 1990.

Gorham, Richard V. "Canada and Cuba: Four and a Half Decades of Cordial Relations." In *Cuba's Ties to a Changing World*, edited by Donna Rich Kaplowitz. Boulder: Lynne Rienner Publishers, 1993.

Grabendorff, Wolf. "The Relationship between the European Community and Cuba." In *Cuba's Ties to a Changing World*, edited by Donna Rich Kaplowitz. Boulder: Lynne Rienner Publishers, 1993.

———. *Cuba: Apertura Economica y Relaciones con Europa*. Madrid: Instituto de Relaciones Europeo-Latino Americanas, 1994.

Greater Miami Chamber of Commerce. *The Trade Impact of a Free Cuba*. Miami: 1992.

Green, Jerrold D. "Strategies for Evading Economic Sanctions." In *Dilemmas of Economic Coercion*, edited by Miroslav Nincic and Peter Wallensteen. New York: Praeger, 1983.

Guevara, Ernesto "Che." "Man and Socialism in Cuba." In *Man and Socialism in Cuba: The Great Debate*, edited by Bertram Silverman. New York: Atheneum, 1973.

Gunn, Gillian. "Will Castro Fall?" *Foreign Policy* 79 (Summer 1990).

Halperin, Maurice. *The Taming of Fidel Castro*. Berkeley: University of California Press, 1981.

Hargrove, Erwin. *Jimmy Carter as President: Leadership and the Politics of the Public Good*. Baton Rouge: Louisiana State University Press, 1989.

Hennessy, Alistair, and George Lambie, eds. *The Fractured Blockade: West European–Cuban Relations During the Revolution*. London: Warwick University Caribbean Studies, 1994.

Heritage Foundation. "Removing Soviet Influence from Cuba." *National Security Record*. Washington, D.C.: Heritage Foundation, 1981.

Hinckle, Warren, and William Turner. *The Fish Is Red: The Story of the Secret War Against Castro*. New York: Harper and Row, 1981.

Hoffmann, Stanley. "The Hell of Good Intentions." *Foreign Policy* 29 (Winter 1977).

Hufbauer, Gary C., and Jeffrey J. Schott. *Economic Sanctions in Support of Foreign Policy Goals*. Washington, D.C.: Institute for International Economics, 1983.

———. *Economic Sanctions Reconsidered*. First Edition. Washington, D.C.: Institute for International Economics, 1985.

Hufbauer, Gary C., Jeffrey J. Schott, and Kimberly Ann Elliott. *Economic Sanctions Reconsidered: History and Current Policy*. Second Edition. Washington, D.C.: Institute for International Economics, 1990.

———. *Economic Sanctions Reconsidered: Supplemental Case Histories*. Second Edition. Washington, D.C.: Institute for International Economics, 1990.

Jenkins, Gareth. "The Fractured Blockade." *Cuba Business* 8 (July/August 1994).

Kaplowitz, Donna Rich. "U.S. Subsidiary Trade with Cuba: Pre and Post the Cuban Democracy Act." In *Cuba in the International System: Integration and Normalization*, edited by Archibald Ritter and John Kirk. MacMillan Press, 1995.

———, ed. *Cuba's Ties to a Changing World*. Boulder: Lynne Rienner Publishers, 1993.

Kaplowitz, Donna Rich, and Michael Kaplowitz. "New Opportunities for U.S.-Cuban Trade." Washington, D.C.: Johns Hopkins University, Cuban Studies Program, 1992.

Kennan, George. *Memoirs, 1925–1950*. London: Hutchinson, 1968.

Kennedy, Robert. *Thirteen Days*. New York: W.W. Norton, 1969.

Kornbluh, Peter, and James G. Blight. "Dialogue with Castro: a Hidden History." *The New York Review of Books*, October 6, 1994.

Kornbluh, Peter, and Sheryl Walter. "History Held Hostage: 30 Years Later, We're Still Learning the Secrets of the Cuban Missile Crisis." *Washington Post*, October 11, 1992.

Koth, Marcia N. *Housing in Latin America*. Cambridge: MIT Press, 1965.

Krinsky, Michael, and David Golove, eds. *United States Economic Measures Against Cuba*. Northampton: Aletheia Press, 1993.

Lake, Anthony. *Somoza Falling: A Case Study of Washington at Work*. Amherst: The University of Massachusetts Press, 1989.

Larson, David. *The Cuban Crisis of 1962: Selected Documents, Chronology and Bibliography*. Landham: University Press of America, 1986.

LeoGrande, William M. "Cuban Dependency: A Comparison of Pre-Revolutionary and Post-Revolutionary International Economic Relations." *Cuban Studies/Estudios Cubanos* 9 (July 1979).

———. *Cuba's Policy in Africa, 1959–1980*. Berkeley: Institute of International Studies, University of California, 1980.

Leontief, Wassily. "The Trouble with Cuban Socialism." *The New York Review of Books*, January 7, 1971.

Levesque, Jacques. *The USSR and the Cuban Revolution: Soviet Ideological and Strategic Perspectives, 1959–1977*. New York: Praeger Publishers, 1978.

Leyton-Brown, David. "Extraterritoriality in U.S. Trade Sanctions." In *The Utility of Economic Sanctions*, edited by David Leyton-Brown. Australia: Croom Helm, 1987.

———, ed. *The Utility of Economic Sanctions*. Australia: Croom Helm, 1987.

Leyva, Ricardo. "Health and Revolution in Cuba." In *Cuba in Revolution*, edited by Rolando E. Bonachea and Nelson P. Valdés. New York: Doubleday, 1972.

Losman, Donald L. *International Economic Sanctions: The Cases of Cuba, Israel and Rhodesia*. Albuquerque: The University of New Mexico Press, 1979.

MacEwan, Arthur. *Revolution and Economic Development*. New York: St Martin's Press, 1981.

Malloy, Michael P. *Economic Sanctions and U.S. Trade*. Boston: Little, Brown, 1990.

Marcum, John A. *The Angolan Revolution: Exile Politics and Guerrilla Warfare, 1962–1976*. Cambridge: MIT Press, 1978.

Márquez, Gabriel García. "Operation Carlotta." *New Left Review* (February-April 1977).

Marshall, Francine. "Cuba's Relations with Africa: The End of an Era." In *Cuba's Ties to a Changing World*, edited by Donna Rich Kaplowitz. Boulder: Lynne Rienner Publishers, 1993.

Matthews, Herbert L. *The Cuban Story*. New York: George Braziller Press, 1961.

———. "The Bay of Pigs." In *The Cuba Reader*, edited by Brenner, et al. New York: Grove Press, 1989.

Mesa-Lago, Carmelo. "The Economy and International Relations." In *Cuba in the World*, edited by Cole Blasier and Carmelo Mesa-Lago. Pittsburgh: University of Pittsburgh Press, 1979.

———. *The Economy of Socialist Cuba: A Two-Decade Appraisal*. Albuquerque: University of New Mexico Press, 1981.

Miyagawa, Makio. *Do Economic Sanctions Work?* New York: St. Martin's Press, 1992.

Morley, Morris. *Imperial State and Revolution: The United States and Cuba, 1952–1986*. Cambridge: Cambridge University Press, 1987.

Nathan, James A., ed. *Cuban Missile Crisis Revisited*. New York: St. Martin's Press, 1992.

Newsom, David D. *The Soviet Brigade in Cuba*. Bloomington: Indiana University Press, 1987.

Nikolayenko, Valery. "An Official Statement of the New Soviet Policy in Latin America." In *The Russians Aren't Coming: New Soviet Policy in Latin America*, edited by Wayne Smith. Boulder: Lynne Rienner Publishers, 1992.

Nincic, Miroslav, and Peter Wallensteen. "Economic Coercion and Foreign Policy." In *Dilemmas of Economic Coercion: Sanctions in World Politics*, edited by Nincic and Wallensteen. New York: Praeger Publishers, 1983.

———, eds. *Dilemmas of Economic Coercion: Sanctions in World Politics*. New York: Praeger Publishers, 1983.

Paterson, Thomas. *Contesting Castro: The United States and the Triumph of the Cuban Revolution*. New York: Oxford University Press, 1994.

Pérez-López, Jorge. "Sugar and Structural Change in the Cuban Economy." *World Development* 17 (1989).

Perez-Stable, Marifeli. "Castro Takes the Economy in Hand." *Nation*, September 26, 1987.

Plant, Steven E. "Economic Warfare: Costs and Benefits?" *Washington Quarterly* (Spring 1981). Center for Strategic and International Studies, Georgetown University.

Preeg, Ernest H. *Cuba and the New Caribbean Economic Order*. Washington, D.C.: Center for Strategic and International Studies, Significant Issues Series, Vol. XV, No. 2 (1993).

Purcell, Susan Kaufman. "Cuba's Cloudy Future." *Foreign Affairs* 69 (Summer 1990).

———. "Collapsing Cuba." *Foreign Affairs* 71 (Winter 1992).

Renwick, Robin. "Economic Sanctions." Harvard Studies in International Affairs, No. 45. Cambridge: Harvard University, Center for International Affairs, 1981.

Rich, Donna. "Brazil and Cuba Strengthening Relations." *InfoBrazil* (May 1988).

———. "The U.S. Embargo Against Cuba: Its Evolution and Enforcement." A study prepared for the British Commonwealth Countries. Washington, D.C.: Johns Hopkins University, Cuba Studies Project, 1988.

———. "Embargo Economics: Keeping Cuba at Bay." *Multinational Monitor* (April 1989).

———. "Lessons for the U.S. Embargo Against Cuba." In *South Africa: The Sanctions Report, Documents and Statistics*, edited by Joseph Hanlon. London: The Commonwealth Secretariat, 1990.

———. "U.S. and Cuba: Trading Partners?" *Cuba Update* (April 1990).

———. "Cuba's Role as Mediator in International Conflict." In *Cuban Foreign Policy Confronts a New International Order*, edited by Michael Erisman and John Kirk. Boulder: Lynne Rienner Publishers, 1991.

Rich, Donna, and Kirby Jones. *Opportunities for U.S. Cuban Trade*. Washington, D.C.: Johns Hopkins University, 1988.

Ritter, Archibald. "The Compensation Question: Who Compensates Whom, Why, How?" Paper presented at the Cuba Symposium, Ottawa, Canada, September 23–25, 1993.

Robbins, Carla Anne. *The Cuban Threat*. Philadelphia: ISHI Publications, 1983.

Roca, Sergio. "Economic Sanctions Against Cuba." In *The Utility of International Economic Sanctions*, edited by David Leyton-Brown. Australia: Croom Helm, 1987.

Rudolph, James D., ed. *Cuba: A Country Study*. Washington, D.C.: Department of the Army, 1987.

Ruiz, Ramon Eduardo. *Cuba: The Making of a Revolution*. New York: W.W. Norton, 1968.

Schlesinger, Arthur M. *Robert Kennedy and His Times*. Boston: Houghton Mifflin, 1978.

Schreiber, Anna P. "Economic Coercion as an Instrument of Foreign Policy: U.S. Economic Measures Against Cuba and the Dominican Republic." *World Politics* XXV (April 1973).

Schulicki, Jaime, and Antonio Jorge. *Investing in Cuba: Problems and Prospects*. New Brunswick: Transaction Publishers, 1994.

Smith, Gaddis. *Morality, Reason and Power: American Diplomacy in the Carter Years*. New York: Hill and Wang, 1986.

Smith, Robert. *The United States and Cuba: Business and Diplomacy, 1917–1960*. New Haven: College and University Press, 1960.

Smith, Wayne S. "Castro's Cuba: Soviet Partner or Nonaligned?" Washington, D.C.: Woodrow Wilson Center, Smithsonian Institution, 1984.

———. *The Closest of Enemies: A Personal and Diplomatic History of the Castro Years*. New York: W.W. Norton, 1987.

———. *Portrait of Cuba*. Kansas City: Turner Publishing Inc., 1991.

———. "Cuba and the Soviet Union, Cuba and Russia." In *Cuba's Ties to a Changing World*, edited by Donna Kaplowitz. Boulder: Lynne Rienner Publishers, 1993.

———, ed. *Subject to Solution: Problems in U.S.-Cuban Relations*. Boulder: Lynne Rienner Publishers, 1988.

———, ed. *The Russians Aren't Coming: New Soviet Policy in Latin America*. Boulder: Lynne Rienner Publishers, 1992.

Sommerfield, Stanley. "Treasury Regulations Affecting Trade with the Sino-Soviet Bloc and Cuba." *The Business Lawyer*, July 1964.

———. "Treasury Regulations of Foreign Assets and Trade." In *A Lawyer's Guide to International Business Transactions*, edited by Walter Surrey and Don Wallace. Philadelphia: American Law Institute, 1977.

Szulc, Tad. "U.S. Curtails Aid to Five Countries that Sell to Cuba." *New York Times*, February 19, 1964.

Tambs, Lewis, ed. "A New Inter-American Policy for the Eighties: Report of the Committee of Santa Fe." Washington, D.C.: Council for Inter-American Security, 1981.

Thomas, Hugh. *Cuba: The Pursuit of Freedom*. New York: Harper and Row, 1971.

———. *The Cuban Revolution*. New York: Harper and Row, 1977.

Thucydides. *The History of the Peloponnesian War*. New York: The Modern Library, 1951.

Valdés, Nelson P. "The Radical Transformation of Cuban Education." In *Cuba in Revolution*, edited by Rolando Bonachea and Nelson P. Valdés. New York: Doubleday, 1972.

———. "Revolutionary Solidarity in Angola." In *Cuba in the World*, edited by Cole Blasier and Carmelo Mesa-Lago. Pittsburgh: University of Pittsburgh Press, 1979.

Vance, Cyrus. *Hard Choices: Critical Years in America's Foreign Policy*. New York: Simon and Schuster, 1983.
Vasconcelos, Luis L. "The Limits and Possibilities of Cuban-Brazilian Relations." In *Cuba's Ties to a Changing World*, edited by Donna Rich Kaplowitz. Boulder: Lynne Rienner Publishers, 1993.
Wallensteen, Peter. "Economic Sanctions: Ten Modern Cases, Three Important Lessons." In *Dilemmas of Economic Coercion: Sanctions in World Politics*, edited by Miroslav Nincic and Peter Wallensteen. New York: Praeger Publishers, 1983.
Welch, Richard E. *Response to Revolution: The United States and the Cuban Revolution*. Chapel Hill: University of North Carolina Press, 1985.
Williams, William A. *The U.S., Cuba and Castro: An Essay in the Dynamics of Revolution and the Dissolution of Empire*. New York: Monthly Review Press, 1962.
Williams, John H. "Havana's Military Machine: On Castro's Island Most of the Population is Under Arms." *The Atlantic Monthly* 262 (August 1988).
Wyden, Peter. *Bay of Pigs: The Untold Story*. New York: Simon and Schuster, 1979.
Zimbalist, Andrew. "Teetering on the Brink: Cuba's Current Economic and Political Crisis." *Journal of Latin American Studies* 24, Part 2 (May 1992).
———. "Impact of Blockade." *Cuba Business* 6 (December 1992).
———. "Dateline Cuba: Hanging On in Havana." *Foreign Policy* 92 (Fall 1993).
Zimbalist, Andrew, and Susan Eckstein. "Patterns of Cuban Development: The First Twenty-Five Years." *World Development* 15 (January 1987).

Government Documents and Reports

Cable from U.S. Embassy, Madrid, to Secretary of State, October 19, 1962. National Security Archive, Cuban Missile Crisis Document Set.
"Chronology of Important Events in U.S.-Cuban Relations, 1957–1962." The White House, from the document collection at the National Security Archive, Cuban Missile Crisis Document Set.
Day, Erin. "Economic Sanctions Imposed by the United States Against Specific Countries: 1979–1992." Congressional Research Service Report for Congress, August 10, 1992.
Department of the Treasury Memorandum. From Raymond W. Konan, Chief Counsel, Foreign Assets Control, to Margery Waxman, Deputy General Counsel, July 27, 1983. Re: Cuban Regulations Chronology.
Foreign Claims Settlement Commission of the United States. *Final Report of the Cuban Claims Program*. Washington, D.C, July 1972.
Mark, Clyde R. Congressional Research Service, Issue Brief 85066, June 27, 1994.
National Security Action Memorandum No. 220, February 5, 1963. National Security Archive, Cuban Missile Crisis Document Set.
Office of Foreign Assets Control. *An Analysis of Licensed Trade with Cuba by Foreign Subsidiaries of U.S. Companies*. Washington, D.C.: U.S. Department of Treasury, July 1989.
———. Special Report, *An Analysis of Licensed Trade with Cuba by Foreign Subsidiaries of U.S. Companies*, Washington, D.C.: U.S. Department of Treasury, April 1990.
———. *An Analysis of Licensed Trade with Cuba by Foreign Subsidiaries of U.S. Companies*. Washington, D.C.: U.S. Department of Treasury, July 1990.

———. *An Analysis of Licensed Trade with Cuba by Foreign Subsidiaries of U.S. Companies*. Washington, D.C.: U.S. Department of Treasury, July 1991.

Pregelj, Vladimir N. "U.S. Foreign Trade Sanctions Imposed for Foreign Policy Reasons in Force as of April 10, 1988." CRS Report for Congress, April 13, 1988, 88–301-E.

Rusk, Dean. "Memorandum for President Kennedy," April 17, 1963. National Security Archive, Cuban Missile Crisis Document Set.

Sklar, Barry. U.S. Congress, Joint Economic Committee. *The Political Economy of the Western Hemisphere: Selected Issues for U.S. Policy*. Prepared for the Subcommittee on International Trade, Finance and Security Economics of the Joint Economic Committee, 97th Congress, 1st Session, September 18, 1981. Washington, D.C.: U.S. Government Printing Office, 1981.

Theriot, Lawrence. U.S. Congress, Joint Economic Committee. *Cuba Faces the Economic Realities of the 1980s*. 97th Congress, 2nd Session, March 22, 1982. Washington, D.C.: U.S. Government Printing Office, 1982.

Theriot, Lawrence and Linda Droker. "Cuban Trade with the Industrialized West, 1974–1979." East West Trade Policy Staff Paper, Project D-76. Department of Commerce, 1981.

U.S. Congress, Senate. Committee on Foreign Relations. Briefing on Cuban Developments, January 25, 1962.

U.S. Congress, Senate. Committee on Foreign Relations. *Nomination of Henry A. Kissinger Part I*. 93rd Congress, 1st Session, September 7, 10, 11, and 14, 1973. Washington, D.C.: U.S. Government Printing Office, 1973.

U.S. Congress, Senate. *Alleged Assassination Plots Involving Foreign Leaders*. 94th Congress, 1st Session, Report No. 94–465, November 20, 1975. Washington, D.C.: U.S. Government Printing Office, 1975.

U.S. Congress, House. Committee on International Relations, Subcommittees on International Trade and Commerce and International Organizations. *U.S. Trade Embargo of Cuba*. 94th Congress, 1st Session. Washington, D.C.: U.S. Government Printing Office, 1975.

U.S. Congress, Senate. Select Committee to Study Governmental Operations with Respect to Intelligence Activities. 94th Congress, 2nd Session. Report No. 94-755, April 23, 1976. Washington, D.C.: U.S. Government Printing Office, 1976.

U.S. Congress, House. Committee on International Relations. *Toward Improved United States–Cuba Relations*. Report of a Special Study Mission to Cuba, February 10–15, 1977. 95th Congress, 1st Session. Washington, D.C.: U.S. Government Printing Office, 1977.

U.S. Congress, House. Committee of Foreign Affairs, Subcommittee on Western Hemisphere Affairs. *Cuba and the United States: Thirty Years of Hostility and Beyond*. 101st Congress, 1st Session, 1989. Washington, D.C.: U.S. Government Printing Office, 1990.

U.S. Congress, House. Committee on Foreign Affairs, Subcommittees on Europe and the Middle East and on Western Hemisphere Affairs. *Cuba in a Changing World: The United States–Soviet–Cuban Triangle*. 102nd Congress, 1st Session, April 30, July 11 and 31, 1991. Washington, D.C.: U.S. Government Printing Office, 1991.

U.S. Congress, House. Committee on Foreign Affairs, Subcommittee on Western Hemisphere Affairs. *Recent Developments in United States–Cuban Relations: Immigration and Nuclear Power.* 102nd Congress, 1st Session, June 5, 1991. Washington, D.C.: U.S. Government Printing Office, 1991.

U.S. Congress, Senate. Committee on Foreign Relations, Subcommittee on Western

Hemisphere and Peace Corps Affairs. *Democracy in Cuba.* 103rd Congress, 1st Session, August 5, 1992. Washington, D.C.: U.S. Government Printing Office, 1992.

U.S. Congress, House. Committee on Ways and Means, Subcommittee on Trade. *Cuban Democracy Act of 1992.* 103rd Congress, 1st Session, August 10, 1992. Washington, D.C.: U.S. Government Printing Office, 1992.

U.S. Congress, House. Committee on Ways and Means, Subcommittee on Trade, 103rd Congress, 2nd Session, March 17, 1994, *Free Trade with Cuba Act* Washington, D.C.: U.S. Government Printing Office, 1994.

U.S. Departments of State and Defense. "The Soviet-Cuban Connection in Central America and the Caribbean," Washington, D.C., March 1985.

Cuban Publications

Anuario Estadistico de Cuba, 1987. Comite Estatal de Estadisticas, Republic of Cuba.

Banco Nacional de Cuba. "Selected Statistical Information of the Cuban Economy." June 1990.

Castro, Fidel. "Main Report to the Third Party Congress of the Communist Party of Cuba." February 4, 1986. *Granma Weekly Review*, February 10, 1986.

Instituto de Investigaciones Económicas, Juceplan. *El Bloqueo Economico a Cuba por los Estados Unidos*. Havana, 1992.

Rodríguez, José Luis. "La economía de Cuba ante la cambiante coyuntura internacional." Boletín de Información Sobre La Economía Cubana, February 1992.

Correspondence received and interviews conducted by the author

In preparation of this work, the author took six trips to Cuba between 1988 and 1992 to interview numerous Cuban officials about the embargo. The trips were funded by travel grants from the Arca and Ford Foundations and by the Johns Hopkins Cuban Studies Program.

Abreu, Raúl. Quimimport, June 24, 1991.

Alexander, Bill. U.S. Congressman, February 1988.

Alfaia, Georgina. Ministry of Foreign Trade, Cuba, March 1992.

Alligood, Arlene. Researcher, December 5, 1988.

Alvaréz, Amado. Cubafrutas, June 24, 1991.

Aruca, Francisco. Marazul Tours, numerous conversations.

B'Hamel, María de la Luz. Ministry of Foreign Trade, Cuba, March 1992.

Blanco, Alfredo. Banco Nacional de Cuba, June 1991.

Brenner, Philip. American University, January 25, 1994, and correspondence with author.

Brito, Ada Prado. Cubatex, February 25, 1992.

Castro, Fidel. President of Cuba, March 1988.

David, Clara. U.S. Treasury Department, August 31, 1993; January 23, 1995.

Fernández, Oscar García. Institute of Advanced International Relations, Cuba, June 1991.

Fretz, Bob. U.S. Department of State, September 7, 1993.
Garcia, Raúl Montes. Ministry of Foreign Relations, Cuba, June 1991.
García, Carlos. Cubanacán, February 24, 1992.
Grabendorff, Wolf. Correspondence, September 10, 1993.
Harrington, Brendan. Cargill International, September 15, 1993.
Hernández, Carlos García. Cubanacán, Cuba, June 25, 1991.
Izquierdo, Emerio. Cubaexport, June 24, 1991.
Jessup, David. British West India Committee, September 14, 1993.
Jones, Kirby. World Bank, January 25, 1988.
Jones, Kirby. Correspondence provided this author among Kirby Jones of Alamar Associates, his attorney Donald Rehm, and the Treasury Department.
Kaminarides, John. Arkansas State University, February 1988.
Kirk, John. Dalhousie University, September 9, 1993.
Krinsky, Michael. U.S. lawyer representing Cuba, September 9, 1993.
Larrinaga, Abeledo. Chamber of Commerce, Cuba, February 24, 1992.
Mann, Catherine. U.S. Treasury Department, June 8, 1988; July 19, 1988.
Moe, Serena. U.S. Treasury Department, September 13, 1993.
Parodi, Ramon Sanchez. Former Chief, Cuban Interests Section, Washington, D.C., ongoing.
Rodriguez, Carlos Rafael. Vice-president of Cuba, March 1988.
Rodriguez, Jose Luis. Former Director, Center of Studies on World Economy, 1988.
Sallot, Jeff. *Globe and Mail*, September 14, 1993.
Scanlan, Kathleen. U.S. Department of Commerce, February 1988.
Sigarroa, Olimpia. Chamber of Commerce, Cuba, March 1992.
Soto, Rodrigo. U.S. Department of Commerce, February 10, 1992.
Taladrid, Raúl. Cuban Agency for Economic Cooperation, February 26, 1992.
Theriot, Lawrence. U.S. Department of Commerce, 1988.
Valdés, Berta Sueiro. University of Havana, June 15, 1991.
Victoria, Aldo. Banco Nacional de Cuba, February 25, 1992.
Zimbalist, Andrew. Smith College, April 15, 1992.

Newspapers and Periodicals Consulted

Atlantic Monthly; Aviation Seek and Space Technology; Bohemia; Business Latin America; Business Lawyer; Business Week; Chemical Week; Chicago Tribune; Christian Science Monitor; Chronicle of Latin American Economic Affairs; Congressional Record; CubaINFO; Cuba Business; Cuba Foreign Trade; Cuba Update; Cuban Studies; The Economist; Esquire; Facts on File; Federal Register; Financial Times; Forbes; Foreign Affairs; Foreign Broadcast Information Service; Foreign Policy; Globe and Mail; Granma; Granma Weekly; Houston Post; International Journal; International Security; International Trade Reporter; Journal of Commerce; Journal of Latin American Studies; Latin American Newsletters; London Times; Los Angeles Times; Miami Herald; Multinational Monitor; The Nation; National Journal; New Left Review; New York Review of Books; New York Times; Newsweek; Problems in Communism; Time; USA Today; US News and World Report; Wall Street Journal; Washington Post; Washington Quarterly; World Development; World Politics.

Note: Some information was obtained via the Lexis-Nexis system on the Internet. Internet citations are marked.

Index

About the Book

Among the most comprehensive and longest-lasting embargoes in the history of U.S. foreign policy, the embargo against Cuba reflects the intricacies of the modern world: struggles for independence, relationships among national, regional, and global sources of power, and both North-South and East-West conflicts. Kaplowitz provides the most comprehensive historical analysis to date of the U.S. embargo and also explains why it has failed to achieve its major objectives—most notably the ouster of Fidel Castro—despite its longevity and exhaustive scope.

Donna Rich Kaplowitz is adjunct professor of political science at Michigan State University and president of Cuba Research Associates, a Michigan-based consulting group. In 1988–1992, she served as deputy director of the Cuban Studies Program at Johns Hopkins University's School of Advanced International Studies, where she was also founder and executive editor of *CubaINFO*. Her publications include *The Cuba Reader* and *Cuba's Ties to a Changing World*.